The Poems of
Phillis Wheatley

PHILLIS WHEATLEY. NEGRO SERVANT to M.ʳ JOHN WHEATLEY, of BOSTON.

THE POEMS OF

Phillis Wheatley

REVISED AND ENLARGED EDITION

Edited with an Introduction by

JULIAN D. MASON, JR.

The University of North Carolina Press
Chapel Hill & London

Library of Congress Cataloging-in-Publication Data

Wheatley, Phillis, 1753–1784.
  [Poems]
  The poems of Phillis Wheatley / edited with an introduction by
Julian D. Mason, Jr.—Rev. and enl. ed.
    p. cm.
  Bibliography: p.
  Includes index.
  ISBN 0-8078-1835-6 (alk. paper). ISBN 0-8078-4245-1 (pbk.)
  I. Mason, Julian D. (Julian Dewey), 1931– . II. Title.
PS866.W5 1989   88-23280
811'.1—dc19   CIP

The paper in this book meets the

guidelines for permanence and durability

of the Committee on Production

Guidelines for Book Longevity of the

Council on Library Resources.

Printed in the United States of America

93 92 91 90   5 4 3 2

In Memory of

C. Hugh Holman
(1914–1981)

Contents

Other Poems and Variants of Poems 113

~

Illustrations

All illustrations are from the 1773 edition of *Poems on Various Subjects, Religious and Moral* in the Louis Round Wilson Library of the University of North Carolina at Chapel Hill.

~

Acknowledgments

G rateful acknowledgment is given to the following for permission to use for this edition the items from each of them indicated below:

The American Antiquarian Society for manuscripts of Wheatley's poems "To the University of Cambridge, Wrote in 1767" and "On the Death of the Rev'd Dr. Sewall. 1769"; handwritten notes in a copy of Wheatley's *Poems on Various Subjects*; and information about a copy of Thomas Amory's *Daily Devotions* once owned by Wheatley and also once owned by the society.

The Beinecke Library of Yale University for the inscription in a copy of John Lathrop's *The Importance of Early Piety* which was once owned by Wheatley.

The Boston Public Library for a manuscript of Wheatley's letter to Samuel Hopkins of 6 May 1774 (in the Chamberlin Collection in Rare Books and Manuscripts).

The Bowdoin College Library for a manuscript of Wheatley's poem "On the Capture of General Lee."

The Cheshunt Foundation, Westminster College, Cambridge, England, for manuscripts of Wheatley's poem "On the Decease of the Rev'd Dr. Sewell"; letters from Phillis Wheatley to the Countess of Huntingdon of 25 October 1770, 27 June 1773, and 17 July 1773; letters from Susanna Wheatley to the Countess of Huntingdon of 20 February 1773 and 30 April 1773; and letters from Richard Cary to the Countess of Huntingdon of 25 May 1772, 3 April 1773, and 3 May 1773—all of the above from the Papers of the Countess of Huntingdon.

The Connecticut Historical Society for manuscripts of Wheatley's poems "On the Death of Dr. Samuel Marshall" and "To the Rev, Mr. Pitkin, on the Death of his Lady," and a letter from Susanna Wheatley to Samson Occom of 29 March 1773.

The Essex Institute for inscriptions in a copy of Granville Sharp's *Remarks on Several Very Important Prophecies, in Five Parts* which was once owned by Wheatley.

The Haverford College Library's Quaker Collection for a manuscript of Wheatley's letter to Arbour Tanner of 19 May 1772.

The Historical Society of Pennsylvania for manuscripts of a letter from Wheatley to Samuel Hopkins of 9 February 1774 and of Wheatley's poem "To the King's Most Excellent Majesty"; and broadsides of Wheatley's poems *To Mrs. Leonard, on the Death of Her Husband, To the Hon'ble Thomas Hubbard,* and *An Elegiac Poem* [on the death of Whitefield].

The Houghton Library of Harvard University for a manuscript of Wheatley's "A Poem on the Death of Charles Eliot."

The Huntington Library for a broadside of Wheatley's *An Ode of Verses on the Death of George Whitefield.*

The Library Company of Philadelphia for manuscripts of Wheatley's poems "Atheism," "Deism," "America," "To the Hon.ble Commodore Hood," "On the Death of Mr. Snider," and "on Atheism."

The Library of Congress (Rare Book and Special Collections Division) for a broadside of Wheatley's poem *To the Rev. Mr. Pitkin, on the Death of his Lady.*

The Massachusetts Historical Society for manuscripts of letters from Wheatley to David Worcester [Wooster] of 18 October 1773 and to Mary Wooster of 15 July 1778 (which includes Wheatley's poem "On the Death of General Wooster"); letters from John Andrews to William Barrell of 29 May 1772, 22 September 1772, 24 and 26 February 1773, 4 June 1773, 28 January 1774, and 7 and 18 February 1774 and ones from Barrell to Andrews of 16 and 22 March 1773; a letter from the Countess of Huntingdon to Mrs. John Wheatley of 13 May 1773; letters from Elizabeth Wallcut to Thomas Wallcut of 30 January and 18 March 1773, from Thomas Wallcut to Elizabeth Wallcut of 20 April 1773, and from Christopher Wallcut to Thomas Wallcut of 8 March 1774; letters from Wheatley to Obour (Arbour) Tanner of 19 July 1772, 30 October 1773, 21 March 1774, 6 May 1774, 29 May 1778, and 10 May 1779; Wheatley's poems "An Address to the Atheist," "An Address to the Deist," "Atheism," "A Poem on the Death of Charles Eliot," and "An Elegy Sacred to the Memory of the Revd. Samuel Cooper D.D.";
and a letter from Wheatley to Lord Dartmouth of 10 October 1772. Also for a broadside of Wheatley's poem *An Elegy to Miss. Mary Moorhead* and a pamphlet of her poem *An Elegy, Sacred to the Memory of... Dr. Samuel Cooper.*

The Medford Historical Society for letters from Timothy Fitch to Peter Gwin of 12 January and 8 November 1760 and 4 September 1761.

The Moorland-Spingarn Research Center at Howard University for a manuscript of Wheatley's poem "On Friendship" (Thomas Gregory Collection, Box 37-12, Folder 362).

The New-York Historical Society for a pamphlet of Wheatley's poem *Liberty and Peace*.

The Rare Book collection of the Louis Round Wilson Library of the University of North Carolina at Chapel Hill for the complete 1773 *Poems on Various Subjects*, including the picture of Wheatley.

The Schomburg Center for Research in Black Culture, New York Public Library, for a manuscript prayer said to have been found in Wheatley's Bible and for inscriptions in books which were owned by her.

The Scottish Record Office, Edinburgh, Scotland, for manuscripts (GD 26/13/663) of letters from Wheatley to John Thornton of 21 April 1772, 1 December 1773, 29 March 1774, and 30 October 1770 [1774]; a letter from Thornton to Wheatley, 1775 [1774]; and letters from Susanna Wheatley to Thornton of 26 October 1771 and 9 February 1773. Permission to use these was granted by the Earl of Leven and Melville, for which thanks is given.

The Staffordshire Record Office, Stafford, England, for manuscripts of a letter from Thomas Wooldridge to Lord Dartmouth of 24 November 1772 and one from Wheatley to Lord Dartmouth of 10 October 1772; Wheatley's poem "To the Right Honl. William Earl of Dartmouth"; and a biographical sketch of Wheatley, signed by Nathaniel Wheatley—all from the Papers of Lord Dartmouth. Permission to use these materials was granted by the Earl of Dartmouth, for which thanks is given.

Warm acknowledgment also is given (concerning the first edition of this book) for the kind assistance of the staff of the library of the University of North Carolina at Chapel Hill (especially of its Rare Book Room and its Interlibrary Center), and (for this edition) to the staffs of the Dalton Rare Book Collection and of the Interlibrary Loan Office of the Atkins Library of the University of North Carolina at Charlotte; and for the willingness of numerous libraries and societies to allow me to use their manuscript and print collections when I visited them and/or to lend books or provide information, advice, assistance, and/or copies of material.

I also gratefully acknowledge (for the first edition) a grant from the Smith Fund of the University of North Carolina at Chapel Hill for assistance with obtaining materials, funds provided by the William A. Whitaker Foundation for purchasing the 1773 edition of *Poems on Various Subjects* for the Wilson

Library of the University of North Carolina at Chapel Hill, and (for this edition) a temporary reduction in teaching load by the Department of English of the University of North Carolina at Charlotte, and reassignment of duties from teaching for a full semester which was made possible by funds from the Foundation of the University of North Carolina at Charlotte.

I also acknowledge, with thanks and respect, the extensive work of my fellow scholars, which my work can only build upon, especially (for the first edition) Dorothy Porter, Vernon Loggins, Justin Winsor, and William B. Sprague and his *Annals of the American Pulpit*, and (for this edition) William Robinson, Ali Isani, and all the other persistent searchers for those fragments so difficult to find, but the hunt for which is so challenging and rewarding. I thank Richard Newman for allowing me access to his copy of *Poems on Comic, Serious, and Moral Subjects*; John Shields for letting me borrow copies of the papers from the Phillis Wheatley Conference at Illinois State University; and Ali Isani for a photocopy of Wheatley's poem "An Elegy on Leaving——" in the *Arminian Magazine*.

I thank the staff and the Board of Governors of the University of North Carolina Press for their help, encouragement, understanding, and patience; and my wife for exceptional amounts of all of those, especially while I was working against the deadline for this book and she was facing the same deadline for a long quilting project, and somehow both things were accomplished in the same household at the same time, without rancor or discouragement on the part of either of us, with more than tolerance, and even with respect, faith, hope, and love.

The Poems of
Phillis Wheatley

Introduction

W hen the first edition of this book was published in 1966, it appropriately spoke of the need to make readily available once more Phillis Wheatley's poems, which had become difficult to obtain despite various printings of them over the decades. Since 1966 her poems have become much more widely available through that edition and also through the work of a respectable body of scholars and critics over only a little more than two decades since that first edition was prepared. Various factors have contributed to increased interest in Phillis Wheatley and her poetry during that time, including the country's bicentennial (focusing on the period when she flourished) and a general heightening of awareness of past and continuing contributions by blacks to American culture as a whole. Another of the catalysts and aids in this interest (as had been intended) was the first edition of this book, making most of her work readily available once more and in context in a scholarly edition. Now, thanks mostly to a handful of persistent scholars whose contributions are obvious in the pages of this new edition, we know of more poems, more variants of poems, and more letters by her, and we know a good bit more about her life and its contexts. Also, much more aesthetic, cultural, and intentional critical attention has been paid to her writings.

Therefore, it is time to enlarge and revise the 1966 book accordingly and to make it even better than it was before by including the additional works and an index and by correcting the first edition's errors (and some of those by others) in text and in facts, while cutting away both some contexts and some suppositions that were appropriate for what was known in 1966 but now have been proven wrong or are no longer needed or no longer appropriate, often superseded by clearer or fuller information or interpretation. Also (to be found primarily in the notes) for this new edition I have been able to add some things that have not been published before. For example, see some new information concerning her personal library which adds a southern connection, in this introduction; two more books she owned, in the notes to her poem to Thomas Amory and her letter to David Wooster; a new way to understand her poem on George Washington, in the note for it; a corrected transcription of a letter from John Andrews, which letter has been used by others to interpret partially incorrectly what happened in response to her 1772 Proposals, in the note for them; and two of her manuscripts previously unnoticed by scholars, with the variants of her poems to Mr. Pitkin and on Samuel Marshall. By providing this new edition, we again offer honor and respect to her and her works, through a much better book, collecting her now available works and putting them in even better contexts; and it is hoped that this new edition will help even more readers find it easier to own and to know her poetry and to understand and appreciate it in context. Written by a young black slave of Boston in the last third of the eighteenth century, her poems, though as a whole not exceptional in quality, are almost as good as any that were published by Americans at that time, even though they are the work of one who had been brought from Africa as a child and who knew no English when she arrived on these shores.

Even though by far we still do not know all we would like to know about Phillis Wheatley, and there are some things concerning her that yet are subject to interpretation, we do know a good bit more than was the case in 1966.[1] She was brought from west Africa[2] to Boston on the slave-trade

---

1. This very brief biographical sketch is distilled from almost twenty-five years of scholarly work on Phillis Wheatley. Some of it is indebted to my own research, in both primary and secondary sources; but the major part of it is indebted (for clues, sources, information, and clarification) to so many sources hither and yon that it would not be feasible to try to list them all here. Some of them are mentioned in the section on her reputation, but more important is the work of numerous scholars whose efforts have now taken us far beyond most of the older biographical sources about her, and whose contributions appear in the list of works near the end of this volume, especially Mukhtar Ali Isani and William H. Robinson. Indeed, special mention should be made of Robinson's very full and helpful essay "On Phillis Wheatley and Her Boston" in his *Phillis Wheatley and Her Writings* (pp. 3–69, hereafter cited as *Her Writings*) and the many notes to that volume.

This brief essay gives only an overview of the broad pattern and important aspects and events of Wheatley's life, as an introduction. In deciding what not to include, it was presumed that the reader will also read the rest of this volume and especially her works themselves and the notes to them. Therefore, an effort has been made to avoid repetition among the various parts of this volume, but also to provide adequate access and awareness at any given point through cross-reference and an index. Therefore, to know all that this book can provide about her life one must go beyond this sketch to the other sections of the book, particularly the chronologically arranged sections of her works and the notes to them, both for supplementing what is in this sketch and for what is not in it. All of that will provide a great deal of information about her and her works, but by no means all there is to know, which one can pursue further with the help of the list of works near the end of this volume (and what will appear in this active field after this book is published).

schooner *Phillis* (owned by Timothy Fitch and captained by Peter Gwin), arriving on July 11, 1761. Later that month the frail child, apparently about eight years old, was personally selected for purchase, through the Boston slave dealer John Avery, by Susanna Wheatley (1709–74), wife of a prominent Boston merchant, John Wheatley (1703–78), for the purpose of assisting Mrs. Wheatley during the remaining years of her life. The child was taken to the Wheatley home on King Street (in the heart of Boston's political, social, book-selling, printing and publishing, and other business activities), into a household of Mr. and Mrs. Wheatley, their eighteen-year-old twins, Mary and Nathaniel, and a few other slaves. Certainly this home and Boston were quite different from the world from which she had been taken. Boston's population was something over fifteen thousand, of which about one thousand were slaves and only about twenty were free blacks. The Wheatley family were members of the New South Congregational Church and firm Christian believers, and Susanna Wheatley was a quite active Christian. She became a great admirer of the Calvinist Methodist evangelist George White-field and engaged in missions work by correspondence, encouragement, accommodating visiting ministers in her home, and (at least occasionally) donations of money. John Wheatley's wholesale business was good and expanding, and he owned some residential real estate, some dockside warehouses, some wharfage, and the three-masted schooner *London Packet*, on which Phillis in 1773 would go to London and return. Increasingly, Nathaniel Wheatley (1743–83) became effective and active in the family business, gradually undertaking more and more responsibility in it. (Sometimes in the years ahead he would call upon the intelligence and good handwriting of Phillis to help him, dictating letters to her.)

Mary Wheatley (1743–78) became Phillis's friend and her tutor in religion and language, and Phillis proved to be an apt pupil with a quick mind, studying the Bible, English (language and literature), Latin (language and literature), history, geography, and Christian principles. Indeed, she gained as good an education as (and probably a better one than) most Boston women had, and her learning and abilities gradually gained the interest of a wider

---

Further notes will be given with this sketch when the directly pertinent complementary or supplementary information in this volume is not otherwise obvious (in poem titles, letter recipients, dates, and so on), or for what is not said elsewhere in this volume.

2. Although there has been some reference to her as a native of the Senegal-Gambia region, that cannot be substantiated. See her poem "To a Gentleman of the Navy" and note 37.

and wider segment of the community, especially after she began writing poetry at about the age of twelve, after having been in Boston only about four years. Apparently she became well acquainted with the Bible and with works of Horace, Vergil, Ovid, Terence, and various contemporary English poets, especially Pope (and through his translations, Homer), and probably Milton. Apparently, hers was an education that would have been prized in many a Boston family, even among its elite; and it was supplemented by contact with persons of status and education, both townspeople and visitors, particularly ministers, who tended to encourage her religious, intellectual, and literary development, apparently sometimes sharing their books with her[3] and occasionally even giving her books to be her own.[4] In her 1767 poem to the students at Harvard College, in nearby Cambridge, she made quite clear her ideas about the purposes for and the value of education (especially in relation to the strong Christian beliefs she had adopted), and the Wheatleys continued to aid and encourage her.

The location of the Wheatley home also provided another education, one about much that was going on in Boston, certainly a leading cultural and business center, experiencing growing friction with the British. From this house she would witness or easily hear much about many of the significant prerevolutionary actions of patriot protest and rebellion (and British response) taking place nearby, and to some of them she responded with early poems. However, despite various evidence in her poems and letters of her sympathy and friendliness (for philosophical and personal reasons, as well as because of local pride and business factors) with the patriots and with the Revolution as it developed, she also maintained loyalist and British friendships and contacts (for both personal and religious reasons). She was young, black, female, a slave, a pious Christian, clever, talented, and astute; and she understood the various aspects of her position in society and the need to be alert, decorous, open, careful, and nimble of mind. She also seems, above party and strife, to have been a loyal friend and a sincere Christian. She was proud to be American in such trying times, but for her there were many types of Americans—and, even more important, there were many types of Christians, all of them children of God, worthy of concern and help, and often capable of giving, and willing to give, help to her. Her principal loyalties were to God, herself, and the Wheatleys, in that order.

3. For example, see Shields, "Phillis Wheatley and Mather Byles."
4. See the note to her poem to Thomas Amory.

Once Phillis began writing poetry, apparently it was Susanna Wheatley who, in addition to providing Phillis social awareness and decorum, encouraged her publication in every way she could, including useful contacts, financial backing, and helping to publicize and distribute her works through letters and in information given to the newspapers and magazines. It is not strange, then, that in such a favorable context (despite her legal slavery) Phillis should have been able to develop her talent for and her inclinations toward poetry. She came to be treated almost as a member of the family and was assigned only very light housekeeping tasks, with permission and encouragement to ignore even these duties when she felt poetically inclined. It is to her credit that such preferential treatment did not make her haughty, but rather fostered in her a strong attachment, respect, and concern for the members of the Wheatley family. However, her fortunate circumstances apparently did not alienate the respect of her fellow slaves, even though she was accepted as a guest in the homes of some of the Wheatleys' friends and was allowed the unusual privilege of having both heat and light in her own room in the Wheatley home at night in deference to her relatively frail health and a memory apparently so untrustworthy as to make it desirable for her to commit her ideas and poems to paper as quickly as possible.

The first poem listed in her 1772 Proposals is dated there 1765, and apparently her earliest poem to be published was "On Messrs Hussey and Coffin" in December 1767 in Newport, Rhode Island. Her literary career can be traced through the poems, letters, and proposals for book publication (and here the notes for them) which give this book its reason for being, for they are why we are interested in knowing about Phillis Wheatley. After she had published a few more poems, including the 1770 poem on the death of George Whitefield which had given her some wide reputation, an attempt was made in 1772 to publish a volume of her poems in Boston. When it did not succeed, efforts for publication of a book of her poems were shifted to England. Meanwhile, Phillis's respiratory problems and generally frail health, which plagued her all of her life and sometimes had caused her to be sent to the country for awhile, were serious enough that a medical decision was made that she needed sea air. In 1771—the same year in which Mary Wheatley had married the Reverend John Lathrop (1740–1816) and Phillis on August 18 had become a member of the Congregationalist Old South Church (not the church of which the Wheatley family had been and still were members)—John Wheatley had retired and Nathaniel had bought his father's business holdings and part ownership of the family home. Now Nathaniel planned a trip to London in the spring of 1773 to expand certain aspects of the family business, and it was decided that Phillis would accompany him. They sailed from Boston in the family's ship *London Packet* on May 8 and arrived in London on June 17.

As plans for a London publication of her book had begun, the contents of the book had been altered by deletion of poems (particularly anti-British ones), addition of poems, and changing the titles and contents of some poems to be more appropriate for an English audience. (Her poem on leaving Boston, "A Farewel to America," was added after she reached London, and perhaps others were added then also.) Captain Robert Calef of the Wheatley-owned *London*, which made regular runs between Boston and London, had already served as the family's representative in first having the manuscript accepted for publication by Archibald Bell, a London bookseller emphasizing religious works (after the book's authenticity had been attested by John Wheatley and by prominent Boston citizens), and then in securing (through Bell) permission to dedicate the book to the Countess of Huntingdon, thereby elevating its status, the notice given of it, and its sales. The Samson Occom Papers at the Connecticut Historical Society contain a letter of March 29, 1773, from Susanna Wheatley to Occom that sheds some light not only on the progress of Phillis's book during this period but also on the state of affairs in the Wheatley household. The letter, which appears to be in Phillis's hand, indicates that she was not the only one with physical problems:

Rev'd Sir   Boston March 29. 1773

I have rec'd both your Letters, and was glad to hear you was so kindly entertain'd upon the Road. & got Safe home. I am glad to embrace this oppy by Dr. Downer [an insertion above this phrase reads: a particular acquaintance of mine & I wish you cou'd See him] who says he Shall come within 5 miles of you to buy Cattle. I importun'd him much to proceed the other 5 miles, but he says he can't go So far but would take care to forward the Letter. I wrote you before of the Sad accident which befel Mr. Wheatley from a fall, who remains in such a Situation, that he has never been able to get out of his Bed without the assistance of 5 or 6 men: and it is now near 5 weeks Since it happen'd.

I am very weak and low, my old indispositions returning upon me, and to Such a degree, as makes me doubtful whether I shall live to See you once more in this World. I must beg your earnest prayers to God for Mr. Wheatley and Me, that when Death comes he may not be a terror, but as the Outward Man decays the inward may be strong in Faith. Don't forget the injunctions upon you to pray for my Son, for when we are gone, I believe You'll be the only praying Freind he will have left.

I have rec'd a Letter from Capt Calef, he had waited upon Mr. Thornton but could not see him, therefore could not write anything upon our affairs; we expect him [Calef] every Day: My Son intends to go home [to England] with him. You Said you'd give him Letters to your freinds when he went. He would be glad as the roads are good and People will be travelling down this way You would Send them as Soon as a convenient opportunity presents. I have wrote to Mrs. Pierce but have not an Oppy to send it. I hope you'll not forget to write to the revd Mr. Moorhead. He is very kind to Mr. Wheatley & visits him almost every Day.—

The following is an Extract from Capt Calef's Letter dated Jan 7th. "Mr. Bell (the printer) Acquaints me that about 5 weeks ago he waited upon the Countess of Huntingdon with the Poems, who was greatly pleas'd with them, and pray'd him to Read them; and often would break in upon him and Say, "is not this, or that, very fine? do read another," and then expressd herself, She found her heart to knit with her and Questiond him much, whether She was Real without a deception? He then Convinc'd her by bringing my Name [Calef] in question. She is expected in Town in a Short time when we are both to wait upon her. I had like to forget to mention to you She is fond of having the Book Dedicated to her; but one thing She desir'd which She Said She hardly tho't would be denied her, that was to have Phillis' picture in the frontispiece. So that, if you would get it done it can be Engrav'd here, I do imagine it can be Easily done, and think would contribute greatly to the Sale of the Book. I am impatient to hear what the Old Countess Says upon the Occasion, & shall take the Earliest Opp,y of waiting upon her when She comes to Town."

My Husband, Sister and Son Join me in their Sincere love to you and your wife. Shall be glad to hear from you pr. first Opp.y and remain your affectionate Friend. Susanna Wheatley[5]

5. I believe that this is the first time that this letter has been published in full, though part of

A picture of Phillis was provided and was added to the book (and even was available for separate purchase).

Preparations for the book's publication continued while Phillis was in London, but it did not appear while she was there because a message that Mrs. Wheatley was seriously ill led to her returning to Boston earlier than she had intended. This change in plans also made her have to refuse an invitation to visit the Countess of Huntingdon in Wales and also forgo any chance of seeing the king. Nevertheless, she had met many people of interest and seen many sights while in London. She sailed near the end of July and arrived back in Boston on September 13. (Nathaniel stayed in England and in November married Mary Enderby, a member of a thriving mercantile family.) Phillis's *Poems on Various Subjects, Religious and Moral* was published in early September, received a good bit of attention in the London press via ads and notices, and was for sale in at least six places in London. It also was noticed and reviewed elsewhere in England and in Scotland. At some point between September 13 and October 18 Phillis Wheatley was freed by her master and legally was a slave no more.[6] It would be early January 1774 before she would receive copies of her book. When she did receive them she immediately began to market them in letters and in person (as she would for some years to come), a free person now and aware of the necessity to be more responsible for herself in every way. On March 3, 1774, Mrs. Wheatley died. Phillis apparently was allowed to remain in the Wheatley home with Mr. Wheatley as long as he was able to stay there.

While Phillis was in London, she had acquired a number of handsome books,[7] each of which (as far as we know) she inscribed and treasured. Later most of these books would be owned by the Pickman family of Salem, Massachusetts, who over the decades preserved them well. The Pickmans also owned two volumes of the works of William Shenstone, which now are at the Schomburg Center in New York. The inscriptions in them say that they were

----

the third paragraph and all of the fifth paragraph have been published several times previously. See the note to her 1772 Proposals. Robert Calef was the captain of the Wheatley-owned *London Packet*, which made regular runs between Boston and London. If Occom did provide letters to his English friends they would have been useful for meeting various important people engaged in the interests supported by the Countess of Huntingdon and John Thornton, both of whom helped support Occom's efforts, as did Lord Dartmouth. See Wheatley's letter to David Wooster, her poem to Mary Moorhead, and "A Note on the Text."

6. See her 1773 letter to David Wooster.

7. See her 1773 letter to David Wooster.

given to Phillis by Mary Eveleigh on September 24, 1774; and in the rare book collection of Duke University there is a copy of Wheatley's *Poems* given to Mary Eveleigh by Wheatley, perhaps in a face-to-face exchange, since Mary Eveleigh was in New England that summer. Earlier that year Mary Shubrick of Charleston, South Carolina, had married Nicholas Eveleigh of South Carolina, who became the first comptroller of the United States Treasury. When he died, Mary married Edward Rutledge of Charleston, a member of the first and second Continental Congresses, a signer of the Declaration of Independence, and a governor of South Carolina (his brother John was a member of the first and second Continental Congresses, a signer of the Constitution, and a member of the United States Supreme Court). The book of her poems which Wheatley had given to Mary Eveleigh also bears the bookplate of Edward Rutledge's law partner, Charles Cotesworth Pinckney of Charleston, another signer of the Constitution and an important figure in many facets of the government of the new nation, including being the Federalist candidate for president in 1804 and 1808. This is a heretofore unanticipated southern connection. Wheatley's poems were indeed known among the prominent families of Charleston during and after the Revolution, as well as among those of Boston, elsewhere in New England, New York, and Philadelphia.

During the British occupation of Boston, John Wheatley apparently left the city and its many difficulties and great confusion and went to Chelsea, to the north. John and Mary Lathrop went to Providence, Rhode Island. Apparently, Phillis joined them there, temporarily a refugee when she sent her poem about George Washington to him from Providence in October 1775, which eventually led to her visiting Washington at his headquarters in Cambridge the following year just before the British left Boston. The publication by others of her poem about Washington in the spring of 1776 gave her some continued visibility and notoriety. But when the war unsettled her residence and her life in general, though she continued writing, this woman, who had been exchanging poems with Royal Navy personnel as late as December 1774, would publish no more poems over the nine years before 1784, during which period her life departed further and further from the encouragement and security she had known during most of the time since her arrival in Boston as a child slave in 1761.

Eventually John Wheatley, Phillis, and the Lathrops returned to Boston, but life would never be the same for them again. John Wheatley died in

March 1778 and Mary on September 24 of the same year. Nathaniel had become a permanent resident of London in 1773 (he would die there in 1783). Phillis's British friends and many of her Tory friends had left, and by 1778 almost half of those who had signed the letter "To the PUBLICK" at the front of her book were dead. However, on April 1, 1778, Phillis married John Peters, about whom the surviving bits and pieces provide no clear picture except that he was free, thought well of himself, tried various occupations, often had financial difficulties, and remains an enigma. It appears that what began as a marriage which was financially and otherwise comfortable gradually deteriorated. She bore three children, and if a prayer that is said to have been found in her Bible is indeed hers, it is in part an expression of concern by her in June 1779 about childbirth.[8] During the early 1780s the Peters family lived for some time in the small town of Wilmington, Massachusetts, north-northwest of Boston. In the fall of 1779 and again in September 1784, proposals for a second book of Phillis's poems appeared in Boston periodicals, but in the difficult financial conditions following the war, the proposals failed.

As circumstances worsened, Phillis seems to have written little until 1784, after the family's return to Boston. Perhaps during these difficult years she sometimes even wondered whether she should have acquiesced to earlier suggestions that she go to Africa as a missionary, which she had rejected as impractical and not suited to one from the contexts to which she had become accustomed.[9] The reports of her circumstances in the period before her death on Sunday, December 5, 1784, seem to agree that her life was then at least one of hardships, personal, financial, and familial. Her children did not survive her; the last surviving one was buried with her. The year had begun with the funeral of Samuel Cooper, who had baptized her in 1771 as a girl of eighteen, and his death had started her publishing again after a nine-year hiatus. The year ended with her own death and her burial in a now lost grave. (Her husband apparently later secured her manuscripts and books and disposed of them to pay debts. At least that is what is written inside of and about

8. The prayer is at the Schomburg Center in New York and is very fragile and torn. Its provenance apparently is unknown, and it is not possible to tell whether Phillis composed it, copied it, or even wrote down what is there. The note above the prayer telling where it was found appears to be in the same handwriting as the prayer itself. It does seem to be from her period. (The prayer is printed in Robinson, *Her Writings*, p. 346, and Shields, *Collected Works*, p. 194.)

9. See her letters to Samuel Hopkins of May 6, 1774, and to John Thornton of October 30, 1774. Samson Occom also had favored such a possibility for her.

the copy of *Paradise Lost* that had been given to her in London and now is at Harvard.)

The last of her poems to be published during her lifetime had been another of the many poems about death which she had written over the almost two decades of her career as a poet (we have twenty such poems; the titles of at least nine others appear in her Proposals; of such poems in her first Proposals, only one was not included in her book, which included fourteen in its thirty-eight poems by her; her 1779 Proposals include at least nine poems on death [of which we have only one] among the thirty-three titles listed; of the forty-six poems we know were published during her lifetime, twenty were on death). Apparently her first poem dealt with death, and her last one may have also; certainly she felt that she needed to write a poem on Cooper's death that last year—it was expected of her, especially for him. She may even have been asked to write it, for people had certainly come to think of her in an elegiac context; and those who had read her last published poem (on death), in the September *Boston Magazine*, probably thought of it when they read of her death in the same magazine for December and found there also an "Elegy on the Death of a Late Celebrated Poetess," twenty-seven couplets memorializing her, by "Horatio." Like so many of her own poems, Horatio's had to have been written quickly, for the occasion, with little, if any, advance notice. Her community now once again thought of her in relation to death, but this time her own. Of course, one of the reasons for her many elegies was the prevalence of the genre in her place and time, and she was good at writing it. However, I suspect that the combination of her firm and forthright religious faith and a lively, pleasing, and gentle personality also contributed to her being called on so much for this service. She understood all of this and accepted it; in fact, one of her poems on death had been chosen as the example poem for yet another try for a second book of her poems only three months before her death. In her elegies, hope and love and faith usually firmly triumph over death—there can be no doubt about that. She knew what was wanted and needed in such circumstances. Her last poem published during her lifetime began:

> O DEATH! whose sceptre, trembling realms obey,
> And weeping millions mourn thy savage sway;
> Say, shall we call thee by the name of friend,
> Who blasts our joys, and bids our glories end?

but it ended with the admonition to the grieving parents of the child: "suppress the clouds of grief that roll, / Invading peace, and dark'ning all the soul." Such suppression of grief should be possible because of the consoling picture of heavenly happiness, free from earthly sin, which the poet presents as the dead infant's present experience.

In her short life, like most of her contemporaries, she had seen death much and thought of it often (in Africa, on the slave ship, in often harsh New England); even if it were not always welcome, it was no stranger and a part of life, readily available as a subject. Now her time had come. According to the obituaries, she was buried on Thursday, December 9: "Phillis Peters formerly Phillis Wheatley aged 31, known to the literary world by her celebrated miscellaneous poems. Her funeral is to be this afternoon, at 4 o'clock, from the house lately repaired by Mr. Todd, nearly opposite Dr. Bullfinch's at West Boston, where her friends and acquaintances are desired to attend" (from the *Boston Independent Chronicle and Universal Advertiser*). Periodicals across New England carried notices of her death, usually identifying her as "known to the literary world by her celebrated miscellaneous poems." At the end, she was to be known to all only for her writing, not as a former slave or in any other context, and I suspect that she would have liked Horatio's poem, which said in part:

> As if by heaven inspir'd, did she relate,
> The souls grand entrance at the sacred gate!
> And shall the honour, which she oft apply'd,
> To other's reliques, be to hers deny'd?
>   O that the muse, dear spirit! own'd thy art,
> To soften grief and captivate the heart,
> Then should these lines in numbers soft array'd
> Preserve thy mem'ry from oblivion's shade;
> But O! how vain the wish that friendship pays,
> Since her own volumes are her greatest praise.[10]

As a poet she would have been pleased with such last praise from another poet, who could best understand what the most important part of her life had

---

10. The *Boston Magazine*, December 1784, p. 630. The poem is reprinted in full in the 1966 edition of this volume, pp. xvii–xviii; and Kaplan, *Black Presence*, p. 169, has a photograph of the original printing of it.

been and why. She had published at least forty-six poems during her lifetime (not counting variants) and had written a good many more (of which nine have now been published). They and her book had been generally well received at home and abroad, and from various quarters she had been praised as a poet. In this regard, in her brief life of thirty-one years she had accomplished a great deal, despite circumstances that would have suggested that she either could not or would not be able to do so. Perhaps if she had lived longer or in more stable times, she would have accomplished even more.

☙

Phillis Wheatley was not the first black American to publish. For example, Briton Hammon preceded her with a fourteen-page pamphlet in 1760 (his only publication); and Jupiter Hammon published an eighty-eight-line broadside poem that same year but would not publish again until 1778 with a poem praising Wheatley after she was already well established as a poet. Certainly she was the first truly significant black American writer, and her 1773 book of poems was probably the first book—and certainly the first book of poetry—published by a black American. Her progress and development as a writer can be followed in her works in this volume, which are arranged with a chronological emphasis. There is no doubt that her 1773 book was her most significant publication. Though she also published poems as pamphlets and broadsides and in newspapers and magazines on both sides of the Atlantic, her book contains the core, the majority, and most of the best of the poems by her which we have. The printing and reprinting history of her book and individual poems and her letters is best followed in Robinson's *Phillis Wheatley: A Bio-Bibliography*, though much of that history is also found in this volume, especially in its notes and in "A Note on Text."

Phillis Wheatley is important historically, and her works are of importance and interest in their own right, especially in the contexts of her time and place—though some of them easily transcend both. Phillis Wheatley, however, was not a great poet. She was not really a poet in the classical Greek sense of maker, seer, creator, nor were her concerns really much with Ralph Waldo Emerson's meter-making argument or Edgar Allan Poe's rhythmical creation of beauty. She had aspirations, but she also knew her shortcomings;

and her concerns usually were not very august or pretentious. Her primary endeavor was to put into rhythmical, poetic forms thoughts that came to her or were brought to her attention by the crises and significant experiences of the people of Boston as they met life, death, and change, from day to day and year to year. Much of what she wrote of was not noted by the world outside of that place, though she occasionally did treat more general topics, particularly relating to the American Revolution, and did try for general pertinence while treating local particulars. While most successful writers strive for such pertinence, in her case it seems too often to have been a secondary goal that emerged most obviously when she revised a poem for a secondary audience, as in her revisions to make some of her Boston or American poems more acceptable, meaningful, or attractive to an English audience. Mostly, first of all she wrote for local audiences and local publication. When she occasionally did turn to more general emphases, she produced some of her best work, as in her hymns to morning and evening.

Nevertheless, on the basis of the poems that have survived her short career, she must be labeled as primarily an occasional poet, one interested in the clever crafting of verse. Such a craftsman is less concerned with selecting topics and creating patterns than with taking a given or obvious topic and fitting it skillfully to an already existing pattern. If she is a good craftsman, she is distinctive in her own right and possesses a gift that is worthy of the world's attention, if not its lasting praise. Such was Phillis Wheatley's gift and her concern, and she was a better craftsman of verse than most of the others attempting the same type of thing in America in the 1770s, a time and place that certainly produced more craftsmen than true poets. Her reward was in immediate praise—not that which echoes through the ages, but which appropriately sounds again from time to time.

Yet some of her poems reveal an exceptional being producing exceptional poetry. Most of her best work is in her nonoccasional poems, certainly in her more philosophic ones. In this regard it is interesting that various commentators have chosen different ones of her small body of poems to praise as the best,[11] and almost all writers on this subject favor to some degree "An Hymn to the Morning" and "An Hymn to the Evening." One would be amiss not to

11. For example, Loggins, *Negro Author*, p. 373 n. 75, calls "A Farewell to America" "perhaps her most graceful achievement in versification"; Benjamin Brawley, *The Negro in Literature and Art in the United States* (New York, 1934), p. 35, calls "On Imagination" her best poem; Redding, *To Make a Poet Black*, p. 12, favors "Thoughts on the Works of Providence."

place in this company "On Virtue" and "Goliath of Gath," and each reader might wish to include yet others; for in certain complete poems and in parts of others, Wheatley was able to surpass to a great degree what was at once both her great asset and her great liability—a favor for and a remarkable spontaneous ability to recreate the neoclassical poetic mode of Alexander Pope and his followers, in diction, meter, rhyme, and syntax. In such happy instances she avoided ordinary subject matter and clichés, using instead striking, appropriate poetic figures in pleasing form, which attracted both the mind and the ear. In these she was more than just an imitator, and she reflected a fortunate influence of the best neoclassicism. Unfortunately, she could not write this well consistently enough for such good poetry to dominate her work, leaving her to be known primarily as a prodigious imitator. For the same poet who wrote the exceptional poems mentioned above also wrote too many run-of-the-mill elegies.

Wheatley seems to have been fascinated with the device of invocation, and her mixing of Christian and classical in the many invocations in her poems (as well as in other parts of the poems) reflects the two greatest influences on her work, religion and neoclassicism. Indeed, this device and a few others remind one of Milton, though she certainly does not use them with his skill. For example, one can see the mixing of the Christian and the neoclassic in "To Mæcenas" and "On Recollection," and she apparently attempts the Miltonic device of vague exactness in measurement in "Thoughts on the Works of Providence" when she says of the sun's distance from the earth, "Of miles twice forty millions is his height." Vernon Loggins has pointed to the influence of English writers on her poems dealing with imagination, recollection, and virtue and to the influence of Milton on her hymns to the morning and evening and her poem about General Lee. He also suggests the specific influence of Gray on her poem on Whitefield's death and of Addison and Watts on "Ode to Neptune" and "Hymn to Humanity."[12]

The strongest influences on her work definitely were religion (including the Bible) and neoclassicism. Wheatley has been called a typical New Englander of the eighteenth century in her pious religious views, which seem to crop up everywhere. She is constantly aware of God, His Son, His beneficence, and His power; and she intends that her readers be aware of them too.

12. Loggins, *Negro Author*, pp. 24, 27, 373 n. 75. Also see the work of John Shields for other suggestions of possible influences on her poems by various English and classical writers.

Almost every poem produces a moral at some point, and the mood and message of her poem to the University of Cambridge sound as if it might have been issued from the pulpit. She had definite, if stereotyped, ideas that Heaven is a place of halos, angels, and reunion with God and His beloved; and she used these ideas with the same seriousness of purpose that surrounds her classical material. It is not at all strange that one who attended Boston's Old South Meeting House should show such firm Christian convictions and concern with the soul, and these facets of her personality made it very appropriate for friends to turn to her for elegies. In this vein we should not overlook her embellishment of biblical accounts in her poems based on Isaiah and on the encounter of David and Goliath (following in an old New England tradition and beginning a long tradition of black writers' embellishing the Bible). In both of these poems she adds to the biblical narrative and couches it in the neoclassical form that was familiar to her from the poems she read most—iambic pentameter couplets, opening invocation of the muse, panoramic view, attempted elevation of language (especially in the august speeches of the characters), eye-catching details, and hyperbole.

It is clear that Wheatley read as much as possible. Her favorite volumes are reported to have been the Bible, a collection of tales from mythology, and Pope's Homer; and we also know that she read at least some of the Latin authors in the original. Although some of her subject matter can be traced to classical origins outside of Pope's translations and although it is difficult to pinpoint clearly indisputable instances of his influence on her, it still is held by most who study her poems that Pope's translation of Homer was the single most important influence on her work. To that view I too subscribe.

Certainly Pope's relatively fixed formulas for neoclassical poetic music found a ready response in this young African girl's natural imitative ability. However, I suspect that what led her back to Pope time and time again was really Homer's grand narrative, which had retained its greatness of concept even when encased in a neoclassic gait. Wheatley was content to take the form she found because she could use it with ease, but it seems that in choosing Snider, Niobe, David and Goliath, Lee, and Washington, she was also feeling the tug of Homer's heroes on her impressionable young mind. I believe it was the classical world which kindled her talent and interest, though she used the neoclassical approach because of its vogue, its availability to her, and her ability to employ it. Her best-treated subject matter tends to support this view. There has been conjecture about what the rising romanticism would have done to her work if she had lived either later or longer. One may with more pertinence wonder what her poems would have been like had she been immersed in Milton sooner, for what he had done seems to suit her basic interests more. Phillis Wheatley was not the wasp that Pope was, but tended to be more compatible with Milton's Christian classicism and its view of life. It is interesting to note that in a poem dated December 5, 1774, she acknowledges her proper place to be but at the feet of such men as Newton and Milton and reserves for Milton, the grand creator—not for Pope, the translator—the title "British Homer."

On the other hand, even in the face of these facts and of the fact that her best poems seem to be those that depart most from neoclassical imitation, the strong influence of neoclassicism on her in her first, formative years as a poet may not have been a bad thing. It certainly gave her a respect for regularity (which even Wordsworth recognized as necessary), happened to be something she had a natural talent to reproduce (thus probably encouraging her in her own eyes and in the eyes of those who made Pope so popular), was readily available, and was usually not too deep philosophically. The pity is that events and her short career did not give her talent time enough to discover if it could broaden, mature, and diversify more.

The neoclassical influence also may have been responsible for the lack of much about Wheatley herself in her poems. She certainly leaves the reader of her poems only here and there aware of her being black and a slave. Saunders Redding has pointed out, "The Wheatleys had adopted her, but she had adopted their terrific New England conscience."[13] She was conscious of her color, but the degree to which she became a New Englander helped moderate this awareness during her most formative years. For her, Heaven was more to be desired than earthly toil, not so much for the physical rewards which many later slaves would emphasize, but rather for its spiritual rewards. Some seem to chide her for her apparent unconcern over slavery in a Boston where it was obviously much discussed, but it was probably better for her poetry that whatever feelings she had about this subject were sublimated in most of her poetry (it emerges more in her letters).

The few thoughts on Africa and slavery's effect on her that are included in her poems are interesting. Her individual situation did not equip her for abolitionism—indeed, her real and necessary poetic patron was the Wheat-

13. Redding, *To Make a Poet Black*, p. 9.

leys, particularly Susanna Wheatley. She came to America too young for that hard experience not to be modified by her being part of the Wheatley household. But she clearly was not entirely unmindful of blacks' delegated place in the popular mind of the time. She makes good use of this knowledge in her poems to the Earl of Dartmouth, to the University at Cambridge, and on Wooster's death, almost turning it to advantage to strengthen her points. She surely was aware that much of her own notoriety was the result of her work's being usually labeled as that of an African (and she is careful to so call herself in several poems and to entitle one poem "To S. M., A Young African Painter, On Seeing His Works").

In her particular case, she seems to have viewed the captivity that brought her to Boston and to the Wheatleys as not entirely unfortunate. Her poem to Dartmouth speaks of "seeming cruel fate" which snatched her "from Afric's fancied happy seat," and she shows concern primarily for the sorrow of her parents. But she immediately makes it clear that she does not endorse slavers, slavery, or the usual results of slavery. Her poem "On Being Brought from Africa to America" sees the event as fortunate because it allowed her to be a Christian, and the poem almost sounds like the product of missionary propaganda (though she specifically refused to be a missionary to Africa). In this same vein she speaks to the students at the University at Cambridge of her not enjoying the advantages they have because of her having so recently come from a land of "errors" and "gloom," brought forth to safety by the "gracious hand" of God. However, in her poem dated December 5, 1774, to the "Gentleman in the Navy," she seems quite taken with western Africa as a place of peace, beauty, and plenty, but this may be simply a reaction to his poem to which this is a reply. At any rate, in "To Mæcenas" she makes it clear that she thinks the muses ought to come to her aid and not give Terence alone claim to being an inspired African poet. (Of course, here is reflected the narrowness of her knowledge.) Incidentally, this also affords us one of the few instances when we learn anything of Phillis herself from her poems.

Although she did not write much of slavery, certain of her poems do reflect an awareness of current events affecting the society in which she lived. For example, see her poems to the king and to the Earl of Dartmouth and her poems on Snider, Lee, Wooster, and Washington and the poems *Liberty and Peace* and "America."

In her worst poems, Wheatley falls prey to the clichés of neoclassical poetic diction, to wrenched syntax, to trite devices, to runaway rhythm, and to an overemphasis on religion. These appear most frequently in her occasional verses. Over one-third of her extant poems are elegies. Loggins points out the long tradition of elegies in Boston and that hers too are impersonal and artificial in feeling, with much use of hyperbole, overuse of personification, and pompousness of ornamentation.[14] Not only is neoclassical tradition to blame here, but also the fact that most of these were written for the occasion, to console loved ones and embellish the memory of the departed. Yet sometimes a genuine note of understanding and concern is found in her elegies, especially for persons who had played a part in her own life, at which times one feels even more the strain resulting from her poetic form. Sometimes her good product is found close by her poor one in the same poem. In "To a Lady and Her Children, On the Death of Her Son and Their Brother," she speaks of the mother's realization of the death: "Th' unhappy mother sees the sanguine rill / Forget to flow, and nature's wheels stand still." However, later in the same poem we are rudely accosted by the cliché and the wrenched syntax of the following: "No more in briny show'rs, ye friends around, / Or bathe his clay, or waste them on the ground." In her better work, she is much more in control of the syntax and rhythm and employs them with unobjectionable diction and figures, if not always fresh or new ones. An example is found in "Thoughts on the Works of Providence," in which she speaks of dawn and sunset: "Or when the morning glows with rosy charms, / Or the sun slumbers in the ocean's arms," and speaks of God "Which round the sun revolves this vast machine, / Though to his eye its mass a point appears," and of the moon, which "True to her course th' impetuous storm derides, / Triumphant o'er the winds, and surging tides." Or note the opening lines of "An Hymn to the Evening": "Soon as the sun forsook the eastern main / The pealing thunder shook the heav'nly plain; / Majestic grandeur! From the zephyr's wing, / Exhales the incense of the blooming spring. / Soft purl the streams, the birds renew their notes, / And through the air their mingled music floats." These are not great lines, but they are good ones.

Of course, her favorite poetic form was the heroic couplet of English neoclassicism. All of her extant poems employ this form, with six exceptions.[15] There are occasional interspersed three-line rhyme sequences, and

14. Loggins, *Negro Author*, p. 22.

15. The exceptions are "On Virtue," which is free verse (although she may have intended it for blank verse) ending with a heroic couplet; "To the University of Cambridge," which is primarily blank verse; "Ode to Neptune," which has two sections of six lines each, with each sec-

"An Answer to the Rebus" departs from the heroic couplet in its last four lines to employ iambic tetrameter. She attempted her most complicated formal poetic pattern in "An Hymn to Humanity," a poor poem; but her one use of ballad stanza was quite successful. However, she apparently found that the heroic couplet came easier, and she did not abandon it in her later poems.

Wheatley only occasionally used such devices as alliteration and onomatopoeia, and they were not significant in her poetic method. However, as with good neoclassicism, the caesura was important as she constantly attempted not just iambic pentameter couplets but the heroic couplet employed by Alexander Pope. Unfortunately, her work was subject to the uncertainties and irregularities of eighteenth-century English spelling and punctuation, and she was too dependent on elision for regulating her meter. She also rhymes in the eighteenth-century manner—for example, "join" with "divine." Nevertheless, the ear will not excuse her occasional lack of consistency in tense, especially noticeable in her poem on Goliath. If she were responsible for the order of the poems in the 1773 edition (which is somewhat chronological in relation to date of composition), we might note that that order is basically a good one. She seems to have preferred the medium-length poem of from forty to fifty lines, with the eight-line poems "On Friendship" and "On Being Brought from Africa to America" being her shortest and her two narrative poems on Goliath and on Niobe being her longest, each having 224 lines. Wheatley seldom employed her talents in narrative; but she was fairly good at it, sustaining the reader's interest with a good mixture of details, action, speech, and pacing.

For a good number of her poems we have variant versions (sometimes more than one) which show that she could improve the diction, poetic figures, syntax, rhythm, tone, rhyme, and general quality of her work through both changes and deletions, sometimes for different audiences. However,

---

tion having four lines of iambic tetrameter couplets, followed by one heroic couplet—with a third six-line section that is mostly iambic tetrameter and has rhyme of ababcc; "An Hymn to Humanity," which has six sections of six lines each, with each section having first an iambic tetrameter couplet, followed by an iambic trimeter line, followed by an iambic tetrameter couplet, followed by an iambic trimeter line that rhymes with the third line of the section; "A Farewell to America," which is in ballad stanza (but the newspaper version, perhaps because of space considerations, is not separated into the usual four-line sections—this is the only one of these six poems that saw newspaper publication); and "An Elegy on leaving," which has seven sections, with iambic pentameter lines, with rhyme of abab in each section (with second and fourth lines indented).

basically Wheatley was a spontaneous poet, not a laborious one. Therefore, the general regularity of her meter is striking.

Her poetic career began early in her life and was sporadic, brief, and in its later stages apparently difficult. Nevertheless, in the community where she lived, Wheatley practiced the art of poetry and was known there for that practice; and Boston in the years before and after the American Revolution was still the literary capital of America, as well qualified to produce, cultivate, encourage, and judge a poet as any community in the land. In part because she was young, in part because she was female, and in part because she was black and nominally a slave, her work has too often been overpraised. On the other hand, she also has been too often dealt with unfairly or not at all because of this overpraising and the reasons for it. The proper position lies somewhere between these extremes, for her work definitely does have some literary merit, despite its obvious shortcomings. It becomes even more significant in any literary-historical or cultural consideration of it.

Her poems are certainly as good as or better than those of most of the poets usually included and afforded fair treatment in a discussion of American poetry before 1800, and this same evaluation holds true when she is compared with most of the minor English poets of the eighteenth century who wrote in the neoclassical tradition. Finding our early literary soil generally unfit for real poetry, Moses Coit Tyler in his *A History of American Literature, 1607–1765* and *The Literary History of the American Revolution* does, however, treat many "verse-writers," especially those of New England. In comparing his appraisals of these writers, as frank and blunt as the statements are, one still cannot help but conclude that his harsh treatment of Phillis Wheatley in the latter volume is unjust. For she certainly deserves as much praise, or as little blame (depending on whether one is measuring by a relative standard or by an absolute one, as Tyler was), as such early poets as Thomas Morton, Benjamin Tompson, Thomas Godfrey, Nathaniel Evans, Nathaniel Niles, Jonathan Odell, Joseph Stansbury, Michael Wigglesworth, Ebenezer Cook, Mather Byles,[16] and perhaps Francis Hopkinson, John

16. Because Byles offers such an apt comparison with Wheatley, one becomes especially impatient with the treatment given him by various authors and editors. (See the Facsimile Text Society edition of Mather Byles, *Poems on Several Occasions*, with introduction by C. Lennart Carlson [New York, 1940].) Similarities extend to volume title, preface, general subject matter, age, and place (Boston, where his volume appeared in 1744). One has only to compare the poem of each on the subject of David and Goliath to note Wheatley's superior imagination, so-

Trumbull, Timothy Dwight, Joel Barlow, and Anne Bradstreet (though Wheatley is not as sustained and consistent as these latter five, her best work certainly is worthy of inclusion with their best). There is no doubt whatever that she was the best black American author before 1800 and the best black American poet until Frances Ellen Watkins Harper in the middle of the nineteenth century.

As I have said, she was not a great poet; but in her way, in her time, and in her locale, she was a fairly good writer of poems generally in imitation of the neoclassical mode made popular by Alexander Pope. She deserves our consideration by either absolute or relative standards—and not just because of her youth, her sex, or her race. As Perry Miller and countless others have reminded us and shown us, it is indeed a mistake to think there is nothing worth reading in American literature before Washington Irving—and this applies to black authors as well, for there stands Phillis Wheatley of Boston, not one of the very best, but far from one of the worst of the many who, in spite of the struggles of establishment, felt the influence of the muses in colonial America.

The reader who wishes to pursue further critical approaches to and evaluations of Wheatley's poems is referred to the list of works near the end of this volume. (Note Robinson's edition of *Critical Essays* and his "On Wheatley's Poetry" in his *Her Writings*.) For various aesthetic emphases (both theoretical and applied) especially see some works by Barksdale, Cook, Holder, Isani, Rigsby, Scruggs, Shields, and Sistrunk. For critical focuses on other than aesthetic concerns in her poems (including some racial, religious, and feminist emphases) especially see some works by Burroughs, Collins, Gates, Huddleston, Isani, Jordan, Levernier, Mason, Matson, O'Neale, Rogal, Smith, and Stetson.

---

phistication, and general poetic ability. She is in command of her subject and is not just adapting a biblical account. Yet most general accounts or collections of early American poetry do not acknowledge the superiority of her poetry to that of Byles. (Shields's "Phillis Wheatley and Mather Byles" has appeared since the first publication of this note in 1966.)

On the Reputation
of Phillis Wheatley, Poet

For several obvious reasons, there has been a continuing, periodically emerging interest in Phillis Wheatley and her works since their first publication. Some indication of this interest can be seen in information given in the notes in this volume, in the Introduction to it, and in "A Note on the Text" (particularly concerning republication of her works). Although there now is Robinson's book-length biobibliographical survey of Phillis Wheatley over the decades, it seems appropriate still to include in the new edition of this volume a by no means exhaustive essay, but a selective, although representative, quick survey of some of the highlights of her reception and continuing reputation over the decades, particularly those of the nineteenth century. This survey will enable the reader of this volume to know something of the pattern of her reputation since the 1770s, especially as many of the eighteenth- and nineteenth-century critiques still are not easy for the average reader to know of or to obtain—much less to see in relation to each other (though Robinson's *Critical Essays* does include a good sampling of them).

A special type of interest in Wheatley is early reflected in the note that usually appeared with her 1770 poem on Whitefield, pointing out that she was a "Servant Girl, of 17 years of Age . . . but 9 Years in this Country from Africa"; and though they were never of the very best quality, her poems soon were good enough to arouse the suspicions of those who did not know her. Therefore, a note to the public appears in the front of her 1773 volume to assure the reader that these are indeed the works of the Wheatleys' slave Phillis. This note was signed by eighteen of "the most respectable Characters in *Boston*, that none might have the least Ground for disputing." The eighteen include the governor and lieutenant governor, seven ministers, and John Wheatley. By the time of her death in 1784 at the age of thirty-one, she was spoken of as talented, celebrated, and a poet.

Among the early tributes to Phillis Wheatley was the second known poem by America's first published black poet, Jupiter Hammon. The poem, *An Address to Miss Phillis Wheatly* [sic], *Ethiopian Poetess, in Boston, who came from Africa at eight years of age, and soon became acquainted with the gospel of Jesus Christ*, was published as a broadside dated Hartford, August 4, 1778.[1] It was twenty-one stanzas of four lines each, printed in double column, at the end of which was an acknowledgment that the poem had been published "by the Author, and a number of his friends, who desire to join with him in their best regards to Miss Wheatly [sic]." Hammon admonishes her to thank God for all the special things He has done for her, and he suggests: "Come you, Phillis, now aspire, / And seek the living God, / So step by step thou mayst go higher, / Till perfect in the word."

It is especially interesting to note how Wheatley's poems have been treated by some of the reviewers for periodicals. The 1773 edition was quickly reviewed by the *London Magazine: Or, Gentleman's Monthly Intelligencer*, a prominent periodical of the time, which had published one of her poems in March of the preceding year. In the September 1773 number (42:456) it quite fairly said:

> These poems display no astonishing power of genius; but when we consider them as the production of a young untutored African, who wrote them after six months [sic] casual study of the English language and of writing, we cannot suppress our admiration of talents so vigorous and lively. We are the more surprised too, as we find her verses interspersed with the poetical names of the ancients, which she has in every instance used with strict propriety. As our readers may be curious enough to wish for a specimen of this Afric Muse's poetry, we subjoin the following ["Hymn to the Morning"].

This was one of the earliest critical notices of her book and was one of the longer portions of that month's section of "An Impartial Review of New Publications."

In December of 1773, the *Monthly Review* of London was less concerned with the poems than with the fact that their author was a Negro slave, saying, among other things, the following (49:457-59):

> If we believed, with the ancient mythologists, that genius is the offspring of the sun, we should rather wonder that the sable race have not been

1. Kaplan, *Black Presence*, p. 172, has a photograph of this broadside in its entirety.

more distinguished by it, than express our surprize at a single instance. . . .

The poems written by this young negro bear no endemial marks of solar fire or spirit. They are merely imitative; and, indeed, most of those people have a turn for imitation, though they have little or none for invention. . . .

She has written many good lines, and now and then one of superior character has dropped from her pen. . . .

We are much concerned to find that this ingenious young woman is yet a slave. The people of Boston boast themselves chiefly on their principles of liberty. One such act as the purchase of her freedom, would, in our opinion, have done them more honor than hanging a thousand trees with ribbons and emblems.

This was a major review that month (not in the "Monthly Catalogue"), approximately one and one-half pages long, in the periodical that has been called "the earliest Review of importance in English literature."[2] (Of note are the review's reflections of the conflicts between England and the colonies and of predominant stereotype ideas about blacks.

The 1834 *Memoir and Poems of Phillis Wheatley* brought forth more periodical notice (as well as a thirty-six-page *Memoir of Phillis Wheatley* by B. B. Thatcher, also published in Boston during the same year). On March 22, 1834 (4: 47), the *Liberator*, an abolition weekly published in Boston, praised the memoir and reminded its readers of the prior publication of most of the poems in its own pages. (Perhaps this publication of the poems by the *Liberator* had been partly responsible for the preparation of the 1834 volume.) It called Phillis the "famous African poetess" and said that her poems "are alike extraordinary, both as to their origin and merit; and deserve a place eminently conspicuous in every private and public library."

The *New-England Magazine* for April 1834 carried a short notice of the *Memoir and Poems* in its "Literary Notices" section (6:344): "This is a republication from the earliest edition, which has now become very rare, of one of the most remarkable works, in some points of view, which the literary world have ever seen—the poems of an African Slave!" After a few more remarks, the notice ends with Phillis's hymn to the morning as a suitable example of "the literary character of these compositions."

2. Walter Graham, *English Literary Periodicals* (New York, 1930), p. 209.

In May 1834, the *Christian Examiner*, a Unitarian magazine published in Boston, carried a five-and-one-half page review of the *Memoir and Poems*. "Contemporary and recent commentators agree that the *Christian Examiner* (1824–1869) contained some of the outstanding literary criticism in an American periodical during its four decades."[3] William Charvat says that it "was the most important [American] magazine of the years 1830–1835. . . . Here was unitarianism at its intellectual best. Here too were the critical standards of the day warmed into life and vitality."[4] This particular review was written by William Joseph Snelling of Boston, a journalist, satirist, poet, author of books in prose, and later an editor of the *Boston Herald*. Snelling's review is honest and interesting, the product of both the reformer and the man of letters. Its first three and one-quarter pages are a summary of and comment on the memoirs; then:

> We turn to her poetry. It seems to us respectable, though not of a high order. Yet many of the white writers of this country have enjoyed a transient reputation on much less intrinsic merit! What proportion of the rhymesters, who enrich our newspapers and magazines with their effusions, can write half so well as Phillis Wheatley? She had no assistance. . . . Accordingly, we find some ill-constructed and harsh and prosaic lines, but not so many by half as in the verses of most of her contemporary American poets. That her lines are full of feeling, no one will deny who has read the extract we have already given. That she had considerable originality will be apparent from her epitaph on Dr. Sewall [which follows]. [16:172.]
>
> Phillis Wheatley, we think, was a precocious genius, destined very rapidly to acquire a certain degree of excellence, and there to stop for ever [sic]. As mediocrity, or even moderate merit in song, is never tolerated, we dare not hope that her works will ever be very popular or generally read; for readers never take into account the disadvantages the writer may have labored under. It is not just that they should. . . . It is little consolation to him who has wasted his time and money in buying

3. Frances Pedigo, "Critical Opinions of Poetry, Drama, and Fiction, in the *Christian Examiner*, 1824–1869" (Ph.D. dissertation, University of North Carolina, Chapel Hill, 1953), p. 301.

4. William Charvat, *The Origins of American Critical Thought, 1810–1835* (New York, 1961), p. 198.

and reading a wretched production, to be told that it was written by an apprentice or a woman. We do not mean by this to express any disapprobation of the publication before us, but merely to say that, singular as its merits are, they are not of the kind that will command admiration. Still the work will live,—there will always be friends enough of liberty and of the cause of negro improvement not to let it sink into oblivion, and many will desire to possess it as a curiosity. . . . As a friend of the African and of mankind at large, we are happy to record our tribute of praise in behalf of one who was an honor and ornament to her race and her kind. [P. 174.]

Among the other things he says, Snelling concludes that "In the midst of obloquy attached to her hue, she reached an intellectual eminence known to few of the females of that day, and not common even now" (p. 174). The most important thing about this review is its appearance. But though it is sympathetic, it finds her poetry wanting when judged against absolute standards.

A fourth review of the *Memoir and Poems* appeared in New York in the *Knickerbocker* in August 1834. It was a ten-and-one-half-page unsigned lead article, entitled "African Anecdotes." It begins: "This is a timely republication of a work [the poems], which has now become so rare, even among the bibliopoles, that it is much to be doubted whether half a dozen copies of it might be found in the country" (4:85). After dealing with several other matters, the reviewer comments on the poems:

The style of the poems is evidently formed, in a great degree, after that of Pope, a writer now in the golden age of his fame; and, indeed, we not unfrequently meet with passages which remind us of the model so closely, that we cannot but think the original editor or printer failed to do the writer the common justice of attaching the usual marks of quotation to matter, here and there, that has very much the air of an extract. [A few lines of the "Address to Imagination" are quoted.]

These lines . . . indicate, perhaps as sufficiently as any thing we can either cite or say, the cultivation of her literary taste and the development of her poetical genius. It must, of course, be remembered under what circumstances she commenced her career [elaborated for five lines]. While passages of her productions, then are characterized by the beautiful and even sublime expression of fine thoughts, and while they are distinguished throughout by an eminent degree of that harmony for which her race are supposed to have a peculiar sensibility, it is surely to be wondered at, if, on the whole, they should rather suggest to the philosophical mind what human, and what African nature is, and what it may accomplish under certain problematical circumstances, than furnish an intrinsic gratification to the mature taste, or a luxury to the mere lover of poetry. [P. 91.]

He then speaks of the anecdotes about the inspired nature of the writing of the poems and cites "the artlessness, in one sense of the word, which is for the most part a recommendation of the poems." This artlessness he speaks of further, not in a derogatory way, as being the result of the poetess' lack of training, so that she "merely *enjoyed*, rather than *employed*, her inventive faculties" (p. 92). Approximately one page of the review is devoted to the poems. This review, also, finds the poems wanting; yet it is willing to couch its few passing remarks of praise in very complimentary terms. The review is almost too apologetic, and yet the book was chosen for review in a prominent place in the magazine, primarily for its biographical-sociological interests. Indeed, it has been contended that this book may have been reviewed because of an absence of abolition sentiment in the poems at a time when generally few works by black authors were being reviewed by major American magazines.[5] After all, the work reviewed presented posthumously the poems of a female black author with some reputation, whose apparent views generally were not in conflict with those of conservative minds, while her deeds and demonstrated intellect appealed to the more liberal minds of the time.

During the abolition decades, Phillis Wheatley, of course, was often brought up in publications and discussions by both sides. There was also significant interest in her on the part of the Massachusetts Historical Society during the 1860s, which resulted in the printing of several important items in the society's *Proceedings* for 1863–64: the first printing of her poem on General Lee (October 1863, 7:165–67); the first printing of her letters to Obour Tanner (November 1863, 7:267–79); Nathaniel B. Shurtleff's short account of her (November 1863, 7:270–72n.) reprinted from the *Boston Daily Advertiser* of December 21, 1863; and in the *Proceedings* for 1864–65,

---

5. Julian D. Mason, Jr., "The Critical Reception of American Negro Authors in American Magazines, 1800–1885" (Ph.D. dissertation, University of North Carolina, Chapel Hill, 1962), pp. 64–65.

the first reprinting of her 1779 Proposals (September 1865, 8:461–62). The letters also were printed separately in 1864.

In July 1884, a fifteen-page article on Phillis by Father John R. Slattery of St. Joseph's Seminary in Baltimore appeared in the *Catholic World*[6] as a sequel to his earlier article on the black mathematician Benjamin Banneker. Most of the article is biographical, but some of it deals with her writing, and there is frequent extensive quotation of her poetry. At one point he says, "The reader will be astonished, no doubt, that a slave-girl should write so many poems from the fifteenth to the twentieth year of her age—a time of life when most girls are given to all giddiness. The lofty sentiments of her mind are still more wonderful when Phillis' race is remembered" (p. 495).

On March 6, 1897, the *Literary Digest* of New York carried an item entitled "Negro Poets" (14:550–51), which had been generated by the recent publication of a volume of verse by Paul Dunbar. The article notes that John Edward Bruce had written in the Boston *Evening Transcript* about black writers before Dunbar. Bruce is quoted:

> The first negro poet to attract the attention of the American public, and whose genius and cleverness won her an international reputation and the friendship of the most distinguished people of her day, on both sides of the Atlantic, was Phillis Wheatly [sic]. . . . No article on negro poets would be complete without some reference to the remarkable young woman, who in that early day did so much to destroy the general impression that the negro was incapable of the higher intellectual development. [P. 550.]

However, from the beginning of her notoriety, attention to Phillis was by no means limited to periodicals. She was cited by numerous writers. Benjamin Rush in 1773 spoke of her: "There is now in the town of Boston a Free Negro Girl, about 18 years of age, who has been but 9 [sic] years in the country, whose singular genius and accomplishments are such as not only do honor to her sex, but to human nature. Several of her poems have been printed, and read with pleasure by the public."[7] This was probably before the

---

6. John R. Slattery, "Phillis Wheatley, the Negro Poetess," *Catholic World* 39 (July 1884): 484–98.

7. Benjamin Rush, *An Address To the Inhabitants of the British Settlement in America, upon Slave-Keeping* (Boston, 1773), p. 2n.

1773 volume of poems appeared, but Rush apparently continued his good opinions after seeing that volume.[8] (Notice that Wheatley listed a letter to Dr. Rush in her 1779 Proposals.) Voltaire, in a 1774 letter to Baron Constant de Rebecq, said of her: "Fontenelle avait tort de dire qu'il n'y aurait jamais de poëtes chez les Nègres: l y a actuellement une Négresse qui fait de très-bons vers anglais."[9]

Another who was ready to say there had never been a Negro poet was Thomas Jefferson, who included Wheatley in the contention; but he also was answered. When he published his *Notes on Virginia* in 1784, "Query XIV" contained the following:

Misery is often the parent of the most affecting touches in poetry. Among the blacks is misery enough, God knows, but no poetry. Love is the peculiar oestrum of the poet. Their love is ardent, but it kindles the senses only, not the imagination. Religion, indeed, has produced a Phyllis Whately [sic]; but it could not produce a poet. The compositions published under her name are below the dignity of criticism. The heroes of the Dunciad are to her, as Hercules to the author of that poem.[10]

(George Washington had been more generous. See his letter in the note to her poem to him.) Gilbert Imlay defended Phillis against Jefferson's charge:

I will transcribe part of her Poem on Imagination, and leave you to judge whether it is poetical or not. It will afford you an opportunity, if you have never met with it, of estimating her genius and Mr. Jefferson's judgment; and I think, without any disparagement to him, that by comparison, Phillis appears much the superior. Indeed, I should be glad to be informed what white upon this continent has written more beautiful lines. [Followed by twenty lines of the poem.][11]

In 1808, in his *De la littérature des nègres*, the noted Frenchman Henri Grégoire very much regretted that such an esteemed man as Jefferson had

---

8. See William Dickson, *Letters on Slavery* (London, 1789), pp. 76–77, 187.
9. Quoted in Edward Derbyshire Seeber, *Anti-Slavery Opinion in France during the Second Half of the Eighteenth Century* (Baltimore, 1937), p. 57 n. 54.
10. Thomas Jefferson, *The Writings of Thomas Jefferson*, ed. Albert Ellery Bergh (Washington, D.C., 1907), 2:196.
11. Gilbert Imlay, *A Topographical Description of the Western Territory of North America* (New York, 1793), 1:185–86.

made such remarks. In his account of Wheatley, he says that he will refute Jefferson with the judgment of the public as shown by the publication of the 1773 volume and with its contents themselves, several of which he includes.[12] In 1810, Samuel Stanhope Smith, president of the College of New-Jersey and a member of the American Philosophical Society, declared, "But I will demand of Mr. Jefferson, or any other man who is acquainted with American planters, how many of those masters could have written poems equal to those of Phillis Whately [sic]?"[13]

In 1878, Jefferson's remarks were still reverberating, and in the November–December 1878 issue of the *North American Review* there was an article by James Parton entitled "Antipathy to the Negro." In the course of the article Parton mentions Jefferson's views on the creativity of blacks and then continues:

> It was this passage in his "Notes on Virginia" that appears to have led a French author (M. Grégoire) to compile a work, in 1808, on the "Literature of the Negroes," a copy of which he sent to Mr. Jefferson during his presidency. . . . Unfortunately the bishop's book possessed no value, because he omitted to ascertain whether his literary negroes were of pure or mixed blood and his desire to make out a case for the Negro made him blindly credulous. The colored poet, Phillis Wheatley, had her admirers a hundred years ago in Boston, where her volume can still occasionally be found. We have carefully looked over it, and cannot deny the justice of Jefferson's remarks upon it. She was a poet very much as "Blind Tom" is a musician, her verses being the merest echo of the common jingle of her day. . . . A fatal facility of imitation stands in the way of this interesting race, and we cannot fairly deny that facts give support to the opinion of an inherent mental inferiority. It is ninety years since Jefferson published his "Notes," and we cannot yet name one negro of pure blood who has taken the first, the second, the third, or the tenth rank in business, politics, art, literature, scholarship, science, or philosophy. To the present hour the negro has contributed nothing to the intellectual resources of man. [127:487–88.]

12. Grégoire, *An Enquiry*, pp. 44–45, 236–41.

13. Samuel Stanhope Smith, *An Essay on the Causes of the Variety of Complexion and Figure in the Human Species* (New-Brunswick and New York, 1810), p. 269n.

In July 1880, the *National Quarterly Review* had a twenty-six-page review article by R. T. Greener, the first black to graduate from Harvard College (1870), where he had won the Boylston Prize in oratory twice and the Bowdoin Prize for a dissertation.[14] Parton's article, Jefferson's writings, and Grégoire's book were reviewed together for the primary purpose of pointing out the ignorance of most Americans concerning the accomplishments of blacks. In the process, he cites Imlay's remarks concerning Wheatley (61: 173–74). (Of course, Greener was not the first black person to refute Jefferson's views of the abilities of blacks, but his was one of the more urbane of the written refutations and one which was assured a somewhat unique audience.)

Some other eighteenth- and nineteenth-century acknowledgments of Wheatley and her poems (usually favorable) are to be found in the following sources: Thomas Clarkson, *An Essay on the Slavery and Commerce of the Human Species, Particularly the Africans* (London, 1788) (e.g., p. 122: "this observation, that if the authoress *was designed for slavery*, . . . the greater part of the inhabitants of Britain must lose their claim to freedom."); Thomas Branagan, *A Preliminary Essay, On the Oppression of the Exiled Sons of Africa* (Philadelphia, 1804) (e.g., p. 102: "Are not her poetical compositions . . . excellent, not only for their piety, but their poetical beauties?"); Joseph Brown Ladd, "The Prospects of America" (a poem in which she is praised along with Freneau and Barlow), *The Literary Remains of Joseph Brown Ladd*, compiled by Elizabeth Haskins (New York, 1832), p. 35; Lydia M. Child, *An Appeal in Favor of That Class of Americans Called Africans* (Boston, 1833), p. 171; Abigail Mott, *Biographical Sketches and Interesting Anecdotes of Persons of Color* (New York, 1838), pp. 15–18; *Chambers' Miscellany of Useful and Entertaining Tracts* (Edinburgh, 1846), vol. 7, no. 63; Caroline May, *The American Female Poets* (Philadelphia, 1848), p. 39; *Wheatley, Banneker, and Horton* (Boston, 1849), compiled by William G. Allen, containing a memoir of Wheatley, a number of her poems, and Washington's letter to her; Evert A. and George L. Duyckinck, *Cyclopedia of American Literature* (New York, 1856), 1:368 (favorably compares her with Anne Bradstreet and says she is a respectable follower of Pope); Benjamin J. Lossing, *Eminent Americans* (New York, 1881) (she is one of the few women treated); Justin Winsor, ed., *The Memorial History of Boston* (Boston, 1881), 3:147 and 4:339; Phebe A. Hanaford,

---

14. For a summary of the various achievements of this distinguished gentleman, see Richard Bardolph, *The Negro Vanguard* (New York, 1959), p. 88; or the *Dictionary of American Biography*.

Daughters of America (Boston, 1883) p. 37; Edmund Clarence Stedman and Ellen M. Hutchinson, eds., *A Library of American Literature from the Earliest Settlement to the Present Time* (New York, 1892), vol. 3; Charles F. Richardson, *American Literature, 1607–1885* (New York, 1895), 2:9 (e.g.: "Some of the poems are of decided excellence; good lines of the prevalent 'classic' style are not hard to find; the general merit of the [1773] collection easily surpasses that of Mrs. Bradstreet's; and when we make allowance for its artificiality, we may readily admit that it equals the average first volume of poems to-day. . . . The book remains the principal literary achievement of the colored race in America."); Katherine Lee Bates, *American Literature* (New York, 1898), p. 79; and S. Austin Allibone, *A Critical Dictionary of English Literature and British and American Authors* (Philadelphia, 1899), 3:2666. Wheatley is, of course, also treated by almost every black author writing about the achievements of the race, including from the nineteenth century William C. Nell, R. B. Lewis, William Wells Brown, George Washington Williams, and Frederick Douglass.

The above listing is by no means exhaustive but only additionally illustrative of the continuing interest in and reputation of Phillis Wheatley and her poems on through the nineteenth century into the present one. This fluctuating reputation continues in the twentieth century, but it has suffered from especially regrettable neglect in at least two instances: she is not even mentioned in *The Cambridge History of American Literature* or in the *Literary History of the United States*.[15] In these she deserves only the meager treatment of a minor author, but she definitely deserves that, along with the scores of other minor authors of comparable ability and reputation who do appear. Fortunately, most reference works and anthologies in which Wheatley's inclusion should be pertinent do now include her, especially if they were published after 1966; and the list of works near the end of this volume reflects some of the continuing and growing (and deepening and broadening) interest in her and her works.

Before this brief overview closes, two gatherings to honor Wheatley should be mentioned. The first was a poetry festival held November 4–7, 1973, at Jackson State College in Mississippi to commemorate the two hundredth

15. In the bibliography volume of the latter, p. 100, there is a single sentence: "The Negro poetaster Phillis Wheatley (*ca.* 1753–1784) achieved something of a vogue with the publication of her *Poems on Various Subjects* (1773), though it received little critical notice."

anniversary of the publication of her book. It primarily featured readings (including a number of poems about Wheatley) by more than a dozen well-known black women poets who had gathered for this occasion. It also had a critical session, a dramatic presentation, and the unveiling of a new bust of Wheatley. The guiding spirit behind the festival and its theme of Phillis Wheatley's continuing pertinence was the writer Margaret Walker.[16] The second gathering was a scholarly conference on Wheatley held September 27–28, 1984, at Illinois State University, marking the two hundredth anniversary of her death. It was organized by John Shields and partially funded by the National Endowment for the Humanities. It is hoped that papers read at the conference will be published, either together or separately, for they contain many insights that could be helpful to us in our appreciation and understanding of Wheatley and in the shaping of her continuing reputation.[17]

16. For accounts of the festival, see *Jackson State Review* 6 (Summer 1974); Rowell and Ward, "Ancestral Memories"; Parks, "Phillis Wheatley Comes Home"; and "Wheatley Wheatley," *Ebony* 29 (March 1974): 94–96 +.

17. Because of their value, near the end of this volume there is a listing of those papers from the conference which its organizer hoped would be published.

❧

A Note on the Text

I n preparing this new edition the emphasis has been on being as accurate as possible in all parts and aspects of the book, and especially on textual accuracy for Wheatley's poems and letters (and on proper sequencing for variants). A strong effort has been made to keep the capitalization, punctuation, spelling, italics, and general format as they are in the best available sources. Therefore, a great deal of effort and time was put into working directly from the actual manuscript of an item if it existed or from an actual copy of the particular printed version when the manuscript was not available. Working from reproductions (of any kind) of manuscripts or printed versions of Wheatley's texts was avoided as much as possible—that is, in most instances. This, of course, meant going to the materials as much as possible, and I am indebted to the helpful staffs of many repositories. (Taking this approach also led to new information and items and better understanding of some previously known material.) Information about textual sources is given in the notes to each of the items not in her 1773 book and below for the book itself. (Also see the acknowledgments section.)

The intention has been to include in this edition all poems and letters that are known definitely to be by Phillis Wheatley and any significant variants thereof for which she might well have been responsible. (Not included are the poem on the birthday of Pompey Stockbridge, a prayer said to be by her, and a few other items for which there is not sufficient evidence of her authorship but which some attribute to her.) Included with her letters are the 1772, 1773, and 1779 Proposals because of the valuable information and insights they provide. Who wrote them is not known, but the chances are good that she wrote the 1772 and 1779 ones—certainly she cooperated in their conception and contents. For context reasons, three of her letters and the 1784 Proposal are printed with the poems they are directly associated with, but they are listed chronologically in the Contents with the other letters and Proposals. The contents of her 1773 book, which has its own integrity, has been placed first among her works because of its importance and centrality in her career. Following it are the other of her poems (and their variants) and also variants of some of the poems in her book—all in one chronological order to illustrate the pattern of her development as a poet (except that within this section all variants for any poem are printed in their chronological order immediately following the earliest of them, regardless of how they might otherwise fit into the chronology of her works as a whole, which is done for convenience in comparing the variants). The section of her prose is in chronological order also.

It is intended that this volume meet standards of scholarly integrity, while at the same time appealing to and being of interest and help to the general reader. The notes usually do not include information generally available in dictionaries, classical dictionaries, encyclopedias, and other widely and readily available reference works. However, within each of the notes and through cross-reference among them an attempt has been made to provide less readily available information which will be helpful in understanding a particular item in itself and in the contexts of her life and her works as a whole. All notes in this volume indicated by asterisks appeared thus in the primary sources used for those particular items, and in the case of solely printed sources it is not known whether such notes were by Wheatley or someone else (though they likely are hers). All numbered notes are by the present editor.

The list of works near the back of this volume does not include every work mentioned in the volume but is selective both in that regard and in regard to the large body of material about Wheatley not mentioned in this volume. Works mentioned in this volume that are not in the list are usually narrowly or obliquely oriented (in relation to the primary and overall concerns of this book), and bibliographical information for them appears where they are mentioned. On the other hand, bibliographical information is truncated at the place of mention in this volume for works that are more broadly or more directly focused upon Phillis Wheatley and her works or their contexts, and the reader is referred to the list at the back for full bibliographical information for them. Also included in the list are other works that have been selected for inclusion on the basis of their being useful to the reader in gaining further knowledge about or understanding of this subject, and the entire list has been both compiled and limited with such usefulness in mind. There is now so much printed material about Wheatley that to attempt a comprehensive list would create one so large as to go beyond the purposes of this volume and perhaps overwhelm the reader; judicious selection has been attempted, with an emphasis on works published since 1960 but including some of the still quite important earlier work. The list does not include the many entries about her in reference works, nor does it include any republication of her book unless there is some supplementary aspect of the work that commends it for this list (but see below concerning some of the republications of her book).

This edition includes fifty-five poems by Wheatley (not counting variants) and twenty-two of her letters. Forty-six of her poems were published during her lifetime, and so were some of the variants. Thirty-eight of her poems are in her 1773 book. This new edition includes nine poems (and a number of variants) that were not in the first edition and eleven letters and two Proposals that were not in it. It also includes many additional facts about her and her works. The composition of the poems spans 1767 (perhaps 1766) to 1784, and the letters span 1770 to 1779. However, we have evidence that she wrote more of both, and others are bound to turn up sooner or later. Here are those we have now, and they tell us a great deal.

The centerpiece of this volume is, of course, Wheatley's 1773 *Poems on Various Subjects, Religious and Moral.* Its poems and front matter (excluding the separate page following the title page with only the line "Entered at Stationers Hall," and the frontispiece—concerning which see below) have been printed here in the order in which they appear in a copy of that first edition which is in the Rare Book collection of the Louis Round Wilson Library of the University of North Carolina at Chapel Hill (the pages of which are the size they were before they were trimmed to the binding size usual for this book, and this copy correlates with a copy of the first edition— with the pages trimmed to the usual binding size—in the Rare Book collection of the Duke University Library and with my own copy). The capitalization, punctuation, spelling, italics, and general format of the 1773 edition have been preserved in this one. They do not present problems that hinder the reader's understanding of and appreciation of the poems which are significant enough to offset the partially retained "flavor" of eighteenth-century publishing. However, the eighteenth-century printed *s* resembling the printed *f* has not been retained, the "tag word" appearing at the bottom of each page anticipating the first word of the next page has not been retained, the numbering of every fifth line of poetry has not been retained, the poem titles have been printed in all capital letters, and the beginning of each poem does not appear at the top of a fresh page as in the original. In other words, this is by no means a facsimile of the 1773 edition (though it does have facsimiles of six pages of the front matter of the 1773 book),[1] although there was a conscious effort, by basing this one on that first edition, to give the reader an experience at least similar to that of the original eighteenth-century readers, while at the same time presenting a text of the poems more faithful to the 1773 edition than some of the subsequent reprintings of them have had.

The frontispiece for this volume is a facsimile of the picture of Wheatley used for the frontispiece of her 1773 book. (For how that picture came to be included, see the Introduction to this volume. Who drew the picture is not known, though some think that it was Scipio Moorhead, to whom she wrote a poem which appears in her book among some other poems written in 1773, though that particular one is not dated.) The frontispiece for that first edition was tipped in facing the title page before the book was bound, and the copy of it in the Chapel Hill volume is on a page smaller than the untrimmed pages of the book itself, though in most copies of that tome the pages of the book have been trimmed to the same size as the frontispiece page. Probably Wheatley carried the drawing to England when she went, and it was engraved and printed there. At the bottom of the frontispiece page was printed: "Published according to Act of Parliament, Septr 1st, 1773 by Arch^d Bell, Bookseller N°. 8 near the Saracens Head Aldgate." This date is not part of the engraved plate with the likeness of her, and I take it to be when the frontispiece page was printed. Sidney Kaplan says, "Hers was the first portrait of a black with a name to be painted in America";[2] and it was an important part of the book and aided its sales.

A reprinting of Wheatley's book with the title *Poems on Comic, Serious, and Moral Subjects* and touted on the title page as "The SECOND EDITION, Corrected" was published by "J. French, Bookseller, No. 164, Fenchurch-Street" in London in 1787, probably early in the year, to be available "in Town and Country," suggesting a continued interest in her poems in London at least two years after her death.[3] The following are among the many

1. Robinson, *Her Writings*, and Shields, *Collected Works*, print the entire 1773 volume in facsimile. (The Robinson printing is more reliable.)

2. Kaplan, *Black Presence*, p. 178.

3. I thank Richard Newman of the New York Public Library for providing me access to his personal copy of this very difficult to find volume.

other publications of Wheatley's 1773 book: Philadelphia, 1786 (first American edition), 1787, and 1789; Albany, 1793; Philadelphia, 1801, as an addendum to Volume 2 of the translation from the French of Joseph Lavallee's *The Negro Equalled by Few Europeans*; Walpole, New Hampshire, 1802; Hartford, 1804; Halifax, 1814, as an addendum to *The Interesting Narrative of the Life of Olaudah Equiano, or Gustavus Vassa, the African*; New England, 1816; in a volume with a memoir of Wheatley by Margaretta Matilda Odell, published in Boston in 1834, 1835, and 1838;[4] and in Denver in 1887, with memoirs by W. H. Jackson. The poems of the 1773 volume (and some of her other poems) also appear in *The Poems of Phillis Wheatley*, Philadelphia, 1909; *Phillis Wheatley (Phillis Peters): Poems and Letters*, edited by Charles F. Heartman, with an appreciation by Arthur Schomburg, New York, 1915; *Life and Works of Phillis Wheatley*, by G. Herbert Renfro, Washington, 1916; and *The Poems of Phillis Wheatley, edited with an Introduction and Notes by Charlotte Ruth Wright*, Philadelphia, 1930. Also, most of the poems of the 1773 volume were printed, one at a time, in the *Liberator* between February 11, 1832, and December 22, 1832.

Each republication has its own distinctiveness and merits, and so does this one, which in one sense is based on all of those that preceded; but in another sense it is not but has bypassed them to the originals, from which each edition of her works (in one way or another) must descend.

---

4. The 1838 volume also contains poems by George Moses Horton at the end. The *Memoir and Poems* in the 1830s stirred new interest in Phillis Wheatley and her poems and may have been inspired by the periodic reprinting of her poems in the *Liberator* in 1832. It was probably the *Memoir and Poems* that the sixteen-year-old Charlotte Forten (herself destined for a remarkable role in establishing the abilities of blacks in America) referred to in her journal on Friday, July 28, 1854: "This evening read 'Poems of Phillis Wheatly [sic],' an African slave, who lived in Boston at the time of the Revolution. She was a wonderfully gifted woman, and many of her poems are very beautiful. Her character and genius afford a striking proof of the falseness of the assertion made by some that hers is an inferior race" (*A Free Negro in the Slave Era: The Journal of Charlotte L. Forten* [New York, 1961], p. 55). The 1838 edition apparently was reissued in 1863. The *Proceedings of the Massachusetts Historical Society* 7 (1863–64): 270 tells of "the issue at this time of some copies remaining on hand of what is called the 'third edition' . . . which had been published in 1838"; and on page 276 further information is given about these "some two hundred copies" brought out, not by the publisher of the "third edition" of the *Memoir and Poems*, but by the publisher of the first and second editions of the same, who had pieced together this "edition" from printing done by both publishers. Odell was a great-grandniece of Susanna Wheatley, Phillis's mistress. The *Liberator* of July 16, 1836, advertised the memoir as a separate pamphlet. Robinson, *Her Writings*, pp. 430–50 has a facsimile of the memoir.

❧

Poems on Various Subjects,
Religious and Moral

P O E M S

ON

VARIOUS   SUBJECTS,

RELIGIOUS AND MORAL.

BY

PHILLIS WHEATLEY,

NEGRO SERVANT to Mr. JOHN WHEATLEY,
of BOSTON, in NEW ENGLAND.

L   O   N   D   O   N:

Printed for A. BELL, Bookseller, Aldgate; and sold by
Messrs. COX and BERRY, King-Street, *BOSTON.*

M DCC LXXIII.

DEDICATION.

To the Right Honourable the

COUNTESS of HUNTINGDON,[1]

THE FOLLOWING

P   O   E   M   S

Are moſt reſpectfully

Inſcribed,

By her much obliged,

Very humble,

And devoted Servant,

Phillis Wheatley.

Boſton, June 12,
1773.

---

1. See Wheatley's letters to the countess. The date of this dedication occurred while Wheatley was at sea en route to England (see her poem "Farewell to America" and the Introduction to this volume).

P R E F A C E.

THE following POEMS were written originally for the Amufement of the Author, as they were the Products of her leifure Moments. She had no Intention ever to have publifhed them; nor would they now have made their Appearance, but at the Importunity of many of her beft, and moft generous Friends; to whom fhe confiders herfelf, as under the greateft Obligations. [2]

As her Attempts in Poetry are now fent into the World, it is hoped the Critic will not feverely fenfure their Defects; and we prefume they have too much Merit to

---

2. This protest is traditional. She had been publishing poems for some years and had tried to publish a book of her poems in Boston in 1772 (see her 1772 Proposals). A number of poems had been revised for publication in this book, mostly to be more appropriate for a British audience. Concerning the circumstances of her life while she had been writing these poems, see the Introduction to this volume.

to be caſt aſide with Contempt, as worthleſs and trifling Effuſions.

As to the Diſadvantages ſhe has laboured under, with Regard to Learning, nothing needs to be of-fered, as her Maſter's Letter in the following Page will ſufficiently ſhew the Difficulties in this Reſpect ſhe had to encounter.

With all their Imperfections, the Poems are now humbly ſubmitted to the Peruſal of the Public.

The following is a Copy of a LETTER sent by the
Author's Master to the Publisher. [3]

PHILLIS was brought from *Africa* to *America*,
in the Year 1761, between Seven and Eight
Years of Age. Without any Assistance from School
Education, and by only what she was taught in the
Family, she, in sixteen Months Time from her Ar-
rival, attained the English Language, to which she
was an utter Stranger before, to such a Degree, as
to read any, the most difficult Parts of the Sacred
Writings, to the great Astonishment of all who
heard her.

As to her WRITING, her own Curiosity led her
to it; and this she learnt in so short a Time, that in
the Year 1765, she wrote a Letter to the Rev.
Mr. OCCOM, the *Indian* Minister, while in *England*.

She has a great Inclination to learn the Latin
Tongue, and has made some Progress in it. This
Relation is given by her Master who bought her,
and with whom she now lives.

JOHN WHEATLEY.

Boston, *Nov.* 14, 1772.

---

3. The first two paragraphs of this letter are primarily the one-paragraph sketch signed by
Nathaniel Wheatley on October 12, 1772 (here expanded only a little). The one-paragraph
version appears to be in her handwriting. (See the notes to her poem to Lord Dartmouth and
to her 1772 Proposals. Robinson, *Her Writings*, p. 403, has a facsimile of the 1772 paragraph.)
Regarding Occom, see her letter to him. Occom had sailed from Boston on December 23,
1765, and he raised money in England and Scotland over a period of about a year and a half
for the education of Indians in New England. As a result of the great success which he and his
companion in the endeavor, the Reverend Nathaniel Whitaker, had in this work, Occom's alma
mater, Moor's Indian Charity School in Lebanon, Connecticut, was moved to New Hanover,
New Hampshire (to Occom's considerable disappointment), and converted into Dartmouth
College, named for the Earl of Dartmouth as a result of his interest in the school and the do-
nation he had made. (We do not have this letter she wrote to Occom.)

To the PUBLICK.

A S it has been repeatedly fuggefted to the Publifher, by Per-
fons, who have feen the Manufcript, that Numbers
would be ready to fufpeft they were not really the Writings of
PHILLIS, he has procured the following Atteftation, from
the moft refpeftable Charaſters in *Boſton*, that none might have
the leaft Ground for difputing their *Original*.

W E whofe Names are under-written, do affure the World,
that the POEMS fpecified in the following Page, * were (as we
verily believe) written by PHILLIS, a young Negro Girl, who
was but a few Years fince, brought an uncultivated Barbarian
from *Africa*, and has ever fince been, and now is, under the
Difadvantage of ferving as a Slave in a Family in this Town.
She has been examined by fome of the beft Judges, and is
thought qualified to write them. 4

His Excellency THOMAS HUTCHINSON, *Governor,*

The Hon. ANDREW OLIVER, *Lieutenant-Governor.*

The Hon. Thomas Hubbard,	*The Rev.* Charles Chauncy, *D. D.*
The Hon. John Erving,	*The Rev.* Mather Byles, *D. D.*
The Hon. James Pitts,	*The Rev* Ed. Pemberton, *D.D.*
The Hon. Harrifon Gray,	*The Rev.* Andrew Elliot, *D.D.*
The Hon. James Bowdoin,	*The Rev.* Samuel Cooper, *D.D.*
John Hancock, *Efq;*	*The Rev. Mr.* Samuel Mather,
Jofeph Green, *Efq;*	*The Rev. Mr.* John Moorhead,
Richard Carey, *Efq;*	*Mr.* John Wheatley, *her Maſter.*

N. B. The original Atteftation, figned by the above Gentle-
men, may be feen by applying to *Archibald Bell*, Bookſeller,
No. 8, *Aldgate-Street.*

---

* The Words "*following Page*," allude to the Contents of
the Manufcript Copy, which are wrote at the Back of the
above Atteftation.

4. Concerning the origins of this statement, see the note to Wheatley's 1772 Proposals. This
statement was also used by the publisher of her book, Archibald Bell, as part of his advertising
campaign in London newspapers in September 1773. (Robinson, *Her Writings*, pp. 404–5, has
a facsimile of one such advertisement.) Apparently because these ads also had some biographi-
cal information about her, according to Robinson, *Her Writings*, p. 404, the first volumes of her
book produced in London did not have the dedication, the preface, the biographical sketch, or
the attestation which are in most copies of the first edition of her book. In one of the newspa-
per ads (in *Lloyd's Evening Post and British Chronicle*, September 10–13) this statement is dated
October 28, 1772. Robinson, *Her Writings*, p. 270, points out that a number of the signers of
this attestation were related by blood or (mostly) by marriage. All were respected persons of
position and influence, although they represented various denominations and diverse political
views. Information about Oliver (1706–74), Hubbard (1702–73), Bowdoin (1726–90), Cooper
(1725–83), and Moorhead (1703–73) can be found with Wheatley's poems having to do with
them. Concerning Richard Cary (1717–90), see the note to Wheatley's first letter to the
Countess of Huntingdon. Concerning Chauncy (1705–87), pastor of the First Unitarian
Church and a respected author on religious subjects, particularly noted for his stand against
Whitefield and emotional religion, see Wheatley's poem to Thomas Amory. Hutchinson
(1711–80), governor of Massachusetts since 1771, would leave Boston in 1774 and live after
that in England. Erving (1728–1816), Gray (1711?–94), and Hancock (1737–93) were promi-

TO MÆCENAS.[5]

MÆCENAS, you, beneath the myrtle shade,
Read o'er what poets sung, and shepherds play'd.
What felt those poets but you feel the same?
Does not your soul possess the sacred flame?
Their noble strains your equal genius shares
In softer language, and diviner airs.

   While *Homer* paints lo! circumfus'd in air,
Celestial Gods in mortal forms appear;
Swift as they move hear each recess rebound,
Heav'n quakes, earth trembles, and the shores resound.
Great Sire of verse, before my mortal eyes,
The lightnings blaze across the vaulted skies,
And, as the thunder shakes the heav'nly plains,
A deep-felt horror thrills through all my veins.
When gentler strains demand thy graceful song,
The length'ning line moves languishing along.
When great *Patroclus* courts *Achilles'* aid,
The grateful tribute of my tears is paid;
Prone on the shore he feels the pangs of love,
And stern *Pelides* tend'rest passions move.

---

nent Boston merchants, and the latter would attain much visibility during the period of the
Revolution as a bold signer of the Declaration of Independence. Green (1705?–80), a Tory,
was known as a merchant, poet, and wit and for his large library. Byles (1707–88) not only was
a Congregational minister but also was known for his poetry and wit (see the Introduction to
this volume). Samuel Mather (1706–85), pastor of the Tenth Congregational Church, was a
son of Cotton Mather. Ebenezer Pemberton (1704–77) was pastor of the Congregational New
Brick Church in the North End (see the notes to her poem on Whitefield). Eliot (1718–78)
was pastor of the Congregational New North Church and was known for his antislavery views,
as was Gray. Concerning John Wheatley, see the Introduction for this volume and throughout
the volume. The five whose names are preceded with "The Hon." were members of the gov-
erning council—including Pitts (1710–76). Some of the signers were owners of slaves. (Note
that in the printed statement the last names of Eliot and Cary are misspelled, as is the abbre-
viation of Pemberton's first name.)
   5. The Roman Gaius Cilnius Mæcenas was the special friend and patron of Horace and
Vergil. This poem was not listed in the 1772 Proposals.

Great *Maro's* strain in heav'nly numbers flows,
The *Nine* inspire, and all the bosom glows.
O could I rival thine and *Virgil's* page,
Or claim the *Muses* with the *Mantuan* Sage;
Soon the same beauties should my mind adorn,
And the same ardors in my soul should burn:
Then should my song in bolder notes arise,
And all my numbers pleasingly surprize;
But here I sit, and mourn a grov'ling mind,
That fain would mount, and ride upon the wind.

Not you, my friend, these plaintive strains become,
Not you, whose bosom is the *Muses* home;
When they from tow'ring *Helicon* retire,
They fan in you the bright immortal fire,
But I less happy, cannot raise the song,
The fault'ring music dies upon my tongue.

The happier *Terence** all the choir inspir'd,
His soul replenish'd, and his bosom fir'd;
But say, ye *Muses*, why this partial grace,
To one alone of *Afric's* sable race;
From age to age transmitting thus his name
With the first glory in the rolls of fame?

Thy virtues, great *Mæcenas*! shall be sung
In praise of him, from whom those virtues sprung:
While blooming wreaths around thy temples spread, ⎫
I'll snatch a laurel from thine honour'd head, ⎬
While you indulgent smile upon the deed. ⎭

As long as *Thames* in streams majestic flows,
Or *Naiads* in their oozy beds repose,
While Phœbus reigns above the starry train,
While bright *Aurora* purples o'er the main,
So long, great Sir, the muse thy praise shall sing,
So long thy praise shall make *Parnassus* ring:

* He was an *African* by birth.

Then grant, *Mæcenas*, thy paternal rays,
Hear me propitious, and defend my lays.

🍂

ON VIRTUE.[6]

O Thou bright jewel in my aim I strive
To comprehend thee. Thine own words declare
Wisdom is higher than a fool can reach.
I cease to wonder, and no more attempt
Thine height t'explore, or fathom thy profound.
But, O my soul, sink not into despair,
Virtue is near thee, and with gentle hand
Would now embrace thee, hovers o'er thine head.
Fain would the heav'n-born soul with her converse,
Then seek, then court her for her promis'd bliss.

   Auspicious queen, thine heav'nly pinions spread,
And lead celestial *Chastity* along;
Lo! now her sacred retinue descends,
Array'd in glory from the orbs above.
Attend me, *Virtue*, thro' my youthful years!
O leave me not to the false joys of time!
But guide my steps to endless life and bliss.
Greatness, or *Goodness*, say what I shall call thee,
To give an higher appellation still,
Teach me a better strain, a nobler lay,
O Thou, enthron'd with Cherubs in the realms of day!

6. This poem was listed in her 1772 Proposals, dated 1766.

TO THE UNIVERSITY OF CAMBRIDGE, IN NEW-ENGLAND.[7]

WHILE an intrinsic ardor prompts to write,
The muses promise to assist my pen;
'Twas not long since I left my native shore
The land of errors, and *Egyptian* gloom:
Father of mercy, 'twas thy gracious hand
Brought me in safety from those dark abodes.

   Students, to you 'tis giv'n to scan the heights
Above, to traverse the ethereal space,
And mark the systems of revolving worlds.
Still more, ye sons of science ye receive
The blissful news by messengers from heav'n,
How *Jesus*' blood for your redemption flows.
See him with hands out-stretcht upon the cross;
Immense compassion in his bosom glows;
He hears revilers, nor resents their scorn:
What matchless mercy in the Son of God!
When the whole human race by sin had fall'n,
He deign'd to die that they might rise again,
And share with him in the sublimest skies,
Life without death, and glory without end.

   Improve your privileges while they stay,
Ye pupils, and each hour redeem, that bears
Or good or bad report of you to heav'n.
Let sin, that baneful evil to the soul,
By you be shunn'd, nor once remit your guard;
Suppress the deadly serpent in its egg.
Ye blooming plants of human race devine,
An *Ethiop* tells you 'tis your greatest foe;
Its transient sweetness turns to endless pain,
And in immense perdition sinks the soul.

7. According to Samuel Eliot Morison, *Three Centuries of Harvard, 1636–1936* (Cambridge, Mass., 1936), pp. 101–32, the students at Harvard during this period had a reputation for

~

TO THE KING'S MOST EXCELLENT MAJESTY. 1768.[8]

YOUR subjects hope, dread Sire—
The crown upon your brows may flourish long,
And that your arm may in your God be strong!
O may your sceptre num'rous nations sway,
And all with love and readiness obey!

   But how shall we the *British* king reward!
Rule thou in peace, our father, and our lord!
Midst the remembrance of thy favours past,
The meanest peasants most admire the last.*
May *George*, belov'd by all the nations round,
Live with heav'ns choicest constant blessings crown'd!
Great God, direct, and guard him from on high,
And from his head let ev'ry evil fly!
And may each clime with equal gladness see
A monarch's smile can set his subjects free!
* The Repeal of the Stamp Act.

~

ON BEING BROUGHT FROM AFRICA TO AMERICA.[9]

'TWAS mercy brought me from my *Pagan* land,
Taught my benighted soul to understand
That there's a God, that there's a *Saviour* too:
Once I redemption neither sought nor knew.
Some view our sable race with scornful eye,
"Their colour is a diabolic die."
Remember, *Christians*, *Negros*, black as *Cain*,
May be refin'd, and join th' angelic train.

---

boisterousness. See the variant version of this poem and its note.
  8. See the variant version of this poem and its note.
  9. This poem was listed in her 1772 Proposals, dated 1768. For possible punning here on
the words "die" and "Cain" in relation to the indigo dye, sugarcane, and slaves of the triangu-

ON THE DEATH OF THE REV. DR. SEWELL. 1769.[10]

ERE yet the morn its lovely blushes spread,
See *Sewell* number'd with the happy dead.
Hail, holy man, arriv'd th' immortal shore,
Though we shall hear thy warning voice no more.
Come, let us all behold with wishful eyes
The saint ascending to his native skies;
From hence the prophet wing'd his rapt'rous way
To the blest mansions in eternal day.
Then begging for the Spirit of our God,
And panting eager for the same abode,
Come, let us all with the same vigour rise,
And take a prospect of the blissful skies;
While on our minds *Christ's* image is imprest,
And the dear Saviour glows in ev'ry breast.
Thrice happy saint! to find thy heav'n at last,
What compensation for the evils past!

   Great God, incomprehensible, unknown
By sense, we bow at thine exalted throne.
O, while we beg thine excellence to feel,
Thy sacred Spirit to our hearts reveal,
And give us of that mercy to partake,
Which thou hast promis'd for the *Saviour's* sake!

   "*Sewell* is dead." Swift-pinion'd *Fame* thus cry'd.   ⎫
"Is *Sewell* dead," my trembling tongue reply'd,   ⎬
O what a blessing in his flight deny'd!   ⎭
How oft for us the holy prophet pray'd!
How oft to us the Word of Life convey'd!
By duty urg'd my mournful verse to close,
I for his tomb this epitaph compose.

---

lar trade among North America, Africa, and the West Indies, see Levernier, "Wheatley's ON
BEING BROUGHT FROM AFRICA TO AMERICA."
  10. See the variant version of this poem and its note.

"Lo, here a Man, redeem'd by *Jesus*' blood,
"A sinner once, but now a saint with God;
"Behold ye rich, ye poor, ye fools, ye wise,
"Nor let his monument your heart surprize;
"'Twill tell you what this holy man has done,
"Which gives him brighter lustre than the sun.
"Listen, ye happy, from your seats above.
"I speak sincerely, while I speak and love,
"He sought the paths of piety and truth,
"By these made happy from his early youth;
"In blooming years that grace divine he felt,
"Which rescues sinners from the chains of guilt.
"Mourn him, ye indigent, whom he has fed,
"And henceforth seek, like him, for living bread;
"Ev'n *Christ*, the bread descending from above,
"And ask an int'rest in his saving love.
"Mourn him, ye youth, to whom he oft has told
"God's gracious wonders from the times of old.
"I, too have cause this mighty loss to mourn,
"For he my monitor will not return.
"O when shall we to his blest state arrive?
"When the same graces in our bosoms thrive."

❧

ON THE DEATH OF THE REV. MR. GEORGE WHITEFIELD. 1770.[11]

HAIL, happy saint, on thine immortal throne,
Possest of glory, life, and bliss unknown;
We hear no more the music of thy tongue,
Thy wonted auditories cease to throng.
Thy sermons in unequall'd accents flow'd,
And ev'ry bosom with devotion glow'd;

11. See the two variant versions of this poem and their notes. (In addition to being printed as a broadside, the earlier version also appeared as an eight-page pamphlet, "Printed and Sold by Ezekiel Russell, in Queen-street, And John Boyles, in Marlboro'-street" in Boston. (Harvard's Houghton Library has a copy of the pamphlet.) Whitefield had a very large following on this side of the Atlantic as well as in Britain.

Thou didst in strains of eloquence refin'd
Inflame the heart, and captivate the mind.
Unhappy we the setting sun deplore,
So glorious once, but ah! it shines no more.

Behold the prophet in his tow'ring flight!
He leaves the earth for heav'n's unmeasur'd height,
And worlds unknown receive him from our sight.
There *Whitefield* wings with rapid course his way,
And sails to *Zion* through vast seas of day.
Thy pray'rs, great saint, and thine incessant cries
Have pierc'd the bosom of thy native skies.
Thou moon hast seen, and all the stars of light,
How he has wrestled with his God by night.
He pray'd that grace in ev'ry heart might dwell,
He long'd to see *America* excel;
He charg'd its youth that ev'ry grace divine
Should with full lustre in their conduct shine;
That Saviour, which his soul did first receive,
The greatest gift that ev'n a God can give,
He freely offer'd to the num'rous throng,
That on his lips with list'ning pleasure hung.

"Take him, ye wretched, for your only good,
"Take him ye starving sinners, for your food;
"Ye thirsty, come to this life-giving stream,
"Ye preachers, take him for your joyful theme;
"Take him my dear *Americans*, he said,
"Be your complaints on his kind bosom laid:
"Take him, ye *Africans*, he longs for you,
"*Impartial Saviour* is his title due:
"Wash'd in the fountain of redeeming blood,
"You shall be sons, and kings, and priests to God."

Great *Countess*,* we *Americans* revere
Thy name, and mingle in thy grief sincere;

* The Countess of *Huntingdon*, to whom Mr. *Whitefield* was Chaplain. [See
  Wheatley's letters to her.]

New England deeply feels, the *Orphans* mourn,
Their more than father will no more return.

But, though arrested by the hand of death,
Whitefield no more exerts his lab'ring breath,
Yet let us view him in th' eternal skies,
Let ev'ry heart to this bright vision rise;
While the tomb safe retains its sacred trust,
Till life divine re-animates his dust.

❧

ON THE DEATH OF A YOUNG LADY OF FIVE YEARS OF AGE.[12]

FROM dark abodes to fair etherial light
Th' enraptur'd innocent has wing'd her flight;
On the kind bosom of eternal love
She finds unknown beatitude above.
This know, ye parents, nor her loss deplore,
She feels the iron hand of pain no more;
The dispensations of unerring grace,
Should turn your sorrows into grateful praise;
Let then no tears for her henceforward flow,
No more distress'd in our dark vale below.

Her morning sun, which rose divinely bright,
Was quickly mantled with the gloom of night;
But hear in heav'n's blest bow'rs your *Nancy* fair,
And learn to imitate her language there.
"Thou, Lord, whom I behold with glory crown'd,
"By what sweet name, and in what tuneful sound
"Wilt thou be prais'd? Seraphic pow'rs are faint
"Infinite love and majesty to paint.

---

12. This poem was listed in her 1772 Proposals, dated 1770. A briefer, variant version of this poem was published during her lifetime, in the London *Arminian Magazine* for December 1781 (see the note to her poem "On Imagination" in this volume). It was slightly altered for re-printing in the Philadelphia *Arminian Magazine* in 1789.

"To thee let all their grateful voices raise,
"And saints and angels join their songs of "praise."

Perfect in bliss she from her heav'nly home
Looks down, and smiling beckons you to come;
Why then, fond parents, why these fruitless groans?
Restrain your tears, and cease your plaintive moans.
Freed from a world of sin, and snares, and pain,
Why would you wish your daughter back again?
No—bow resign'd. Let hope your grief control,
And check the rising tumult of the soul.
Calm in the prosperous, and adverse day,
Adore the God who gives and takes away;
Eye him in all, his holy name revere,
Upright your actions, and your hearts sincere,
Till having sail'd through life's tempestuous sea,
And from its rocks, and boist'rous billows free,
Yourselves, safe landed on the blissful shore,
Shall join your happy babe to part no more.

❧

ON THE DEATH OF A YOUNG GENTLEMAN.[13]

WHO taught thee conflict with the pow'rs of night,
To vanquish Satan in the fields of fight?
Who strung thy feeble arms with might unknown,
How great thy conquest, and how bright thy crown!
War with each princedom, throne, and pow'r is o'er,
The scene is ended to return no more.
O could my muse thy seat on high behold,
How deckt with laurel, how enrich'd with gold!
O could she hear what praise thine harp employs,
How sweet thine anthems, how divine thy joys!

13. This poem was listed in her 1772 Proposals but was undated. A variant version of this poem was published during her lifetime, in the London *Arminian Magazine* for December 1781 (see the note to her poem "On Imagination" in this volume).

What heav'nly grandeur should exalt her strain!
What holy raptures in her numbers reign!
To sooth the troubles of the mind to peace,
To still the tumult of life's tossing seas,
To ease the anguish of the parents heart,
What shall my sympathizing verse impart?
Where is the balm to heal so deep a wound?
Where shall a sov'reign remedy be found?
Look, gracious Spirit, from thine heav'nly bow'r,
And thy full joys into their bosoms pour;
The raging tempest of their grief control,
And spread the dawn of glory through the soul,
To eye the path the saint departed trod,
And trace him to the bosom of his God.

❧

TO A LADY ON THE DEATH OF HER HUSBAND.[14]

GRIM monarch! see, depriv'd of vital breath,
A young physician in the dust of death:
Dost thou go on incessant to destroy,
Our griefs to double, and lay waste our joy?
Enough thou never yet wast known to say,
Though millions die, the vassals of thy sway:
Nor youth, nor science, nor the ties of love,
Nor aught on earth thy flinty heart can move.
The friend, the spouse from his dire dart to save,
In vain we ask the sovereign of the grave.
Fair mourner, there see thy lov'd *Leonard* laid,
And o'er him spread the deep impervious shade;
Clos'd are his eyes, and heavy fetters keep
His senses bound in never-waking sleep,
Till time shall cease, till many a starry world

14. See the variant version of this poem, *To Mrs. Leonard, on the Death of Her Husband,* and
its note.

Shall fall from heav'n, in dire confusion hurl'd,
Till nature in her final wreck shall lie,
And her last groan shall rend the azure sky:
Not, not till then his active soul shall claim
His body, a divine immortal frame.

But see the softly-stealing tears apace
Pursue each other down the mourner's face;
But cease thy tears, bid ev'ry sigh depart,
And cast the load of anguish from thine heart:
From the cold shell of his great soul arise,
And look beyond, thou native of the skies;
There fix thy view, where fleeter than the wind
Thy *Leonard* mounts, and leaves the earth behind.
Thyself prepare to pass the vale of night
To join for ever on the hills of light:
To thine embrace his joyful spirit moves
To thee, the partner of his earthly loves;
He welcomes thee to pleasures more refin'd,
And better suited to th' immortal mind.

&

GOLIATH OF GATH.[15]

I Sam. Chap. XVII.

YE martial pow'rs, and all ye tuneful nine,
Inspire my song, and aid my high design.
The dreadful scenes and toils of war I write,
The ardent warriors, and the fields of fight:
You best remember, and you best can sing
The acts of heroes to the vocal string:
Resume the lays with which your sacred lyre,
Did then the poet and the sage inspire.

15. This poem was listed in her 1772 Proposals but was undated.

Now front to front the armies were display'd,
Here *Israel* rang'd, and there the foes array'd;
The hosts on two opposing mountains stood,
Thick as the foliage of the waving wood;
Between them an extensive valley lay,
O'er which the gleaming armour pour'd the day,
When from the camp of the *Philistine* foes,
Dreadful to view, a mighty warrior rose;
In the dire deeds of bleeding battle skill'd,
The monster stalks the terror of the field.
From *Gath* he sprung, *Goliath* was his name,
Of fierce deportment, and gigantic frame:
A brazen helmet on his head was plac'd,
A coat of mail his form terrific grac'd,
The greaves his legs, the targe his shoulders prest:
Dreadful in arms high-tow'ring o'er the rest
A spear he proudly wav'd, whose iron head,
Strange to relate, six hundred shekels weigh'd;
He strode along, and shook the ample field,
While *Phœbus* blaz'd refulgent on his shield:
Through *Jacob's* race a chilling horror ran,
When thus the huge, enormous chief began:

"Say, what the cause that in this proud array
"You set your battle in the face of day?
"One hero find in all your vaunting train,
"Then see who loses, and who wins the plain;
"For he who wins, in triumph may demand
"Perpetual service from the vanquish'd land:
"Your armies I defy, your force despise,
"By far inferior in *Philistia's* eyes:
"Produce a man, and let us try the fight,
"Decide the contest, and the victor's right."

Thus challeng'd he: all *Israel* stood amaz'd,
And ev'ry chief in consternation gaz'd;
But *Jesse's* son in youthful bloom appears,
And warlike courage far beyond his years:

He left the folds, he left the flow'ry meads,
And soft recesses of the sylvan shades.
Now *Israel's* monarch, and his troops arise, ⎫
With peals of shouts ascending to the skies; ⎬
In *Elah's* vale the scene of combat lies. ⎭

When the fair morning blush'd with orient red,
What *David's* sire enjoin'd the son obey'd,
And swift of foot towards the trench he came,
Where glow'd each bosom with the martial flame.
He leaves his carriage to another's care,
And runs to greet his brethren of the war.
While yet they spake the giant-chief arose,
Repeats the challenge, and insults his foes:
Struck with the sound, and trembling at the view,
Affrighted *Israel* from its post withdrew.
"Observe ye this tremendous foe, they cry'd,
"Who in proud vaunts our armies hath defy'd:
"Whoever lays him prostrate on the plain,
"Freedom in *Israel* for his house shall gain;
"And on him wealth unknown the king will pour,
"And give his royal daughter for his dow'r."

Then *Jesse's* youngest hope: "My brethren say,
"What shall be done for him who takes away
"Reproach from *Jacob*, who destroys the chief,
"And puts a period to his country's grief.
"He vaunts the honours of his arms abroad,
"And scorns the armies of the living God."

Thus spoke the youth, th' attentive people ey'd
The wond'rous hero, and again reply'd:
"Such the rewards our monarch will bestow,
"On him who conquers, and destroys his foe."

Eliab heard, and kindled into ire
To hear his shepherd-brother thus inquire,
And thus begun? "What errand brought thee? say
"Who keeps thy flock? or does it go astray?

"I know the base ambition of thine heart,
"But back in safety from the field depart."

   Eliab thus to *Jesse's* youngest heir,
Express'd his wrath in accents most severe.
When to his brother mildly he reply'd,
"What have I done? or what the cause to chide?"

   The words were told before the king, who sent
For the young hero to his royal tent:
Before the monarch dauntless he began,
"For this *Philistine* fail no heart of man:
"I'll take the vale, and with the giant fight:
"I dread not all his boasts, nor all his might."
When thus the king: "Dar'st thou a stripling go,
"And venture combat with so great a foe?
"Who all his days has been inur'd to fight,
"And made its deeds his study and delight:
"Battles and bloodshed brought the monster forth,
"And clouds and whirlwinds usher'd in his birth."
When *David* thus: "I kept the fleecy care,
"And out there rush'd a lion and a bear;
"A tender lamb the hungry lion took,
"And with no other weapon than my crook
"Bold I pursu'd, and chas'd him o'er the field,
"The prey deliver'd, and the felon kill'd:
"As thus the lion and the bear I slew,
"So shall *Goliath* fall, and all his crew:
"The God, who sav'd me from these beasts of prey,
"By me this monster in the dust shall lay."
So *David* spoke. The wond'ring king reply'd;
"Go thou with heav'n and victory on thy side:
"This coat of mail, this sword gird on," he said,
And plac'd a mighty helmet on his head:
The coat, the sword, the helm he laid aside,
Nor chose to venture with those arms untry'd,
Then took his staff, and to the neighb'ring brook
Instant he ran, and thence five pebbles took.

Mean time descended to *Philistia's* son
A radiant cherub, and he thus begun:
"Goliath, well thou know'st thou hast defy'd
"Yon Hebrew armies, and their God deny'd:
"Rebellious wretch! audacious worm! forbear,
"Nor tempt the vengeance of their God too far:
"Them, who with his omnipotence contend,
"No eye shall pity, and no arm defend:
"Proud as thou art, in short liv'd glory great,
"I come to tell thee thine approaching fate.
"Regard my words. The judge of all the gods,
"Beneath whose steps the tow'ring mountain nods,
"Will give thine armies to the savage brood,
"That cut the liquid air, or range the wood.
"Thee too a well-aim'd pebble shall destroy,
"And thou shalt perish by a beardless boy:
"Such is the mandate from the realms above, ⎫
"And should I try the vengeance to remove, ⎬
"Myself a rebel to my king would prove. ⎭
"*Goliath* say, shall grace to him be shown,
"Who dares heav'ns monarch, and insults his throne?"

"Your words are lost on me," the giant cries, ⎫
While fear and wrath contended in his eyes, ⎬
When thus the messenger from heav'n replies: ⎭
"Provoke no more *Jehovah's* awful hand
"To hurl its vengeance on thy guilty land:
"He grasps the thunder, and, he wings the storm,
"Servants their sov'reign's orders to perform."

The angel spoke, and turn'd his eyes away,
Adding new radiance to the rising day.

Now *David* comes: the fatal stones demand
His left, the staff engag'd his better hand:
The giant mov'd, and from his tow'ring height
Survey'd the stripling, and disdain'd the sight,
And thus began: "Am I a dog with thee?

"Bring'st thou no armour, but a staff to me?
"The gods on thee their vollied curses pour,
"And beasts and birds of prey thy flesh devour."

    David undaunted thus, "Thy spear and shield
"Shall no protection to thy body yield:
"*Jehovah's* name —— no other arms I bear,
"I ask no other in this glorious war.
"To-day the Lord of Hosts to me will give
"Vict'ry, to-day thy doom thou shalt receive;
"The fate you threaten shall your own become,
"And beasts shall be your animated tomb,
"That all the earth's inhabitants may know
"That there's a God, who governs all below:
"This great assembly too shall witness stand,
"That needs nor sword, nor spear, th' Almighty's hand:
"The battle his, the conquest he bestows,
"And to our pow'r consigns our hated foes."

    Thus *David* spoke; *Goliath* heard and came
To meet the hero in the field of fame.
Ah! fatal meeting to thy troops and thee,
But thou wast deaf to the divine decree;
Young *David* meets thee, meets thee not in vain;
'Tis thine to perish on th' ensanguin'd plain.

    And now the youth the forceful pebble flung,
Philistia trembled as it whizz'd along:
In his dread forehead, where the helmet ends,
Just o'er the brows the well-aim'd stone descends,
It pierc'd the skull, and shatter'd all the brain,
Prone on his face he tumbled to the plain:
Goliath's fall no smaller terror yields
Than riving thunders in aerial fields:
The soul still ling'red in its lov'd abode,
Till conq'ring *David* o'er the giant strode:
Goliath's sword then laid its master dead,
And from the body hew'd the ghastly head;

The blood in gushing torrents drench'd the plains,
The soul found passage through the spouting veins.

And now aloud th' illustrious victor said,
"Where are your boastings now your champion's dead?"
Scarce had he spoke, when the *Philistines* fled:
But fled in vain; the conqu'ror swift persu'd:
What scenes of slaughter! and what seas of blood!
There *Saul* thy thousands grasp'd th' impurpled sand
In pangs of death the conquest of thine hand;
And *David* there were thy ten thousands laid:
Thus *Israel's* damsels musically play'd.

Near *Gath* and *Ekron* many an hero lay,
Breath'd out their souls, and curs'd the light of day:
Their fury, quench'd by death, no longer burns,
And *David* with *Goliath's* head returns,
To *Salem* brought, but in his tent he plac'd
The load of armour which the giant grac'd.
His monarch saw him coming from the war,
And thus demanded of the son of *Ner.*
"Say, who is this amazing youth?" he cry'd,
When thus the leader of the host reply'd;
"As lives thy soul I know not whence he sprung,
"So great in prowess though in years so young:"
"Inquire whose son is he," the sov'reign said,
"Before whose conq'ring arm *Philistia* fled."
Before the king behold the stripling stand,
Goliath's head depending from his hand:
To him the king: "Say of what martial line
"Art thou, young hero, and what sire was thine?"
He humbly thus; "the son of *Jesse* I:
"I came the glories of the field to try.
"Small is my tribe, but valiant in the fight;
"Small is my city, but thy royal right."
"Then take the promis'd gifts," the monarch cry'd,
Conferring riches and the royal bride:

"Knit to my soul for ever thou remain
"With me, nor quit my regal roof again."

&

THOUGHTS ON THE WORKS OF PROVIDENCE.[16]

ARISE, my soul, on wings enraptur'd, rise
To praise the monarch of the earth and skies,
Whose goodness and beneficence appear
As round its centre moves the rolling year,
Or when the morning glows with rosy charms,
Or the sun slumbers in the ocean's arms:
Of light divine be a rich portion lent
To guide my soul, and favour my intent.
Celestial muse, my arduous flight sustain,
And raise my mind to a seraphic strain!

Ador'd for ever be the God unseen,
Which round the sun revolves this vast machine,
Though to his eye its mass a point appears:
Ador'd the God that whirls surrounding spheres,
Which first ordain'd that mighty *Sol* should reign
The peerless monarch of th' ethereal train:
Of miles twice forty millions is his height,
And yet his radiance dazzles mortal sight
So far beneath—from him th' extended earth
Vigour derives, and ev'ry flow'ry birth:
Vast through her orb she moves with easy grace
Around her *Phœbus* in unbounded space;

16. This poem was not listed in her 1772 Proposals. It was later published by E. Gay in
Halifax in 1805 as an eight-page pamphlet. The title page of the pamphlet read *A Beautiful
Poem on Providence*, but at the head of the poem was the title given here. (The Library of Con-
gress has a copy, in fragile condition.) The poem was well chosen for a separate printing; it has
some good passages and suggests an influence from Milton. A briefer, variant version of this
poem was published during her lifetime, in the London *Arminian Magazine* for December
1781 (see the note to her poem "On Imagination" in this volume).

True to her course th' impetuous storm derides,
Triumphant o'er the winds, and surging tides.

Almighty, in these wond'rous works of thine,
What *Pow'r*, what *Wisdom*, and what *Goodness* shine?
And are thy wonders, Lord, by men explor'd,
And yet creating glory unador'd!

Creation smiles in various beauty gay,
While day to night, and night succeeds to day:
That *Wisdom*, which attends *Jehovah's* ways,
Shines most conspicuous in the solar rays:
Without them, destitute of heat and light,
This world would be the reign of endless night:
In their excess how would our race complain,
Abhorring life! how hate its length'ned chain!
From air adust what num'rous ills would rise?
What dire contagion taint the burning skies?
What pestilential vapours, fraught with death,
Would rise, and overspread the lands beneath?

Hail, smiling morn, that from the orient main
Ascending dost adorn the heav'nly plain!
So rich, so various are thy beauteous dies,
That spread through all the circuit of the skies,
That, full of thee, my soul in rapture soars,
And thy great God, the cause of all adores.

O'er beings infinite his love extends,
His *Wisdom* rules them, and his *Pow'r* defends.
When tasks diurnal tire the human frame,
The spirits faint, and dim the vital flame,
Then too that ever active bounty shines,
Which not infinity of space confines.
The sable veil, that *Night* in silence draws,
Conceals effects, but shews th' *Almighty Cause*;
Night seals in sleep the wide creation fair,
And all is peaceful but the brow of care.
Again, gay *Phœbus*, as the day before,

Wakes ev'ry eye, but what shall wake no more;
Again the face of nature is renew'd,
Which still appears harmonious, fair, and good.
May grateful strains salute the smiling morn,
Before its beams the eastern hills adorn!

Shall day to day, and night to night conspire
To show the goodness of the Almighty Sire?
This mental voice shall man regardless hear,
And never, never raise the filial pray'r?
To-day, O hearken, nor your folly mourn
For time mispent, that never will return.

But see the sons of vegetation rise,
And spread their leafy banners to the skies.
All-wise Almighty providence we trace
In trees, and plants, and all the flow'ry race;
As clear as in the nobler frame of man,
All lovely copies of the Maker's plan.
The pow'r the same that forms a ray of light,
That call'd creation from eternal night.
"Let there be light," he said: from his profound
Old *Chaos* heard, and trembled at the sound:
Swift as the word, inspir'd by pow'r divine,
Behold the light around its maker shine,
The first fair product of th' omnific God,
And now through all his works diffus'd abroad.

As reason's pow'rs by day our God disclose,
So we may trace him in the night's repose:
Say what is sleep? and dreams how passing strange!
When action ceases, and ideas range
Licentious and unbounded o'er the plains,
Where *Fancy's* queen in giddy triumph reigns.
Hear in soft strains the dreaming lover sigh
To a kind fair, or rave in jealousy;
On pleasure now, and now on vengeance bent,
The lab'ring passions struggle for a vent.

What pow'r, O man! thy *reason* then restores,
So long suspended in nocturnal hours?
What secret hand returns the mental train,
And gives improv'd thine active pow'rs again?
From thee, O man, what gratitude should rise!
And, when from balmy sleep thou op'st thine eyes,
Let thy first thoughts be praises to the skies.
How merciful our God who thus imparts
O'erflowing tides of joy to human hearts,
When wants and woes might be our righteous lot,
Our God forgetting, by our God forgot!

    Among the mental pow'rs a question rose,
"What most the image of th' Eternal shows?"
When thus to *Reason* (so let *Fancy* rove)
Her great companion spoke immortal *Love*.

    "Say, mighty pow'r, how long shall strife prevail,
"And with its murmurs load the whisp'ring gale?
"Refer the cause to *Recollection's* shrine,
"Who loud proclaims my origin divine,
"The cause whence heav'n and earth began to be,
"And is not man immortaliz'd by me?
"*Reason* let this most causeless strife subside."
Thus *Love* pronounc'd, and *Reason* thus reply'd.

    "Thy birth, celestial queen! 'tis mine to own,
"In thee resplendent is the Godhead shown;
"Thy words persuade, my soul enraptur'd feels
"Resistless beauty which thy smile reveals."
Ardent she spoke, and, kindling at her charms,
She clasp'd the blooming goddess in her arms.

    Infinite *Love* wher'er we turn our eyes
Appears: this ev'ry creature's wants supplies;
This most is heard in *Nature's* constant voice,
This makes the morn, and this the eve rejoice;
This bids the fost'ring rains and dews descend
To nourish all, to serve one gen'ral end,

The good of man: yet man ungrateful pays
But little homage, and but little praise.
To him, whose works array'd with mercy shine,
What songs should rise, how constant, how divine!

&

TO A LADY ON THE DEATH OF THREE RELATIONS.[17]

WE trace the pow'r of Death from tomb to tomb,
And his are all the ages yet to come.
'Tis his to call the planets from on high,
To blacken *Phœbus*, and dissolve the sky;
His too, when all in his dark realms are hurl'd,
From its firm base to shake the solid world;
His fatal sceptre rules the spacious whole,
And trembling nature rocks from pole to pole.

Awful he moves, and wide his wings are spread:
Behold thy brother number'd with the dead!
From bondage freed, the exulting spirit flies
Beyond *Olympus*, and these starry skies.
Lost in our woe for thee, blest shade, we mourn
In vain; to earth thou never must return.
Thy sisters too, fair mourner, feel the dart
Of Death, and with fresh torture rend thine heart.
Weep not for them, who wish thine happy mind
To rise with them, and leave the world behind.

As a young plant by hurricanes up torn,
So near its parent lies the newly born—
But 'midst the bright ethereal train behold
It shines superior on a throne of gold:
Then, mourner, cease; let hope thy tears restrain,
Smile on the tomb, and sooth the raging pain.

17. This poem was not listed in her 1772 Proposals.

On yon blest regions fix thy longing view,
Mindless of sublunary scenes below;
Ascend the sacred mount, in thought arise,
And seek substantial and immortal joys;
Where hope receives, where faith to vision springs,
And raptur'd seraphs tune th' immortal strings
To strains extatic. Thou the chorus join,
And to thy father tune the praise divine.

❧

TO A CLERGYMAN ON THE DEATH OF HIS LADY.[18]

WHERE contemplation finds her sacred spring,
Where heav'nly music makes the arches ring,
Where virtue reigns unsully'd and divine,
Where wisdom thron'd, and all the graces shine,
There sits thy spouse amidst the radiant throng,
While praise eternal warbles from her tongue;
There choirs angelic shout her welcome round,
With perfect bliss, and peerless glory crown'd.

While thy dear mate, to flesh no more confin'd,
Exults a blest, an heav'n-ascended mind,
Say in thy breast shall floods of sorrow rise?
Say shall its torrents overwhelm thine eyes?
Amid the seats of heav'n a place is free,
And angels ope their bright ranks for thee;
For thee they wait, and with expectant eye
Thy spouse leans downward from th' empyreal sky:
"O come away, her longing spirit cries,
"And share with me the raptures of the skies.
"Our bliss divine to mortals is unknown;
"Immortal life and glory are our own.
"There too may the dear pledges of our love

18. See the variant version of this poem, "To the Rev. Mr. Pitkin, on the Death of His Lady,"
and its note. This poem was written after the publication of her 1772 Proposals.

"Arrive, and taste with us the joys above;
"Attune the harp to more than mortal lays,
"And join with us the tribute of their praise
"To him, who dy'd stern justice to atone,
"And make eternal glory all our own.
"He in his death slew ours, and, as he rose,
"He crush'd the dire dominion of our foes;
"Vain were their hopes to put the God to flight,
"Chain us to hell, and bar the gates of light."

She spoke, and turn'd from mortal scenes her eyes,
Which beam'd celestial radiance o'er the skies.

Then thou, dear man, no more with grief retire, ⎫
Let grief no longer damp devotion's fire, ⎬
But rise sublime, to equal bliss aspire. ⎭
Thy sighs no more be wafted by the wind,
No more complain, but be to heav'n resign'd.
'Twas thine t' unfold the oracles divine,
To sooth our woes the task was also thine;
Now sorrow is incumbent on thy heart,
Permit the muse a cordial to impart;
Who can to thee their tend'rest aid refuse?
To dry thy tears how longs the heav'nly muse!

❧

AN HYMN TO THE MORNING.[19]

ATTEND my lays, ye ever honour'd nine,
Assist my labours, and my strains refine;
In smoothest numbers pour the notes along,
For bright *Aurora* now demands my song.

Aurora hail, and all the thousand dies,
Which deck thy progress through the vaulted skies:

19. This poem was not listed in her 1772 Proposals.

The morn awakes, and wide extends her rays,
On ev'ry leaf the gentle zephyr plays;
Harmonious lays the feather'd race resume,
Dart the bright eye, and shake the painted plume.

Ye shady groves, your verdant gloom display
To shield your poet from the burning day:
Calliope awake the sacred lyre,
While thy fair sisters fan the pleasing fire:
The bow'rs, the gales, the variegated skies
In all their pleasures in my bosom rise.

See in the east th' illustrious king of day!
His rising radiance drives the shades away—
But Oh! I feel his fervid beams too strong,
And scarce begun, concludes th' abortive song.

&

AN HYMN TO THE EVENING.[20]

SOON as the sun forsook the eastern main
The pealing thunder shook the heav'nly plain;
Majestic grandeur! From the zephyr's wing,
Exhales the incense of the blooming spring.
Soft purl the streams, the birds renew their notes,
And through the air their mingled music floats.

Through all the heav'ns what beauteous dies are spread!
But the west glories in the deepest red:
So may our breasts with ev'ry virtue glow,
The living temples of our God below!

Fill'd with the praise of him who gives the light,
And draws the sable curtains of the night,
Let placid slumbers sooth each weary mind,
At morn to wake more heav'nly, more refin'd;

20. This poem was not listed in her 1772 Proposals.

So shall the labours of the day begin
More pure, more guarded from the snares of sin.

Night's leaden sceptre seals my drousy eyes,
Then cease, my song, till fair *Aurora* rise.

෴

ISAIAH LXIII. 1–8.[21]

SAY, heav'nly muse, what king, or mighty God,
That moves sublime from *Idumea's* road?
In *Bozrah's* dies, with martial glories join'd,
His purple vesture waves upon the wind.
Why thus enrob'd delights he to appear
In the dread image of the *Pow'r* of war?

Compres'd in wrath the swelling wine-press groan'd,
It bled, and pour'd the gushing purple round.

"Mine was the act," th' Almighty Saviour said,
And shook the dazzling glories of his head,
"When all forsook I trod the press alone,
"And conquer'd by omnipotence my own;
"For man's release sustain'd the pond'rous load,
"For man the wrath of an immortal God:
"To execute th' Eternal's dread command
"My soul I sacrific'd with willing hand;
"Sinless I stood before the avenging frown,
"Atoning thus for vices not my own."

His eye the ample field of battle round
Survey'd, but no created succours found;
His own omnipotence sustain'd the fight,
His vengeance sunk the haughty foes in night;
Beneath his feet the prostrate troops were spread,
And round him lay the dying, and the dead.

21. This poem was not listed in her 1772 Proposals.

Great God, what light'ning flashes from thine eyes?
What pow'r withstands if thou indignant rise?

Against thy *Zion* though her foes may rage,
And all their cunning, all their strength engage,
Yet she serenely on thy bosom lies,
Smiles at their arts, and all their force defies.

❧

ON RECOLLECTION.[22]

MNEME begin. Inspire, ye sacred nine,
Your vent'rous *Afric* in her great design.
Mneme, immortal pow'r, I trace thy spring:
Assist my strains, while I thy glories sing:
The acts of long departed years, by thee
Recover'd, in due order rang'd we see:
Thy pow'r the long-forgotten calls from night,
That sweetly plays before the *fancy's* sight.

Mneme in our nocturnal visions pours
The ample treasure of her secret stores;
Swift from above she wings her silent flight
Through *Phœbe's* realms, fair regent of the night;
And, in her pomp of images display'd,
To the high-raptur'd poet gives her aid,
Through the unbounded regions of the mind,
Diffusing light celestial and refin'd.
The heav'nly *phantom* paints the actions done
By ev'ry tribe beneath the rolling sun.

Mneme, enthron'd within the human breast,
Has vice condemn'd, and ev'ry virtue blest.
How sweet the sound when we her plaudit hear?

22. See the variant version of this poem and its note. The "eighteen years" is indicated with the earlier version as her age when the poem was written, which must have been in 1771.

Sweeter than music to the ravish'd ear,
Sweeter than *Maro's* entertaining strains
Resounding through the groves, and hills, and plains.
But how is *Mneme* dreaded by the race,
Who scorn her warnings and despise her grace?
By her unveil'd each horrid crime appears,
Her awful hand a cup of wormwood bears.
Days, years mispent, O what a hell of woe!
Hers the worst tortures that our souls can know.

Now eighteen years their destin'd course have run,
In fast succession round the central sun.
How did the follies of that period pass
Unnotic'd, but behold them writ in brass!
In Recollection see them fresh return,
And sure 'tis mine to be asham'd, and mourn.

O *Virtue*, smiling in immortal green,
Do thou exert thy pow'r, and change the scene;
Be thine employ to guide my future days,
And mine to pay the tribute of my praise.

Of *Recollection* such the pow'r enthron'd
In ev'ry breast, and thus her pow'r is own'd.
The wretch, who dar'd the vengeance of the skies,
At last awakes in horror and surprize,
By her alarm'd, he sees impending fate,
He howls in anguish, and repents too late.
But O! what peace, what joys are hers t' impart
To ev'ry holy, ev'ry upright heart!
Thrice blest the man, who, in her sacred shrine,
Feels himself shelter'd from the wrath divine!

~

ON IMAGINATION.[23]

THY various works, imperial queen, we see,
How bright their forms! how deck'd with pomp by thee!
Thy wond'rous acts in beauteous order stand,
And all attest how potent is thine hand.

From *Helicon's* refulgent heights attend,
Ye sacred choir, and my attempts befriend:
To tell her glories with a faithful tongue,
Ye blooming graces, triumph in my song.

Now here, now there, the roving *Fancy* flies,
Till some lov'd object strikes her wand'ring eyes,
Whose silken fetters all the senses bind,
And soft captivity involves the mind.

Imagination! who can sing thy force?
Or who describe the swiftness of thy course?
Soaring through air to find the bright abode,
Th' empyreal palace of the thund'ring God,
We on thy pinions can surpass the wind,
And leave the rolling universe behind:

---

23. This poem was not listed in her 1772 Proposals. A variant version was published in the last month of her life, in John Wesley's *Arminian Magazine* for December 1784, in London. During 1781 and 1784 this magazine of the Methodist movement published variants of a total of eight previously published Wheatley poems ("On the Death of a Child, five years of Age"; "On the Death of a young Gentleman"; "Thoughts on the Works of Providence"; "To T. H[ubbard] Esq; on the Death of his Daughter"; "To S. M. a young African Painter, on seeing his Works"; "To the Right Honourable William, Earl of D——t——th, when Secretary of State for North America"; "On the Death of J. C. an Infant"; and "On Imagination") and one previously unpublished poem ("An Elegy on leaving ——"). That such a magazine would find her poems appropriate for inclusion is not strange given the religious aspects of her works and her friendships with several persons prominent in the general movement, particularly the Countess of Huntingdon. Rogal ("Wheatley's Methodist Connection") believes that the changes made in at least four of the variants ("To T. H.," "To S. M.," "On . . . J. C.," and "To . . . D[ar]t[mou]th"—he seems not to be aware of the other variants) were made by John Wesley in an editorial capacity to make them even more suitable for his Methodist readers. However, Isani ("Methodist Connection") believes that the *Arminian* had access to changes either made or authorized by Wheatley herself, supporting that contention partly by its printing of a previously unknown poem by her. In some of the poems there was little change of significance.

From star to star the mental optics rove,
Measure the skies, and range the realms above.
There in one view we grasp the mighty whole,
Or with new worlds amaze th' unbounded soul.

Though *Winter* frowns to *Fancy's* raptur'd eyes
The fields may flourish, and gay scenes arise;
The frozen deeps may break their iron bands,
And bid their waters murmur o'er the sands.
Fair *Flora* may resume her fragrant reign,
And with her flow'ry riches deck the plain;
Sylvanus may diffuse his honours round,
And all the forest may with leaves be crown'd:
Show'rs may descend, and dews their gems disclose,
And nectar sparkle on the blooming rose.

Such is thy pow'r, nor are thine orders vain,
O thou the leader of the mental train:
In full perfection all thy works are wrought,
And thine the sceptre o'er the realms of thought.
Before thy throne the subject-passions bow,
Of subject-passions sov'reign ruler Thou,
At thy command joy rushes on the heart,
And through the glowing veins the spirits dart.

Fancy might now her silken pinions try
To rise from earth, and sweep th' expanse on high;

In others the change was significant, especially in lengthy omissions. Nevertheless, for both the variants and the new poem we do not know if she even knew that they were going to be published, much less had some direct hand in bringing that about or making the changes; and the large number of changes made by others in her poems (including truncating and word changes) in reprinting them in book form or in selection over the following decades (see Robinson, *Her Writings* and *Bio-Bibliography*) gives one pause about these changes too, even though they occurred while she was still alive (but in America, not England). On the other hand, there is the new poem printed by the *Arminian*; and Isani suggests several persons who might have been intermediaries. He also considers the possibility that these versions of the poems and the new poem might have been left over (in England after she left) from publishing her book. I would add the possibility of involvement by Nathaniel Wheatley, with whom she had gone to England and who had become a permanent resident there after their arrival and who did not die till the spring of 1783. At any rate, it is fact that no other of her poems were published in the London *Arminian* after her death in December 1784.

From *Tithon's* bed now might *Aurora* rise,
Her cheeks all glowing with celestial dies,
While a pure stream of light o'erflows the skies. }
The monarch of the day I might behold,
And all the mountains tipt with radiant gold,
But I reluctant leave the pleasing views,
Which *Fancy* dresses to delight the *Muse*;
Winter austere forbids me to aspire,
And northern tempests damp the rising fire;
They chill the tides of *Fancy's* flowing sea,
Cease then, my song, cease the unequal lay.

❧

A FUNERAL POEM ON THE DEATH OF C. E. AN INFANT OF
TWELVE MONTHS.[24]

THROUGH airy roads he wings his instant flight
To purer regions of celestial light;
Enlarg'd he sees unnumber'd systems roll,
Beneath him sees the universal whole,
Planets on planets run their destin'd round,
And circling wonders fill the vast profound.
Th' ethereal now, and now th' empyreal skies
With growing splendors strike his wond'ring eyes:
The angels view him with delight unknown,
Press his soft hand, and seat him on his throne;
Then smiling thus. "To this divine abode,
"The seat of saints, of seraphs, and of God,
"Thrice welcome thou." The raptur'd babe replies,
"Thanks to my God, who snatch'd me to the skies,
"E'er vice triumphant had possess'd my heart,

24. See the variant version of this poem about Charles Eliot and its note. This poem was
written after the publication of her 1772 Proposals.

"E'er yet the tempter had beguil'd my heart,
"E'er yet on sin's base actions I was bent,
"E'er yet I knew temptation's dire intent;
"E'er yet the lash for horrid crimes I felt,
"E'er vanity had led my way to guilt,
"But, soon arriv'd at my celestial goal,
"Full glories rush on my expanding soul."
Joyful he spoke: exulting cherubs round
Clapt their glad wings, the heav'nly vaults resound.

    Say, parents, why this unavailing moan?
Why heave your pensive bosoms with the groan?
To *Charles*, the happy subject of my song,
A brighter world, and nobler strains belong.
Say would you tear him from the realms above
By thoughtless wishes, and prepost'rous love?
Doth his felicity increase your pain?
Or could you welcome to this world again
The heir of bliss? with a superior air
Methinks he answers with a smile severe,
"Thrones and dominions cannot tempt me there."
But still you cry, "Can we the sigh forbear,
"And still and still must we not pour the tear?
"Our only hope, more dear than vital breath,
"Twelve moons revolv'd, becomes the prey of death;
"Delightful infant, nightly visions give
"Thee to our arms, and we with joy receive,
"We fain would clasp the *Phantom* to our breast,
"The *Phantom* flies, and leaves the soul unblest."

    To yon bright regions let your faith ascend,
Prepare to join your dearest infant friend
In pleasures without measure, without end.

TO CAPTAIN H——D, OF THE 65TH REGIMENT.[25]

SAY, muse divine, can hostile scenes delight
The warrior's bosom in the fields of fight?
Lo! here the christian, and the hero join
With mutual grace to form the man divine.
In H——d see with pleasure and surprize,
Where *valour* kindles, and where *virtue* lies:
Go, hero brave, still grace the post of fame,
And add new glories to thine honour'd name,
Still to the field, and still to virtue true:
Britannia glories in no son like you.

TO THE RIGHT HONOURABLE WILLIAM, EARL OF DARTMOUTH, HIS MAJESTY'S PRINCIPAL SECRETARY OF STATE FOR NORTH-AMERICA, &C.[26]

HAIL, happy day, when, smiling like the morn,
Fair *Freedom* rose *New-England* to adorn:
The northern clime beneath her genial ray,
Dartmouth, congratulates thy blissful sway:
Elate with hope her race no longer mourns,
Each soul expands, each grateful bosom burns,
While in thine hand with pleasure we behold
The silken reins, and *Freedom's* charms unfold.
Long lost to realms beneath the northern skies

---

25. Robinson, *Her Writings*, p. 273, identifies the subject of this poem as Captain John Hanfield and suggests that the poem was not listed in her 1772 Proposals because of growing antagonism toward British troops on the part of Boston patriots, but was found to be more appropriate for a book to be published in England.

26. See the variant version of this poem and its note. This poem was written after the publication of her 1772 Proposals.

She shines supreme, while hated *faction* dies:
Soon as appear'd the *Goddess* long desir'd,
Sick at the view, she lanquish'd and expir'd;
Thus from the splendors of the morning light
The owl in sadness seeks the caves of night.

No more, *America*, in mournful strain
Of wrongs, and grievance unredress'd complain,
No longer shalt thou dread the iron chain,
Which wanton *Tyranny* with lawless hand
Had made, and with it meant t' enslave the land.

Should you, my lord, while you peruse my song,
Wonder from whence my love of *Freedom* sprung,
Whence flow these wishes for the common good,
By feeling hearts alone best understood,
I, young in life, by seeming cruel fate
Was snatch'd from *Afric's* fancy'd happy seat:
What pangs excruciating must molest,
What sorrows labour in my parent's breast?
Steel'd was that soul and by no misery mov'd
That from a father seiz'd his babe belov'd:
Such, such my case. And can I then but pray
Others may never feel tyrannic sway?

For favours past, great Sir, our thanks are due,
And thee we ask thy favours to renew,
Since in thy pow'r, as in thy will before,
To sooth the griefs, which thou did'st once deplore.
May heav'nly grace the sacred sanction give
To all thy works, and thou for ever live
Not only on the wings of fleeting *Fame*,
Though praise immortal crowns the patriot's name,
But to conduct to heav'ns refulgent fane,
May fiery coursers sweep th' ethereal plain,
And bear thee upwards to that blest abode,
Where, like the prophet, thou shalt find thy God.

ꝰ

ODE TO NEPTUNE.[27]

On Mrs. W—'s Voyage to England.

I.

WHILE raging tempests shake the shore,
While *Æ'lus'* thunders round us roar,
And sweep impetuous o'er the plain
Be still, O tyrant of the main;
Nor let thy brow contracted frowns betray,
While my *Susannah* skims the wat'ry way.

II.

The *Pow'r* propitious hears the lay,
The blue-ey'd daughters of the sea
With sweeter cadence glide along,
And *Thames* responsive joins the song.
Pleas'd with their notes *Sol* sheds benign his ray,
And double radiance decks the face of day.

III.

To court thee to *Britannia's* arms
  Serene the climes and mild the sky,
Her region boasts unnumber'd charms,
  Thy welcome smiles in ev'ry eye.
Thy promise, *Neptune* keep, record my pray'r,
Nor give my wishes to the empty air.

Boston, October 10 1772.

27. This poem was written after the publication of her 1772 Proposals. A copy of Wheatley's book at the American Antiquarian Society has a number of notes written in it. One of those is with "A Farewell to America. To Mrs. S. W.," and it says in ink, "Mrs. Susannah Wright." This is followed by "eminent for her Wax Works etc." in pencil in another hand. Clearly, the farewell poem is Phillis's farewell to her mistress and friend, Susanna Wheatley, who, as far as we know, never traveled to England herself. Probably the note regarding Susannah Wright was intended instead for the poem above. (On the other hand, not all of those notes are accurate, as the Congregational minister Joseph Sewall is identified as a Presbyterian minister, and the Wright who was widely known for her wax figures was Mrs. Patience Wright, who sailed to England in February 1772 on the *Nancy*. Regarding Wright see Paul Engle, *Women in the American Revolu-*

TO A LADY ON HER COMING TO NORTH-AMERICA WITH HER SON, FOR THE RECOVERY OF HER HEALTH.[28]

INdulgent muse! my grov'ling mind inspire,
And fill my bosom with celestial fire.

See from *Jamaica's* fervid shore she moves,
Like the fair mother of the blooming loves,
When from above the *Goddess* with her hand
Fans the soft breeze, and lights upon the land;
Thus she on *Neptune's* wat'ry realm reclin'd
Appear'd, and thus invites the ling'ring wind.

"Arise, ye winds, *America* explore,
"Waft me, ye gales, from this malignant shore;
"The *Northern* milder climes I long to greet,
"There hope that health will my arrival meet."
Soon as she spoke in my ideal view
The winds assented, and the vessel flew.

Madam, your spouse bereft of wife and son,
In the grove's dark recesses pours his moan;
Each branch, wide-spreading to the ambient sky,
Forgets its verdure, and submits to die.

From thence I turn, and leave the sultry plain,
And swift pursue thy passage o'er the main:
The ship arrives before the fav'ring wind,
And makes the *Philadelphian* port assign'd,
Thence I attend you to *Bostonia's* arms,
Where gen'rous friendship ev'ry bosom warms:
Thrice welcome here! may health revive again,
Bloom on thy cheek, and bound in ev'ry vein!

---

tion [Chicago, 1976], pp. 195–206, 282–83.) This particular copy of Wheatley's book was given to the American Antiquarian Society by K. B. Stratford, a relative of Thomas Wallcut (see the note for Wheatley's poem to Thomas Amory).

28. This poem was listed in her 1772 Proposals but was undated.

Then back return to gladden ev'ry heart,
And give your spouse his soul's far dearer part,
Receiv'd again with what a sweet surprize,
The tear in transport starting from his eyes!
While his attendant son with blooming grace
Springs to his father's ever dear embrace.
With shouts of joy *Jamaica's* rocks resound,
With shouts of joy the country rings around.

❧

TO A LADY ON HER REMARKABLE PRESERVATION IN AN HURRICANE IN *NORTH-CAROLINA.*[29]

THOUGH thou did'st hear the tempest from afar,
And felt'st the horrors of the wat'ry war,
To me unknown, yet on this peaceful shore
Methinks I hear the storm tumultuous roar,
And how stern *Boreas* with impetuous hand
Compell'd the *Nereids* to usurp the land.
Reluctant rose the daughters of the main,
And slow ascending glided o'er the plain,
Till *Æolus* in his rapid chariot drove
In gloomy grandeur from the vault above:
Furious he comes. His winged sons obey
Their frantic sire, and madden all the sea.
The billows rave, the wind's fierce tyrant roars,
And with his thund'ring terrors shakes the shores:
Broken by waves the vessel's frame is rent,
And strows with planks the wat'ry element.

But thee, *Maria*, a kind *Nereid's* shield

---

29. This poem was listed in her 1772 Proposals but was undated. Since the Proposals were first published in February 1772, I looked for a hurricane before that date and found that the next one in North Carolina earlier than that date was on September 7–8, 1769 (David M. Ludlum, *Early American Hurricanes* [Boston, 1963]) and that it "was among the severest of the century" (p. 48) and "must be placed among the more destructive storms of the century" (p. 25), with exceptionally rapid and high flooding and much damage to shipping.

Preserv'd from sinking, and thy form upheld:
And sure some heav'nly oracle design'd
At that dread crisis to instruct thy mind
Things of eternal consequence to weigh,
And to thine heart just feelings to convey
Of things above, and of the future doom,
And what the births of the dread world to come.

From tossing seas I welcome thee to land.
"Resign her, *Nereid*," 'twas thy God's command.
Thy spouse late buried, as thy fears conceiv'd,
Again returns, thy fears are all reliev'd:
Thy daughter blooming with superior grace
Again thou see'st, again thine arms embrace;
O come, and joyful show thy spouse his heir,
And what the blessings of maternal care!

❧

TO A LADY AND HER CHILDREN, ON THE DEATH OF HER SON
AND THEIR BROTHER.[30]

O'Erwhelming sorrow now demands my song:
From death the overwhelming sorrow sprung.
What flowing tears? What hearts with grief opprest?
What sighs on sighs heave the fond parent's breast?
The brother weeps, the hapless sisters join
Th' increasing woe, and swell the crystal brine;
The poor, who once his gen'rous bounty fed,
Droop, and bewail their benefactor dead.
In death the friend, the kind companion lies,
And in one death what various comfort dies!

Th' unhappy mother sees the sanguine rill
Forget to flow, and nature's wheels stand still,

---

30. This poem was listed in her 1772 Proposals but was undated. The lady's name is given
there as Mrs. Boylston.

But see from earth his spirit far remov'd,
And know no grief recals your best-belov'd:
He, upon pinions swifter than the wind,
Has left mortality's sad scenes behind
For joys to this terrestrial state unknown,
And glories richer than the monarch's crown.
Of virtue's steady course the prize behold!
What blissful wonders to his mind unfold!
But of celestial joys I sing in vain:
Attempt not, muse, the too advent'rous strain.

   No more in briny show'rs, ye friends around,
Or bathe his clay, or waste them on the ground:
Still do you weep, still wish for his return?
How cruel thus to wish, and thus to mourn?
No more for him the streams of sorrow pour,
But haste to join him on the heav'nly shore,
On harps of gold to tune immortal lays,
And to your God immortal anthems raise.

❧

TO A GENTLEMAN AND LADY ON THE DEATH OF THE LADY'S
BROTHER AND SISTER, AND A CHILD OF THE NAME *AVIS*, AGED
ONE YEAR.[31]

ON *Death's* domain intent I fix my eyes,
Where human nature in vast ruin lies:
With pensive mind I search the drear abode,
Where the great conqu'ror has his spoils, bestow'd;
There there the offspring of six thousand years
In endless numbers to my view appears:
Whole kingdoms in his gloomy den are thrust,
And nations mix with their primeval dust:

31. This poem was listed in her 1772 Proposals but was undated. The gentleman's name is
given there as James Sullivan.

Insatiate still he gluts the ample tomb;
His is the present, his the age to come.
See here a brother, here a sister spread,
And a sweet daughter mingled with the dead.

But, *Madam*, let your grief be laid aside,
And let the fountain of your tears be dry'd,
In vain they flow to wet the dusty plain,
Your sighs are wafted to the skies in vain,
Your pains they witness, but they can no more,
While *Death* reigns tyrant o'er this mortal shore.

The glowing stars and silver queen of light
At last must perish in the gloom of night:
Resign thy friends to that Almighty hand,
Which gave them life, and bow to his command;
Thine *Avis* give without a murm'ring heart,
Though half thy soul be fated to depart.
To shining guards consign thine infant care
To waft triumphant through the seas of air:
Her soul enlarg'd to heav'nly pleasure springs,
She feeds on truth and uncreated things.
Methinks I hear her in the realms above,
And leaning forward with a filial love,
Invite you there to share immortal bliss
Unknown, untasted in a state like this.
With tow'ring hopes, and growing grace arise,
And seek beatitude beyond the skies.

❧

ON THE DEATH OF DR. SAMUEL MARSHALL. 1771.[32]

THROUGH thickest glooms look back, immortal shade,
On that confusion which thy death has made;

32. See the two variant versions of this poem and their notes.

Or from *Olympus'* height look down, and see
A *Town* involv'd in grief bereft of thee.
Thy *Lucy* sees thee mingle with the dead,
And rends the graceful tresses from her head,
Wild in her woe, with grief unknown opprest
Sigh follows sigh deep heaving from her breast.

   Too quickly fled, ah! whither art thou gone?
Ah! lost for ever to thy wife and son!
The hapless child, thine only hope and heir,
Clings round his mother's neck, and weeps his sorrows there.
The loss of thee on *Tyler's* soul returns,
And *Boston* for her dear physician mourns.

   When sickness call'd for *Marshall's* healing hand,
With what compassion did his soul expand?
In him we found the father and the friend:
In life how lov'd! how honour'd in his end!

   And must not then our *Æsculapius* stay
To bring his ling'ring infant into day?
The babe unborn in the dark womb is tost,
And seems in anguish for its father lost.

   Gone is *Apollo* from his house of earth,
But leaves the sweet memorials of his worth:
The common parent, whom we all deplore,
From yonder world unseen must come no more,
Yet 'midst our woes immortal hopes attend
The spouse, the sire, the universal friend.

~

TO A GENTLEMAN ON HIS VOYAGE TO *GREAT-BRITAIN* FOR THE
RECOVERY OF HIS HEALTH.[33]

WHILE others chant the gay *Elysian* scenes,
Of balmy zephyrs, and of flow'ry plains,
My song more happy speaks a greater name,
Feels higher motives and a nobler flame.
For thee, O R—, the muse attunes her strings,
And mounts sublime above inferior things.

I sing not now of green embow'ring woods,
I sing not now the daughters of the floods,
I sing not of the storms o'er ocean driv'n,
And how they howl'd along the waste of heav'n,
But I to R— would paint the *British* shore,
And vast *Atlantic*, not untry'd before:
Thy life impair'd commands thee to arise,
Leave these bleak regions and inclement skies,
Where chilling winds return the winter past,
And nature shudders at the furious blast.

O thou stupendous, earth-enclosing main
Exert thy wonders to the world again!
If ere thy pow'r prolong'd the fleeting breath,

---

33. This poem is not listed in her 1772 Proposals. Daniel Ricketson, *The History of New Bed-ford* (New Bedford, 1858), p. 262, says that this poem is addressed to Joseph Rotch, Jr., brother of William Rotch, Sr., both members of the prominent Quaker merchant family of the same name of New Bedford and Nantucket (pp. 108–12 and passim). "The fervent wish of the gentle Phillis was not granted. The subject of her invocation died in Bristol, England, soon after his arrival" (p. 263). William Rotch places the date of his brother's death in 1767 ("Autobiographical Memoir of William Rotch," *New-England Historical and Genealogical Register* 32 [April 1878]: 154–55). From other sources Robinson, *Her Writings*, p. 273, gives Joseph Rotch's years as 1743–73 and says that he sailed for England at the end of 1772, dying in London. Ricketson apparently printed this poem (pp. 262–63) from the manuscript of it (judging from the end-line dashes preserved there, which are usual in Wheatley's manuscripts, but not usually preserved in her book), with some nineteenth-century "modernization" of spelling and punctuation. In addition, he apparently misread "case" and wrote "care," which also might suggest that he was reading from manuscript.

Turn'd back the shafts, and mock'd the gates of death,
If ere thine air dispens'd an healing pow'r,
Or snatch'd the victim from the fatal hour,
This equal case demands thine equal care,
And equal wonders may this patient share.
But unavailing, frantic is the dream
To hope thine aid without the aid of him
Who gave thee birth, and taught thee where to flow,
And in thy waves his various blessings show.

    May R— return to view his native shore
Replete with vigour not his own before,
Then shall we see with pleasure and surprize,
And own thy work, great Ruler of the skies!

❧

TO THE REV. DR. THOMAS AMORY ON READING HIS SERMONS
ON DAILY DEVOTION, IN WHICH THAT DUTY IS RECOMMENDED
AND ASSISTED.[34]

TO cultivate in ev'ry noble mind
Habitual grace, and sentiments refin'd,
Thus while you strive to mend the human heart,
Thus while the heav'nly precepts you impart,
O may each bosom catch the sacred fire,
And youthful minds to *Virtue's* throne aspire!

    When God's eternal ways you set in sight,

34. Amory (1701–74) was an English minister and religious writer. According to a catalog
card at the American Antiquarian Society, it once owned a copy of Amory's *Daily Devotion As-
sisted and Recommended, in Four Sermons . . . ; The Second Edition Corrected and Improved* (London
[1770], Boston [reprinted and sold by E. Russell] [1772]), which had been given to Wheatley
by the Reverend Dr. Charles Chauncy of Boston (one of those who signed the letter "To the
PUBLICK" used at the front of her book) on October 14, 1772 (after the publication of her
1772 Proposals). She gave the book to Thomas Wallcut (1758–1840) on March 26, 1774
(along with a copy of John Lathrop's *The Importance of Early Piety*, published in Boston by Isa-
iah Thomas in 1771, which is now at Yale's Beinecke Library). (See the notes to her poem to
the students at Cambridge, her 1779 Proposals, and her ode to Neptune.)

And *Virtue* shines in all her native light,
In vain would *Vice* her works in night conceal,
For *Wisdom's* eye pervades the sable veil.

    Artists may paint the sun's effulgent rays,
But *Amory's* pen the brighter God displays:
While his great works in *Amory's* pages shine,
And while he proves his essence all divine,
The Atheist sure no more can boast aloud
Of chance, or nature, and exclude the God;
As if the clay without the potter's aid
Should rise in various forms, and shapes self-made,
Or worlds above with orb o'er orb profound
Self-mov'd could run the everlasting round.
It cannot be—unerring *Wisdom* guides
With eye propitious, and o'er all presides.

    Still prosper, *Amory*! still may'st thou receive
The warmest blessings which a muse can give,
And when this transitory state is o'er,
When kingdoms fall, and fleeting *Fame's* no more,
May *Amory* triumph in immortal fame,
A noble title, and superior name!

   ❧

ON THE DEATH OF J. C. AN INFANT.[35]

NO more the flow'ry scenes of pleasure rise,
Nor charming prospects greet the mental eyes,
No more with joy we view that lovely face
Smiling, disportive, flush'd with ev'ry grace.

---

35. This poem was not listed in her 1772 Proposals. A briefer, variant version of this poem
was published during her lifetime, in the London *Arminian Magazine* for November 1784 (see
the note for her poem "On Imagination" in this volume). It was slightly altered for reprinting
in the Philadelphia *Methodist Magazine* for September 1797.

The tear of sorrow flows from ev'ry eye,
Groans answer groans, and sighs to sighs reply;
What sudden pangs shot thro' each aching heart,
When, *Death*, thy messenger dispatch'd his dart?
Thy dread attendants, all-destroying *Pow'r*,
Hurried the infant to his mortal hour.
Could'st thou unpitying close those radiant eyes?
Or fail'd his artless beauties to surprize?
Could not his innocence thy stroke controul,
Thy purpose shake, and soften all thy soul?

The blooming babe, with shades of *Death* o'erspread,
No more shall smile, no more shall raise its head,
But, like a branch that from the tree is torn,
Falls prostrate, wither'd, languid, and forlorn.
"Where flies my *James?*" 'tis thus I seem to hear }
The parent ask, "Some angel tell me where }
"He wings his passage thro' the yielding air?" }
Methinks a cherub bending from the skies
Observes the question, and serene replies,
"In heav'ns high palaces your babe appears:
"Prepare to meet him, and dismiss your tears."
Shall not th' intelligence your grief restrain,
And turn the mournful to the chearful strain?
Cease your complaints, suspend each rising sigh,
Cease to accuse the Ruler of the sky.
Parents, no more indulge the falling tear:
Let *Faith* to heav'n's refulgent domes repair,
There see your infant, like a seraph glow:
What charms celestial in his numbers flow
Melodious, while the soul-enchanting strain
Dwells on his tongue, and fills th'ethereal plain?
Enough—for ever cease your murm'ring breath;
Not as a foe, but friend converse with *Death*,
Since to the port of happiness unknown
He brought that treasure which you call your own.

The gift of heav'n intrusted to your hand
Chearful resign at the divine command:
Not at your bar must sov'reign *Wisdom* stand. }

❧

AN HYMN TO HUMANITY.[36]
TO S. P. G. ESQ;

I.
LO! for this dark terrestrial ball
Forsakes his azure-paved hall
   A prince of heav'nly birth!
Divine *Humanity* behold.
What wonders rise, what charms unfold
   At his descent to earth!

II.
The bosoms of the great and good
With wonder and delight he view'd,
   And fix'd his empire there:
Him, close compressing to his breast,
The sire of gods and men address'd,
   "My son, my heav'nly fair!

III.
"Descend to earth, there place thy throne;
"To succour man's afflicted son
   "Each human heart inspire:
"To act in bounties unconfin'd
"Enlarge the close contracted mind,
   "And fill it with thy fire."

IV.
Quick as the word, with swift career
He wings his course from star to star,

36. This poem was not listed in her 1772 Proposals.

And leaves the bright abode.
The *Virtue* did his charms impart;
Their G——y! then thy raptur'd heart
    Perceiv'd the rushing God:

V.

For when thy pitying eye did see
The languid muse in low degree,
    Then, then at thy desire
Descended the celestial nine;
O'er me methought they deign'd to shine,
    And deign'd to string my lyre.

VI.

Can *Afric's* muse forgetful prove?
Or can such friendship fail to move
    A tender human heart?
Immortal *Friendship* laurel-crown'd
The smiling *Graces* all surround
    With ev'ry heav'nly *Art*.

❧

TO THE HONOURABLE T. H. ESQ; ON THE DEATH OF HIS
DAUGHTER.[37]

WHILE deep you mourn beneath the cypress-shade
The hand of Death, and your dear daughter laid
In dust, whose absence gives your tears to flow,
And racks your bosom with incessant woe,
Let *Recollection* take a tender part,
Assuage the raging tortures of your heart,
Still the wild tempest of tumultuous grief,
And pour the heav'nly nectar of relief:
Suspend the sigh, dear Sir, and check the groan,

37. See the variant version of this poem and its note.

Divinely bright your daughter's *Virtues* shone:
How free from scornful pride her gentle mind,
Which ne'er its aid to indigence declin'd!
Expanding free, it sought the means to prove
Unfailing charity, unbounded love!

   She unreluctant flies to see no more
Her dear-lov'd parents on earth's dusky shore:
Impatient heav'n's resplendent goal to gain,
She with swift progress cuts the azure plain,
Where grief subsides, where changes are no more,
And life's tumultuous billows cease to roar;
She leaves her earthly mansion for the skies,
Where new creations feast her wond'ring eyes.

   To heav'n's high mandate chearfully resign'd
She mounts, and leaves the rolling globe behind;
She, who late wish'd that *Leonard* might return,
Has ceas'd to languish, and forgot to mourn;
To the same high empyreal mansions come,
She joins her spouse, and smiles upon the tomb:
And thus I hear her from the realms above:
"Lo! this the kingdom of celestial love!
"Could ye, fond parents, see our present bliss,
"How soon would you each sigh, each fear dismiss?
"Amidst unutter'd pleasures whilst I play
"In the fair sunshine of celestial day,
"As far as grief affects an happy soul
"So far doth grief my better mind controul,
"To see on earth my aged parents mourn,
"And secret wish for T——l to return:
"Let brighter scenes your ev'ning-hours employ:
"Converse with heav'n, and taste the promis'd joy."

NIOBE IN DISTRESS FOR HER CHILDREN SLAIN BY APOLLO,
FROM *OVID's* METAMORPHOSES, BOOK VI. AND FROM A VIEW OF
THE PAINTING OF MR. *RICHARD WILSON.*[38]

APOLLO's wrath to man the dreadful spring
Of ills innum'rous, tuneful goddess, sing!
Thou who did'st first th' ideal pencil give,
And taught'st the painter in his works to live,
Inspire with glowing energy of thought,
What *Wilson* painted, and what *Ovid* wrote.
Muse! lend thy aid, nor let me sue in vain,
Tho' last and meanest of the rhyming train!
O guide my pen in lofty strains to show
The *Phrygian* queen, all beautiful in woe.

'Twas where *Mæonia* spreads her wide domain
Niobe dwelt, and held her potent reign:
See in her hand the regal sceptre shine,
The wealthy heir of *Tantalus* divine,
He most distinguish'd by *Dodonean Jove*,
To approach the tables of the gods above:
Her grandsire *Atlas*, who with mighty pains
Th' ethereal axis on his neck sustains:
Her other gran sire on the throne on high
Rolls the loud-pealing thunder thro' the sky.

Her spouse, *Amphion*, who from *Jove* too springs,
Divinely taught to sweep the sounding strings.

Seven sprightly sons the royal bed adorn,
Seven daughters beauteous as the op'ning morn,
As when *Aurora* fills the ravish'd sight,
And decks the orient realms with rosy light

38. This poem was not listed in her 1772 Proposals. Richard Wilson (1714–82) was a Welsh painter noted for his landscapes. He used the Niobe story for three paintings, two of which were engraved during the time Wheatley lived in Boston. It is uncertain to which she refers here.

From their bright eyes the living splendors play,
Nor can beholders bear the flashing ray.

Wherever, *Niobe*, thou turn'st thine eyes,
New beauties kindle, and new joys arise!
But thou had'st far the happier mother prov'd,
If this fair offspring had been less belov'd:
What if their charms exceed *Aurora's* teint,
No words could tell them, and no pencil paint,
Thy love too vehement hastens to destroy
Each blooming maid, and each celestial boy.

Now *Manto* comes, endu'd with mighty skill,
The past to explore, the future to reveal.
Thro' *Thebes'* wide streets *Tiresia's* daughter came,
Divine *Latona's* mandate to proclaim:
The *Theban* maids to hear the orders ran,
When thus *Mæonia's* prophetess began:

"Go *Thebans*! great *Latona's* will obey,
"And pious tribute at her altars pay:
"With rights divine, the goddess be implor'd,
"Nor be her sacred offspring unador'd."
Thus *Manto* spoke. The *Theban* maids obey,
And pious tribute to the goddess pay.
The rich perfumes ascend in waving spires,
And altars blaze with consecrated fires;
The fair assembly moves with graceful air,
And leaves of laurel bind the flowing hair.

Niobe comes with all her royal race,
With charms unnumber'd, and superior grace:
Her *Phrygian* garments of delightful hue,
Inwove with gold, refulgent to the view,
Beyond description beautiful she moves
Like heav'nly *Venus*, 'midst her smiles and loves:
She views around the supplicating train,
And shakes her graceful head with stern disdain,
Proudly she turns around her lofty eyes,

And thus reviles celestial deities:
"What madness drives the *Theban* ladies fair
"To give their incense to surrounding air?
"Say why this new sprung deity preferr'd?
"Why vainly fancy your petitions heard?
"Or say why *Cœus'* offspring is obey'd,
"While to my goddesship no tribute's paid?
"For me no altars blaze with living fires,
"No bullock bleeds, no frankincense transpires,
"Tho' *Cadmus'* palace, not unknown to fame,
"And *Phrygian* nations all revere my name.
"Where'er I turn my eyes vast wealth I find.
"Lo! here an empress with a goddess join'd.
"What, shall a *Titaness* be deify'd,
"To whom the spacious earth a couch deny'd?
"Nor heav'n, nor earth, nor sea receiv'd your queen,
"'Till pitying *Delos* took the wand'rer in.
"Round me what a large progeny is spread!
"No frowns of fortune has my soul to dread.
"What if indignant she decrease my train
"More than *Latona's* number will remain?
"Then hence, ye *Theban* dames, hence haste away,
"Nor longer off'rings to *Latona* pay?
"Regard the orders of *Amphion's* spouse,
"And take the leaves of laurel from your brows."
Niobe spoke. The *Theban* maids obey'd,
Their brows unbound, and left the rights unpaid.

   The angry goddess heard, then silence broke
On *Cynthus'* summit, and indignant spoke;
"*Phœbus*! behold, thy mother in disgrace,
"Who to no goddess yields the prior place
"Except to *Juno's* self, who reigns above,
"The spouse and sister of the thund'ring *Jove*.
"*Niobe* sprung from Tantalus inspires
"Each *Theban* bosom with rebellious fires;
"No reason her imperious temper quells,

"But all her father in her tongue rebels;
"Wrap her own sons for her blaspheming breath,
"*Apollo*! wrap them in the shades of death."
Latona ceas'd and ardent thus replies,
The God, whose glory decks th' expanded skies.

　"Cease thy complaints, mine be the task assign'd
"To punish pride, and scourge the rebel mind."
This *Phœbe* join'd.—They wing their instant flight;
Thebes trembled as th' immortal pow'rs alight.

　With clouds incompass'd glorious *Phœbus* stands;
The feather'd vengeance quiv'ring in his hands.

　Near *Cadmus'* walls a plain extended lay,
Where *Thebes'* young princes pass'd in sport the day:
There the bold coursers bounded o'er the plains,
While their great masters held the golden reins.
Ismenus first the racing pastime led,
And rul'd the fury of his flying steed.
"Ah me," he sudden cries, with shrieking breath,
While in his breast he feels the shaft of death;
He drops the bridle on his courser's mane,
Before his eyes in shadows swims the plain,
He, the first-born of great *Amphion's* bed,
Was struck the first, first mingled with the dead.

　Then didst thou, *Sipylus*, the language hear
Of fate portentous whistling in the air:
As when th' impending storm the sailor sees
He spreads his canvas to the fav'ring breeze,
So to thine horse thou gav'st the golden reins,
Gav'st him to rush impetuous o'er the plains:
But ah! a fatal shaft from *Phœbus'* hand
Smites through thy neck, and sinks thee on the sand.

　Two other brothers were at *wrestling* found,
And in their pastime claspt each other round:
A shaft that instant from *Apollo's* hand

Transfixt them both, and stretcht them on the sand:
Together they their cruel fate bemoan'd,
Together languish'd, and together groan'd:
Together too th' unbodied spirits fled,
And sought the gloomy mansions of the dead.

   Alphenor saw, and trembling at the view,
Beat his torn breast, that chang'd its snowy hue.
He flies to raise them in a kind embrace;
A brother's fondness triumphs in his face:
Alphenor fails in this fraternal deed,
A dart dispatch'd him (so the fates decreed:)
Soon as the arrow left the deadly wound,
His issuing entrails smoak'd upon the ground.

   What woes on blooming *Damasichon* wait!
His sighs portend his near impending fate.
Just where the well-made leg begins to be,
And the soft sinews form the supple knee,
The youth sore wounded by the *Delian* god
Attempts t' extract the crime-avenging rod,
But, whilst he strives the will of fate t' avert,
Divine *Apollo* sends a second dart;
Swift thro' his throat the feather'd mischief flies,
Bereft of sense, he drops his head, and dies.

   Young *Ilioneus*, the last, directs his pray'r,
And cries, "My life, ye gods celestial! spare."
Apollo heard, and pity touch'd his heart,
But ah! too late, for he had sent the dart:
Thou too, O *Ilioneus*, art doom'd to fall,
The fates refuse that arrow to recal.

   On the swift wings of ever-flying *Fame*
To *Cadmus'* palace soon the tidings came:
Niobe heard, and with indignant eyes
She thus express'd her anger and surprize:
"Why is such privilege to them allow'd?
"Why thus insulted by the *Delian* god?

"Dwells there such mischief in the pow'rs above?
"Why sleeps the vengeance of immortal *Jove?*"
For now *Amphion* too, with grief oppress'd,
Had plung'd the deadly dagger in his breast.
Niobe now, less haughty than before,
With lofty head directs her steps no more.
She, who late told her pedigree divine,
And drove the *Thebans* from *Latona's* shrine,
How strangely chang'd!—yet beautiful in woe,
She weeps, nor weeps unpity'd by the foe.
On each pale corse the wretched mother spread
Lay overwhelm'd with grief, and kiss'd her dead,
Then rais'd her arms, and thus, in accents slow,
"Be sated cruel *Goddess*! with my woe;
"If I've offended, let these streaming eyes,
"And let this sev'nfold funeral suffice:
"Ah! take this wretched life you deign'd to save,
"With them I too am carried to the grave.
"Rejoice triumphant, my victorious foe,
"But show the cause from whence your triumphs flow?
"Tho' I unhappy mourn these children slain,
"Yet greater numbers to my lot remain."
She ceas'd, the bow string twang'd with awful sound,
Which struck with terror all th' assembly round,
Except the queen, who stood unmov'd alone,
By her distresses more presumptuous grown.
Near the pale corses stood their sisters fair
In sable vestures and dishevell'd hair;
One, while she draws the fatal shaft away,
Faints, falls, and sickens at the light of day.
To sooth her mother, lo! another flies,
And blames the fury of inclement skies,
And, while her words a filial pity show,
Struck dumb—indignant seeks the shades below.
Now from the fatal place another flies,
Falls in her flight, and languishes, and dies.
Another on her sister drops in death;

A fifth in trembling terrors yields her breath;
While the sixth seeks some gloomy cave in vain,
Struck with the rest, and mingled with the slain.

One only daughter lives, and she the least;
The queen close clasp'd the daughter to her breast:
"Ye heav'nly pow'rs, ah spare me one," she cry'd,
"Ah! spare me one," the vocal hills reply'd:
In vain she begs, the Fates her suit deny,
In her embrace she sees her daughter die.

* "The queen of all her family bereft,
"Without or husband, son, or daughter left,
"Grew stupid at the shock. The passing air
"Made no impression on her stiff'ning hair.
"The blood forsook her face: amidst the flood
"Pour'd from her cheeks, quite fix'd her eye-balls stood.
"Her tongue, her palate both obdurate grew,
"Her curdled veins no longer motion knew;
"The use of neck, and arms, and feet was gone,
"And ev'n her bowels hard'ned into stone:
"A marble statue now the queen appears,
"But from the marble steal the silent tears."
  * This Verse to the End is the Work of another Hand.

❧

TO S. M. A YOUNG *AFRICAN* PAINTER, ON SEEING HIS WORKS.[39]

TO show the lab'ring bosom's deep intent,
And thought in living characters to paint,
When first thy pencil did those beauties give,

39. This poem was not listed in her 1772 Proposals. In a copy of Wheatley's book at the American Antiquarian Society (see the note for her ode to Neptune) there is a notation which identifies S. M. as: "Scipio Moorhead—Negro Servant to the Revd Mr. Moorhead of Boston, whose Genius inclined him that way." (See the note for her poem to Mary Moorhead.) John Moorhead's wife, Sarah (1712–74), was well known in Boston as an art instructor. (Also see

And breathing figures learnt from thee to live,
How did those prospects give my soul delight,
A new creation rushing on my sight?
Still, wond'rous youth! each noble path pursue,
On deathless glories fix thine ardent view:
Still may the painter's and the poet's fire
To aid thy pencil, and thy verse conspire!
And may the charms of each seraphic theme
Conduct thy footsteps to immortal fame!
High to the blissful wonders of the skies
Elate thy soul, and raise thy wishful eyes.
Thrice happy, when exalted to survey
That splendid city, crown'd with endless day,
Whose twice six gates on radiant hinges ring:
Celestial *Salem* blooms in endless spring.

Calm and serene thy moments glide along,
And may the muse inspire each future song!
Still, with the sweets of contemplation bless'd,
May peace with balmy wings your soul invest!
But when these shades of time are chas'd away,
And darkness ends in everlasting day,
On what seraphic pinions shall we move,
And view the landscapes in the realms above?
There shall thy tongue in heav'nly murmurs flow,
And there my muse with heav'nly transport glow:
No more to tell of *Damon's* tender sighs,
Or rising radiance of *Aurora's* eyes,
For nobler themes demand a nobler strain,
And purer language on th' ethereal plain.
Cease, gentle muse! the solemn gloom of night
Now seals the fair creation from my sight.

Robinson, *Her Writings*, pp. 274–75.) A briefer, variant version of this poem was published
during Wheatley's lifetime, in the London *Arminian Magazine* for April 1784 (see the note for
her poem "On Imagination" in this volume). Some think that Scipio Moorhead drew the pic-
ture of Wheatley that was used for the frontispiece of her book (see "A Note on the Text").

TO HIS HONOUR THE LIEUTENANT-GOVERNOR, ON THE DEATH OF HIS LADY. *MARCH* 24, 1773.[40]

ALL-conquering Death! by thy resistless pow'r,
Hope's tow'ring plumage falls to rise no more!
Of scenes terrestrial how the glories fly,
Forget their splendors, and submit to die!
Who ere escap'd thee, but the saint* of old
Beyond the flood in sacred annals told,
And the great sage,† whom fiery courses drew
To heav'n's bright portals from *Elisha's* view;
Wond'ring he gaz'd at the refulgent car,
Then snatch'd the mantle floating on the air.
From *Death* these only could exemption boast,
And without dying gain'd th' immortal coast.
Not falling millions sate the tyrant's mind,
Nor can the victor's progress be confin'd.
But cease thy strife with *Death*, fond *Nature*, cease:
He leads the *virtuous* to the realms of peace;
His to conduct to the immortal plains,
Where heav'n's Supreme in bliss and glory reigns.

There sits, illustrious Sir, thy beauteous spouse;
A gem-blaz'd circle beaming on her brows.
Hail'd with acclaim among the heav'nly choirs,
Her soul new-kindling with seraphic fires,
To notes divine she tunes the vocal strings,
While heav'n's high concave with the music rings.
Virtue's rewards can mortal pencil paint?
No—all descriptive arts, and eloquence are faint;

* Enoch.
† Elijah.

40. This poem was written after the publication of her 1772 Proposals and was a response to the death of Mary Sanford Oliver on March 17. Andrew Oliver was a Harvard graduate (1724) and was appointed provincial secretary in 1756 and lieutenant governor of Massachusetts in 1771. He was primarily a loyalist and was disliked by the patriots. He was one of those who signed the letter "To the PUBLICK" that was printed at the front of her book.

Nor canst thou, *Oliver*, assent refuse
To heav'nly tidings from the *Afric* muse.

   As soon may change thy laws, eternal *fate*,
As the saint miss the glories I relate;
Or her *Benevolence* forgotten lie,
Which wip'd the trick'ling tear from *Mis'ry's* eye.
Whene'er the adverse winds were known to blow,
When loss to loss* ensu'd, and woe to woe,
Calm and serene beneath her father's hand
She sat resign'd to the divine command.

   No longer then, great Sir, her death deplore,
And let us hear the mournful sigh no more,
Restrain the sorrow streaming from thine eye,
Be all thy future moments crown'd with joy!
Nor let thy wishes be to earth confin'd,
But soaring high pursue th' unbodied mind.
Forgive the muse, forgive th' advent'rous lays,
That fain thy soul to heav'nly scenes would raise.

* Three amiable Daughters who died when just arrived to Womens Estate.

~

A FAREWEL TO AMERICA. TO MRS. S.W.[41]

I.

ADIEU, *New-England's* smiling meads,
   Adieu, the flow'ry plain:
I leave thine op'ning charms, O spring,
   And tempt the roaring main.

41. See the variant version of this poem and its note. It was written after the publication of
her 1772 Proposals.

II.

In vain for me the flow'rets rise,
  And boast their gaudy pride,
While here beneath the northern skies
  I mourn for *health* deny'd.

III.

Celestial maid of rosy hue,
  O let me feel thy reign!
I languish till thy face I view,
  Thy vanish'd joys regain.

IV.

Susannah mourns, nor can I bear
  To see the crystal show'r,
Or mark the tender falling tear
  At sad departure's hour;

V.

Not unregarding can I see
  Her soul with grief opprest:
But let no sighs, no groans for me,
  Steal from her pensive breast.

VI.

In vain the feather'd warblers sing,
  In vain the garden blooms,
And on the bosom of the spring
  Breathes out her sweet perfumes,

VII.

While for *Britannia's* distant shore
  We sweep the liquid plain,
And with astonish'd eyes explore
  The wide-extended main.

VIII.

Lo! *Health* appears! celestial dame!
  Complacent and serene,

With *Hebe's* mantle o'er her Frame,
  With soul-delighting mein.

IX.

To mark the vale where *London* lies
  With misty vapours crown'd,
Which cloud *Aurora's* thousand dyes,
  And veil her charms around,

X.

Why, *Phœbus*, moves thy car so slow?
  So slow thy rising ray?
Give us the famous town to view
  Thou glorious king of day!

XI.

For thee, *Britannia*, I resign
  New-England's smiling fields;
To view again her charms divine,
  What joy the prospect yields!

XII.

But thou! Temptation hence away,
  With all thy fatal train
Nor once seduce my soul away,
  By thine enchanting strain.

XIII.

Thrice happy they, whose heav'nly shield
  Secures their souls from harms,
And fell *Temptation* on the field
  Of all its pow'r disarms!

Boston, May 7, 1773.

~

A REBUS, BY *I. B.*[42]

I.

A BIRD delicious to the taste,
On which an army once did feast,
  Sent by an hand unseen;
A creature of the horned race,
Which *Britain's* royal standards grace;
  A gem of vivid green;

II.

A town of gaiety and sport,
Where beaux and beauteous nymphs resort,
  And gallantry doth reign;
A *Dardan* hero fam'd of old
For youth and beauty, as we're told,
  And by a monarch slain;

III.

A peer of popular applause,
Who doth our violated laws,
  And grievances proclaim.
The' initials[43] show a vanquish'd town,
That adds fresh glory and renown
  To old *Britannia's* fame.

42. Although this poem was not written by Wheatley, it was included in her 1773 volume and is included here because of her response, which follows. It was probably written by James Bowdoin (see her poem on General Lee and her 1779 Proposals). Bowdoin was an important statesman and merchant of the period of the Revolution and a member of several learned societies, both American and foreign. He would become governor of Massachusetts in 1785. He was always actively interested in science and literature, was the first president of the American Academy of Arts and Sciences, and received honorary degrees from Harvard (from which he had graduated in 1745) and Edinburgh. (Bowdoin College is named for him.) He was one of those who signed the letter "To the PUBLICK," which was printed at the front of her book.
43. Of the identities of the six items above.

THE poet asks, and *Phillis* can't refuse
To shew th'obedience of the Infant muse.
She knows the *Quail* of most inviting taste
Fed *Israel's* army in the dreary waste;
And what's on *Britain's* royal standard borne,
But the tall, graceful, rampant *Unicorn?*
The *Emerald* with a vivid verdure glows
Among the gems which regal crowns compose;
Boston's a town, polite and debonair,
To which the beaux and beauteous nymphs repair,
Each *Helen* strikes the mind with sweet surprise,
While living lightning flashes from her eyes.
See young *Euphorbus* of the *Dardan* line
By *Menelaus'* hand to death resign:
The well known peer of popular applause
Is *C——m* zealous to support our laws.[45]
    Quebec now vanquish'd must obey,
    She too must annual tribute pay
    To *Britain* of immortal fame,
    And add new glory to her name.

FINIS.

44. This poem was not listed in her 1772 Proposals. See the preceding poem.
45. William Pitt, the Earl of Chatham (1708–78), in general a friend to the colonies. (For some anonymous verse in praise of Pitt, see Robinson, *Her Writings*, p. 456.)

Other Poems and
Variants of Poems

Here are poems that were not in Wheatley's 1773 book, variants of some of the poems that are in the book, and variants of some of those not in the book. All are in one chronological order (except that variants of the same poem are placed immediately together, following the earliest of them, in chronological order in relation to each other—to aid comparison—without regard for other chronological positions that might be pertinent for them). It is hoped that this chronological order will aid one in seeing the movement of her career as a whole. Of course, we know that she wrote poems which we do not have because they are mentioned here and there or are listed in her Proposals. However, fortunately these we do have; and perhaps some of the others will turn up yet.

❧

TO THE PRINTER.[1]

Please to insert the following Lines, composed by a Negro Girl (belonging to one Mr. Wheatley of Boston) on the following Occasion, viz. Messrs Hussey and Coffin, as undermentioned, belonging to Nantucket, being bound from thence to Boston, narrowly escaped being cast away on Cape-Cod, in one of the late Storms; upon their Arrival, being at Mr. Wheatley's, and, while at Dinner, told of their narrow Escape, this Negro Girl at the same Time 'tending Table, heard the Relation, from which she composed the following Verses.

ON MESSRS HUSSEY AND COFFIN.

Did Fear and Danger so perplex your Mind,
As made you fearful of the Whistling Wind?
Was it not Boreas knit his angry Brow
Against you? or did Consideration bow?
To lend you Aid, did not his Winds combine?
To stop your passage with a churlish Line,

---

1. From the *Newport* [Rhode Island] *Mercury* for December 21, 1767. It apparently is the first poem by Phillis Wheatley to be published. This is undoubtedly the poem which in her 1772 Proposals is called "On two friends, who were cast away," which is there dated 1766. This poem was first republished in Carl Bridenbaugh, "The Earliest-Published Poem of Phillis Wheatley," *New England Quarterly* 42 (December 1969): 583–84.

Did haughty Eolus with Contempt look down
With Aspect windy, and a study'd Frown?
Regard them not;—the Great Supreme, the Wise,
Intends for something hidden from our Eyes.
Suppose the groundless Gulph had snatch'd away
Hussey and Coffin to the raging Sea;
Where wou'd they go? where wou'd be their Abode?
With the supreme and independent God,
Or made their Beds down in the Shades below,
Where neither Pleasure nor Content can flow.
To Heaven their Souls with eager Raptures soar,
Enjoy the Bliss of him they wou'd adore.
Had the soft gliding Streams of Grace been near,
Some favourite Hope their fainting hearts to cheer,
Doubtless the Fear of Danger far had fled:
No more repeated Victory crown their Heads.

Had I the Tongue of a Seraphim, how would I exalt thy
Praise; thy Name as Incense to the Heavens should fly, and
the Remembrance of thy Goodness to the shoreless Ocean of
Beatitude!—Then should the Earth glow with seraphick
Ardour.
Blest Soul, which sees the Day while Light doth shine,
To guide his Steps to trace the Mark divine.

Phillis Wheatley.

❧

TO THE UNIVERSITY OF CAMBRIDGE, WROTE IN 1767—[2]

While an intrinsic ardor bids me write
The muse doth promise to assist my pen.
'Twas but e'en now I left my native Shore

2. From the manuscript at the American Antiquarian Society, which has written on it in the hand of Thomas Wallcut, a friend of Wheatley (see her 1779 Proposals) and also the grandnephew of Susanna Wheatley (Phillis's mistress), that he received two poems from Wheatley on February 2, 1773 (while he was a student at Dartmouth College). Letters at the

The sable Land of error's darkest night
There, sacred Nine! for you no place was found,
Parent of mercy, 'twas thy Powerfull hand
Brought me in Safety from the dark abode.
   To you, Bright youths! he points the heights of
     Heav'n
To you, the knowledge of the depths profound.
Above, contemplate the ethereal Space
And glorious Systems of revolving worlds.
   Still more, ye Sons of Science! you've reciev'd
The pleasing Sound by messengers from heav'n,
The Saviour's blood, for your Redemption flows.
S[ee] Him, with hands stretch'd out upon the Cross!
Divine compassion in his bosom glows.
He hears revilers with oblique regard.
What Condescention in the Son of God!
When the whole human race, by Sin had fal'n;
He deign'd to Die, that they might rise again,
To live with him beyond the Starry Sky
Life without death, and Glory without End.—
   Improve your privileges while they Stay:
Caress, redeem each moment, which with haste
Bears on its rapid wing Eternal bliss.
Let hateful vice so baneful to the Soul,
Be still avoided with becoming care;
Suppress the sable monster in its growth,
Ye blooming plants of human race, divine
An Ethiop tells you, tis your greatest foe
Its present sweetness turns to endless pain
And brings eternal ruin on the Soul.

Massachusetts Historical Society reveal that his mother, Elizabeth Wallcut, on January 30 had
sent him "Dr Sewalls picture and the Verses on his Death composd by Phillis . . . which with a
pi[e]ce She made on our Colledg She Sends as a present to you." This poem to students at
Harvard College in Cambridge, Massachusetts, is listed in Wheatley's 1772 Proposals and was
revised and included in her book. Robinson, *Her Writings*, pp. 354–55, has a facsimile of this
manuscript. Kaplan, *Black Presence*, p. 152, also has a copy of the manuscript. (See the note for
her poem to Dr. Thomas Amory.)

Where now shall I begin this Spacious Feild
To tell what curses unbeleif doth yield
Thou that dost daily feel his hand and rod
And dare deny the essence of a god
If there's no god from whence did all things spring
He made the greatest and minutest thing
If there's no heaven whither wilt thou go
Make thy Elysium in the Shades below
With great astonishment any soul is struck
O rashness great hast thou thy sense forsook
Hast thou forgot the preterperfect days
They are recorded in the Book of praise
If twas not written by the hand of God
Why was it sealed with Immanuel's blood
Tho 'tis a second point thou dost deny
Unmeasur'd vengeance Scarlet sins do cry
Turn now I pray thee from the dangerous road
Rise from the dust and seek the mighty God
By whose great mercy we do move and live
Whose Loving kindness doth our sins forgive
Tis Beelzebub our adversary great
Withholds from us the kingdom and the seat

3. From the manuscript owned by the Library Company of Philadelphia, now in the collections of the Historical Society of Pennsylvania. This appears to be a first draft, perhaps evidence of her haste in putting on paper one of those spontaneous inspirations that needed to be written down quickly while she could still remember them. It is part of a four-page, three-poem, continuous manuscript that begins with "America" and ends with the poem to Commodore Hood. "Atheism ——" begins in the middle of page 2 and ends near the top of page 4. The Historical Society of Pennsylvania also houses a significantly different manuscript copy of this poem, apparently in the hand of Hannah Griffitts, a Philadelphia poet, and entitled "on Atheism," which is the source of the version used in Lorenzo Greene, *The Negro in Colonial New England* (New York, 1942), p. 245, which contains only the sixteen lines on page 1 of that three-page manuscript. Both "Atheism ——" and "on Atheism" (in full) were first published in Kuncio, "Some Unpublished Poems," which contains a side-by-side comparison of the two versions. See the more polished version that follows this. (At the Massachusetts Historical So-

Bliss weeping waits us in her arms to fly
To the vast regions of Felicity
Perhaps thy Ignorance will ask us where
Go to the corner stone it will declare
Thy heart in unbeleif will harder grow
Altho thou hidest it for pleasure now
Thou tak'st unusual means, the path forbear
Unkind to Others to thyself severe
Methinks I see the consequence thou art blind
Thy unbeleif disturbs the peaceful mind
The endless Scene too far for me to tread
Too great to Accomplish from so weak a head
If men Such wise inventions then should know
In the high Firmament who made the bow
That covenant was made for to ensure
Made to establish lasting to endure
Who made the heavens and earth a lasting Spring
Of Admiration. to whom dost thou bring
Thy thanks, and tribute, Adoration pay,
To heathen Gods, can wise Apollo say
Tis I that saves thee from the deepest hell
Minerva teach thee all thy days to tell
Doth Pluto tell thee thou shalt see the Shade
Of fell perdition for thy learning made
Doth Cupid in thy breast that warmth inspire
To Love thy brother which is Gods desire
Look thou above and see who made the sky
Nothing more Lucid to an Atheist's eye
Look thou beneath, behold each purling stream
It surely can not a Delusion Seem
Mark rising Pheobus when he spreads his ray

ciety there is another copy of this poem, in Wheatley's hand, which differs slightly from the
version printed above but shares a few of the things which differentiate the Griffitts copy from
the version above. The Massachusetts Historical Society copy is dated July 1769 and probably
is a stage between the version printed above and that which follows.) For a facsimile of the
manuscript printed above, see Robinson, *Her Writings*, pp. 358–60.

And his commission for to guide the day
At night keep watch, and see a Cynthia bright
And her commission for to guide the night
See how the stars when the[y] do sing his praise
Witness his essence in celestial Lays

❧

AN ADDRESS TO THE ATHEIST, BY P. WHEATLEY AT THE AGE OF
14 YEARS——1767——4

Muse! where shall I begin the spacious feild
To tell what curses unbeleif doth yeild?
Thou who dost daily feel his hand, and rod
Darest thou deny the Essence of a God!—
If there's no heav'n, ah! whither wilt thou go
Make thy Ilysium in the shades below?
If there's no God from whom did all things Spring
He made the greatest and minutest Thing
Angelic ranks no less his Power display
Than the least mite scarce visible to Day
With vast astonishment my soul is struck
Have Reason'g powers thy darken'd breast forsook?
The Laws deep Graven by the hand of God,
Seal'd with Immanuel's all-redeeming blood:
This second point thy folly dares deny
On thy devoted head for vengeance cry—
Turn then I pray thee from the dangerous road
Rise from the dust and seek the mighty God.
His is bright truth without a dark disguise

4. From the manuscript at the Massachusetts Historical Society. This poem is included in
her 1772 Proposals. See the preceding version. The manuscript of "An Address to the Atheist"
is on the same sheet of paper as that of "An Address to the Deist." Eight lines from the end of
the above version the rhyme word "skies" has been written over "sky," which was the compara-
ble rhyme word in the earlier "Atheism"; and "eyes," the rhyme pair word with "skies," shows
no revision on the above manuscript—which helps to support the manuscript sequence pre-
sumed above.

And his are wisdom's all beholding Eyes:
With labour'd snares our Adversary great
Withholds from us the Kingdom and the seat.
Bliss weeping waits thee, in her Arms to fly
To her own regions of felicity—
Perhaps thy ignorance will ask us where?
Go to the Corner stone he will declare.
Thy heart in unbeleif will harden'd grow
Tho' much indulg'd in vicious pleasure now—
Thou tak'st unusual means; the path forbear
Unkind to others to thy self Severe—
Methinks I see the consequence thou'rt blind
Thy unbeleif disturbs the peaceful Mind.
The endless scene too far for me to tread
Too great to utter from so weak a head.
That man his maker's love divine might know
In heavens high firmament he placed his Bow
To shew his covenant for ever sure
To endless Age unchanging to endure—
He made the Heavens and earth that lasting Spring
Of admiration! To whom dost thou bring
Thy grateful tribute? Adoration pay
To heathen Gods? Can wise Apollo say
Tis I that saves thee from the deepest hell;
Minerva teach thee all thy days to tell?
Doth Pluto tell thee thou Shalt see the shade
Of fell perdition for transgression made?
Doth Cupid in thy breast that warmth inspire
To love thy Brother, which is God's desire?
Atheist! behold the wide extended skies
And wisdom infinite shall strike thine eyes
Mark rising Sol when far he spreads his Ray
And his Commission read—To rule the Day
At night behold that silver Regent bright
And her command to lead the train of Night
Lo! how the Stars all vocal in his praise
Witness his Essence in celestial lays!

ॾ

DEISM[5]

Must Ethiopians be imploy'd for you
Greatly rejoice if any good I do
I ask O unbeleiver satan's child
Has not thy saviour been to meek & mild
The auspicious rays that round his head do shine
Do still declare him to be christ divine
Doth not the Omnipotent call him son?
And is well pleas'd with his beloved One
How canst thou thus divide the trinity
What can'st thou take up for to make the three
Tis satan snares a Fluttering in the wind
Whereby he hath ensnar'd thy Foolish mind
God the eternal Orders this to be
Sees thy vain arg'ments to divide the three
Canst thou not see the consequence in store
Begin the Omnipotent to adore
Arise the pinions of Persuasions here
Seek the Eternal while he is so near
At the last day where wilt thou hide thy face
The day approaching is no time for grace
Then wilt thou cry thyself undone and lost
Proclaiming Father, Son, and Holy Ghost
Who trod the wine press of Jehovahs wrath

5. From the manuscript owned by the Library Company of Philadelphia, now in the collections of the Historical Society of Pennsylvania. Apparently a quick first draft of the poem that follows, the above was first published in Lapsansky, *"Deism."* At the end of the poem above, the following prayer and two trial lines are written in her hand on the same page:

May I O Eternal salute aurora to begin thy Praise, shall mortal dust do that which Immortals scarcely can comprehend, then O omnipotent I will humbly ask, after imploring thy pardon for this presumpsion, when shall we approach thy majestys presence crown'd with celestial Dignities When shall we see the resting place of the great Supreme When shall we behold thee. O redeemer in all the resplendent Graces of a Suffering God,
ye 6 wise men Sent from the Orient clime
Now led by seraphs to the bless'd abode

For a facsimile of this manuscript, see Robinson, *Her Writings*, pp. 361–63.

Who taught us prayer and gave us grace and faith
Who but the great and the Supreme who bless'd
Ever and ever in Immortal rest
The meanest prodigal that comes to God
Is not cast off, but brought by Jesus Blood
When to the faithless Jews he oft did cry
One call'd him Teacher some made him a lye
He came to you in mean apparell clad
He came to save you from your sins and had
Far more Compassion than I can express
Pains his companions, and his Friends Distress
Immanuel God with us these pains did bear
Must the Eternal our Petitions hear?
Ah! cruel distiny his life he Laid
Father Forgive them thus the saviour said
They nail'd King Jesus to the cross for us
For our Transgressions he did bear the curse.

❧

AN ADDRESS TO THE DEIST——1767——[6]

Must Ethiopians be employ'd for you?
Much I rejoice if any good I do.
I ask O unbeleiver, Satan's child
Hath not thy Saviour been too much revil'd
Th' auspicious rays that round his temples shine
Do still declare him to be Christ divine
Doth not the great <u>Eternal</u> call him Son
Is he not pleas'd with his beloved One—?
How canst thou thus divide the Trinity—

6. From the manuscript at the Massachusetts Historical Society. This poem was listed in her 1772 Proposals. It is a more polished version of the preceding poem, and this presumed order of composition is supported by the fact that the next-to-last line in the manuscript above clearly shows that she first wrote "Th" as if to repeat the first word of the earlier version, before changing to the "Nail'd" above. The above version of the poem is on the same sheet of paper as "An Address to the Atheist" and was first published in Robinson, *Black American Beginnings*, pp. 79–80.

The blest the Holy the eternal three
Tis Satan's Snares are fluttering in the wind
Whereby he doth insnare thy foolish mind
God, the Eternal Orders this to be
Sees thy vain arg'ments to divide the three
Cans't thou not see the Consequence in store?
Begin th' Almighty monarch to adore
Attend to Reason whispering in thine ear
Seek the Eternal while he is so near.
Full in thy view I point each path I know
Lest to the vale of black dispair I go.
At the last day where wilt thou hide thy face
That Day approaching is no time for Grace.
Too late percieve thyself undone and lost
To late own Father, Son, and Holy Ghost.
Who trod the wine-press of Jehovah's wrath?
Who taught us prayer, and promis'd grace and faith—?
Who but the Son, who reigns supremely blest
Ever, and ever, in immortal rest.? [sic]
The vilest prodigal who comes to God
Is not cast out but bro't by Jesus' blood.
When to the faithless Jews he oft did cry
Some own'd this teacher Some made him a lye
He came to you in mean apparel clad
He came to Save us from our Sins, and had
Compassion more than language can express.
Pains his companions, and his friends distress
Immanuel on the cross those pains did bear—
Will the eternal our petitions hear?
Ah! wondrous Distiny his life he laid.
"Father forgive them," thus the Saviour pray'd
Nail'd was King Jesus on the cross for us.
For our transgressions he sustain'd the Curse.

❧

AMERICA[7]

New England first a wilderness was found
Till for a continent 'twas destin'd round
From feild to feild the savage monsters run
E'r yet Brittania had her work begun
Thy Power, O Liberty, makes strong the weak
And (wond'rous instinct) Ethiopians speak
Sometimes by Simile, a victory's won
A certain lady had an only son
He grew up daily virtuous as he grew
Fearing his Strength which she undoubted knew
She laid some taxes on her darling son
And would have laid another act there on
Amend your manners I'll the task remove
Was said with seeming Sympathy and Love
By many Scourges she his goodness try'd
Untill at length the Best of Infants cry'd
He wept, Brittania turn'd a senseless ear
At last awaken'd by maternal fear
Why weeps americus why weeps my Child
Thus spake Brittania, thus benign and mild
My dear mama said he, shall I repeat—
Then Prostrate fell, at her maternal feet
What ails the rebel, great Brittania Cry'd
Indeed said he, you have no cause to Chide
You see each day my fluent tears my food.
Without regard, what no more English blood?
Has length of time drove from our English viens.
The kindred he to Great Brittania deigns?
Tis thus with thee O Brittain keeping down
New English force, thou fear'st his Tyranny and thou didst frown

7. From the manuscript owned by the Library Company of Philadelphia, now in the collections of the Historical Society of Pennsylvania, part of the same manuscript that contains "Atheism." It was first published in Kuncio, "Some Unpublished Poems." This is undoubtedly

He weeps afresh to feel this Iron chain
Turn, O Brittania claim thy child again
Riecho Love drive by thy powerful charms
Indolence Slumbering in forgetful arms
See Agenoria diligent imploy's
Her sons, and thus with rapture she replys
Arise my sons with one consent arise
Lest distant continents with vult'ring eyes
Should charge America with Negligence
They praise Industry but no pride commence
To raise their own Profusion, O Brittain See
By this, New England will increase like thee

༅

TO THE KING'S MOST EXCELLENT MAJESTY[8] ON HIS REPEALING
THE AMERICAN STAMP ACT

Your Subjects hope
The crown upon your head may flourish long
And in great wars your royal arms be strong
May your Sceptre many nations sway
Resent it on them that dislike Obey
But how shall we exalt the British king

---

the poem listed in her 1772 Proposals as "On America, 1768," though this manuscript appears
to be only a rough first draft. This may be the earliest poem we have which shows her aware-
ness of general public affairs and events. It also suggests an awareness of the public press and
its satiric methods. The poem seems to be a response to the deteriorating relations between
America (particularly Massachusetts) and Britain in 1768 following the Townshend Acts of
1767. "Riecho" probably has the intent of "re-echo," with here the import of "return" or "re-
spond to." "Agenoria" is derived from Latin "Agenor," here suggesting "homeland" (i.e.,
Britain).

8. From the manuscript at the Historical Society of Pennsylvania. The last seven words of
the title above seem to stand apart and appear to have been added by her later than the writing
of this draft. This poem was first published in Kuncio, "Some Unpublished Poems." This is
undoubtedly the poem listed in her 1772 Proposals as "On the King" and dated there 1768. It
was revised and included in her book. The changes and excisions for the book version (to be
published in England) result in a poem even more favorable toward the king. Robinson, *Her
Writings*, p. 364, contains a facsimile of this manuscript.

Who ruleth france Possessing every thing
The sweet remembrance of whose favours past
The meanest peasants bless the great the last
May George belov'd of all the nations round
Live and by earths and heavens blessings crownd
May heaven protect and Guard him from on high
And at his presence every evil fly
Thus every clime with equal gladness See
When kings do Smile it sets their Subjects free
When wars came on the proudest rebel fled
God thunder'd fury on their guilty head

Phillis

❧

ON FRIENDSHIP[9]

Let amicitia[10] in her ample reign
Extend her notes to a Celestial strain
Benevolent far more divinely Bright
Amor[11] like me doth triumph at the sight
When my thoughts in gratitude imploy
Mental Imaginations give me Joy
Now let my thoughts in Contemplation steer
The Footsteps of the Superlative fair

Written by   Phillis Wheatley
               Boston July 15
               1769

9. From the manuscript in the Moorland-Spingarn Research Center at Howard University, which came there in the Thomas M. Gregory Collection in 1966. In a letter to me of November 16, 1967, Howard librarian and bibliographer Dorothy Porter said, "Mr. Gregory is not certain how he obtained it. He states, 'that [Arthur] Schomburg got the manuscript for me either from London, or the noted book-seller in Metuchen, N.J. It may be that it was enclosed in the volume of poems by her.'" In her 1772 Proposals this poem is listed as having been written in 1768, though this seems to be a 1769 draft, especially as on the manuscript at the beginning of line five she has changed "To let" to "When." This poem was first published in William H. Robinson, ed., *Early Black American Poets* (Dubuque, Iowa, 1969), pp. 111–12.
    10. Latin for "friendship."
    11. Latin for "love."

TO THE HON.^{ble} COMMODORE HOOD ON HIS PARDONING A
DESERTER[12]

It was thy noble soul and high desert
That caus'd these breathings of my grateful heart
You sav'd a soul from Pluto's dreary shore
You sav'd his body and he asks no more
This generous act Immortal wreaths shall bring
To thee for meritorious was the Spring
From whence from whence, [sic] this candid ardor flow'd
To grace thy name, and Glorify thy God
The Eatherial spirits in the realms above
Rejoice to see thee exercise thy Love
Hail: Commodore may heaven delighted pour
Its blessings plentious in a silent shower
The voice of pardon did resound on high
While heaven consented, and he must not die
On thee, fair victor be the Blessing shed
And rest for ever on thy matchless Head

                                                        Phillis

ON THE DEATH OF THE REV'D DR. SEWALL. 1769.—[13]

E'er yet the morning heav'd its Orient head
Behold him praising with the happy dead.

12. From the manuscript owned by the Library Company of Philadelphia, now in the collections of the Historical Society of Pennsylvania, part of the same manuscript that contains "Atheism." It was first published in Kuncio, "Some Unpublished Poems." In her 1772 Proposals this poem is dated 1769. From 1767 through 1770, Commodore Samuel Hood (1724–1816) was commander of the North American station of the British, based at Boston. The *London Gentleman's Magazine, and Historical Chronicle* for February 1769 on page 105 reported, under a dateline of Boston, December 2, that there had been a court-martial aboard the *Mermaid* and two sailors had been sentenced to be flogged and one to be hanged, but that just as the death penalty was about to be carried out a pardon had arrived from Hood.
13. From the manuscript at the American Antiquarian Society. This poem is in her 1772

Hail! happy Saint, on the immortal Shore,
We hear thy warnings and advice no more:
Then let each one behold with wishful eyes
The saint ascending to his native Skies,
From hence the Prophet wing'd his rapturous way
To mansions pure, to fair celestial day.—
    Then begging for the Spirit of his God
And panting eager for the bless'd abode,
Let every one, with the Same vigour Soar
To bliss, and happiness, unseen before
Then be Christ's image on our minds impress'd
And plant a Saviour in each glowing Breast.
Thrice happy thou, arriv'd to Joy at last;
What compensation for the evil past!
    Thou Lord, incomprehensible, unknown,
To Sense, we bow, at thy exalted Throne!
While thus we beg thy excellence to feel,
Thy Sacred Spirit, in our hearts reveal
And make each one of us, that grace partake
Which thus we ask for the Redeemer's Sake
    "Sewall is dead." Swift pinion'd fame thus cry'd. ⎫
Is Sewall dead?" my trembling heart reply'd   ⎬
O what a blessing in thy flight deny'd!   ⎭
But when our Jesus had ascended high,
With Captive bands he led Captivity;

Proposals. A shortened and much revised version was included in her book. There also is a
manuscript of this poem in the Countess of Huntingdon's Papers of the Cheshunt Foundation
at Westminster College in Cambridge, England. (Robinson, *Her Writings*, pp. 365–67, prints a
facsimile of that manuscript, omitting the first word of the title.) It is very similar to the manu-
script version above, except that line 25 reads, "Behold, to us, a benefit deny'd"; lines 30 and
31 read, "O ruin'd world, my mournful tho'ts reply'd / And ruin'd continent the ecco cry'd";
and the title reads, "On the Decease of the rev'd Dr. Sewell." I take the manuscript in England
to be earlier than the manuscript above, which has more punctuation and has added the
bracket for the three-line rhyme, which also is used in the 1773 book version. The version of
line 25 above also is reflected in the printed version (lines 30 and 31 above are among those
excised in the printed version). The brackets that she put into some of her manuscripts suggest
that she also might have been responsible for the frequent use of such bracketing in her book.
Robinson, *Her Writings*, pp. 368–69, has a facsimile of the manuscript above. (See the note to
her poem to the students at Cambridge.)
    Joseph Sewall (b. 1688) died on June 27, 1769, at the age of eighty-one. (Wheatley's poems

And gifts reciev'd for such as knew not God
Lord! Send a Pastor, for thy Churche's [good]¹⁴
O ruin'd world! bereft of thee, we cryd,
(The rocks responsive to the voice, reply'd.)
How oft for us this holy Prophet pray'd;
But ah! behold him in his Clay-cold bed
By duty urg'd, my weeping verse to close,
I'll on his Tomb, an Epitaph compose.
   Lo! here, a man bought with Christ's precious blood
Once a poor Sinner, now a Saint with God.—
Behold ye rich and poor, and fools and wise;
Nor Let this monitor your hearts Surprize!
I'll tell you all, what this great Saint has done
Which makes him Brighter¹⁵ than the Glorious Sun.—
Listen ye happy from your Seats above
I Speak Sincerely and with truth and Love.
He Sought the Paths of virtue and of Truth
Twas this which made him happy in his Youth.
In Blooming years he found that grace divine
Which gives admittance to the sacred Shrine.
Mourn him, ye Indigent, Whom he has fed,
Seek yet more earnest for the living Bread:
E'en Christ your Bread, who cometh from above

---

consistently misspell his name except in the manuscript above.) He was the son of Chief Justice Samuel Sewall, author of the 1700 antislavery appeal *The Selling of Joseph*. Elected president of Harvard College in 1724, he declined, wishing to remain a pastor of Boston's famous Old South Church (Congregational), where he was known for his fervor and devotion and where Phillis Wheatley would become a member of the congregation by baptism on August 18, 1771 (thus her personal reference near the end of the poem). Sewall had many of the same missionary interests as did Susanna Wheatley (Phillis's mistress) and the Countess of Huntingdon and her friends. His death ended a pastorate of fifty-six years in the Old South Church. (See James Schmotter, "Joseph Sewall," *American Writers before 1800: A Biographical and Critical Dictionary*, ed. James Levernier and Douglas Wilmes, 3 vols. [Westport, Conn., 1983], pp. 1303–5.)

   14. This word is not in this manuscript but is in the one in England (which also lends support to the sequence of the manuscripts presumed in the note above).

   15. In the manuscript the word "greater" is crossed through and replaced by "Brighter" written above it in the same handwriting.

Implore his pity and his grace and Love.
Mourn him ye Youth, whom he hath often told
God's bounteous Mercy from the times of Old.
I too, have cause this mighty loss to mourn
For this my monitor will not return.
  Now this faint Semblance of his life complete
He is, thro' Jesus, made divinely great
And left a glorious pattern to repeat
  But when Shall we, to this bless'd State arrive?
When the same graces in our hearts do thrive.

❧

ON THE DEATH OF MR SNIDER MURDER'D BY RICHARDSON[16]

In heavens eternal court it was decreed
How the first martyr for the cause should bleed
To clear the country of the hated brood
He whet his courage for the common good
Long hid before, a vile infernal here
Prevents Achilles in his mid career
Where'er this fury darts his Pois'nous breath
All are endanger'd to the shafts of death
The generous Sires beheld the fatal wound
Saw their young champion gasping on the ground
They rais'd him up. but to each present ear
What martial glories did his tongue declare

16. From the manuscript owned by the Library Company of Philadelphia, now in the collections of the Historical Society of Pennsylvania. It was first published in Kuncio, "Some Unpublished Poems." It may be a draft, as in the fifth line from the end she clearly wrote "it" before changing the word to "no." In her 1772 Proposals she dates this poem 1770. On February 23, 1770, Christopher Snider, an eleven-year-old boy, was shot and killed by Ebenezer Richardson, a Tory, during an assault by patriots against Tory premises in Richardson's neighborhood, thus making Snider the first martyr in the patriot cause (as she points out) and not those who died in the Boston Massacre of March 5. The events provoked much strong reaction and publicity and a very large funeral. For a fuller presentation of the contexts, see Robinson, *Her Writings*, p. 139. Robinson calls this poem "the strongest of several pro-American and anti-British statements by Wheatley."

The wretch appal'd no longer can despise
But from the Striking victim turns his eyes—
When this young martial genius did appear
The Tory cheifs no longer could forbear.
Ripe for destruction, see the wretches doom
He waits the curses of the age to come
In vain he flies, by Justice Swiftly chaced
With unexpected infamy disgraced
Be Richardson for ever banish'd here
The grand Usurpers bravely vaunted Heir.
We bring the body from the watry bower
To lodge it where it shall remove no more.
Snider behold with what Majestic Love
The Illustrious retinue begins to move
With Secret rage fair freedoms foes beneath
See in thy corse[17] ev'n Majesty in Death

Phillis

❧

AN ELEGIAC POEM, On the DEATH of that celebrated Divine, and
eminent Servant of JESUS CHRIST, the late Reverend, and pious GEORGE
WHITEFIELD,[18] Chaplain to the Right Honourable the Countess of
Huntingdon, &c &c. Who made his Exit from this transitory State, to dwell
in the celestial Realms of Bliss, on LORD'S-DAY, 30th of September,
1770, when he was seiz'd with a Fit of the Asthma, at NEWBURY-PORT,
near BOSTON, in NEW-ENGLAND.   In which is a Condolatory
Address to His truly noble Benefactress the worthy and pious Lady

17. Corpse.
18. From a broadside at the Historical Society of Pennsylvania. The poem is listed in her
1772 Proposals, and an altered version is in her book. Whitefield (1714–70) was quite well
known, and there were a number of special sermons and broadsides on the occasion of his
death (see Broadsides, Ballads, Etc., pp. 209–11), though Wheatley's poem seems to have been
reprinted more than the others. Whitefield was an evangelist and leader of Calvinistic Method-
ism in Britain and America. He was much interested in orphans and other unfortunates. How-
ever, though sympathetic with the plight of blacks, he defended slavery on biblical grounds and
even owned slaves.

HUNTINGDON,—and the Orphan-Children in GEORGIA; who, with many Thousands, are left, by the Death of this great Man, to lament the Loss of a Father, Friend, and Benefactor.
By PHILLIS, a Servant Girl of 17 Years of Age, belonging to Mr. J. WHEATLEY, of Boston:—And has been but 9 Years in this Country from Africa.

Hail happy Saint on thy immortal throne!
To thee complaints of grievance are unknown;
We hear no more the music of thy tongue,
Thy wonted auditories cease to throng.
Thy lessons in unequal'd accents flow'd!
While emulation in each bosom glow'd;
Thou didst, in strains of eloquence refin'd,
Inflame the soul, and captivate the mind.
Unhappy we, the setting Sun deplore!
Which once was splendid, but it shines no more;
He leaves this earth for Heaven's unmeasur'd height:
And worlds unknown, receive him from our sight;
There WHITEFIELD wings, with rapid course his way,
And sails to Zion, through vast seas of day.

When his AMERICANS were burden'd sore,
When streets were crimson'd with their guiltless gore!
Unrival'd friendship in his breast now strove:
The fruit thereof was charity and love

This poem was first published in Boston in 1770 as a broadside. The *Massachusetts Spy* for October 11, 1770, advertised it as "this day published," but it may have been published even sooner. It was also published in 1770 as a broadside once in Newport, four more times in Boston, once in New York, and once in Philadelphia. It also appeared as an addendum to the printing of Ebenezer Pemberton's *Heaven the Residence of the Saints,* a sermon on the death of Whitefield, which he preached on the same Thursday that the *Spy* advertised Wheatley's broadside for sale and which was published in Boston and London in 1771. (Pemberton was one of those who later would sign the letter "To the PUBLICK" printed at the front of her book in 1773.) Further information about most of these printings can be found in Porter, "Early American Negro Writings," pp. 261–63. The version given here apparently is the original, which was used in most of the early broadsides with only very minor variations, which were probably printers' errors or changes. The poem's various printings gave Wheatley her first wide fame as a poet. (Also see the Introduction to this volume, the note to her poem to the Earl of Dartmouth, the poem which follows this one, and the dedication to her book.)

Towards *America*—couldst thou do more
Than leave thy native home, the *British* shore,
To cross the great Atlantic's wat'ry road,
To see *America's* distress'd abode?
Thy prayers, great Saint, and thy incessant cries,
Have pierc'd the bosom of thy native skies!
Thou moon hast seen, and ye bright stars of light
Have witness been of his requests by night!
He pray'd that grace in every heart might dwell:
He long'd to see *America* excell;
He charg'd its youth to let the grace divine
Arise, and in their future actions shine;
He offer'd THAT he did himself receive,
A greater gift not GOD himself can give:
He urg'd the need of HIM to every one;
It was no less than GOD's co-equal SON!
Take HIM ye wretched for your only good;
Take HIM ye starving souls to be your food.
Ye thirsty, come to his life giving stream:
Ye Preachers, take him for your joyful theme:
Take HIM, "my dear AMERICANS," he said,
Be your complaints in his kind bosom laid:
Take HIM ye *Africans*, he longs for you;
Impartial SAVIOUR, is his title due;
If you will chuse to walk in grace's road,
You shall be sons, and kings, and priests to GOD.

Great COUNTESS! we *Americans* revere
Thy name, and thus condole thy grief sincere:
We mourn with thee, that TOMB obscurely plac'd,
In which thy Chaplain undisturb'd doth rest.
New-England sure, doth feel the ORPHAN's smart;[19]
Reveals the true sensations of his heart:
Since this fair Sun, withdraws his golden rays,
No more to brighten these distressful days!

19. The countess was willed Whitefield's orphanage, Bethesda (about twelve miles from Savannah, Georgia) and its more than fifty slaves.

His lonely *Tabernacle*, sees no more
A WHITEFIELD landing on the *British* shore:
Then let us view him in yon azure skies:
Let every mind with this lov'd object rise.
No more can he exert his lab'ring breath,
Seiz'd by the cruel messenger of death.
What can his dear AMERICA return?
But drop a tear upon his happy urn,
Thou tomb, shalt safe retain thy sacred trust,
Till life divine re-animate his dust.

Sold by EZEKIEL RUSSELL, in Queen-Street, and JOHN BOYLES, in Marlboro-Street.

&

AN ODE OF VERSES[20]   On the much-lamented Death of the REV. MR. GEORGE WHITEFIELD, Late Chaplain to the Countess of *Huntingdon;* Who departed this Life, at *Newberry* near *Boston* in *New England*, on the Thirtieth of *September*, 1770, in the Fifty-seventh Year of his Age. Compos'd in *America* by a Negro Girl Seventeen Years of Age, and sent over to a Gentleman of Character in *London*.

HAIL Happy Saint, on thy Immortal Throne!
To thee Complaints of Grievance are unknown.
We hear no more the Music of thy Tongue,
Thy wonted Auditories cease to throng.

20. From a broadside in the Huntington Library. The version of this poem in Wheatley's 1773 book differs from the earlier versions, most of which were quite similar in text, but with varying pictorial, typographical, and artistic embellishments on the individual broadsides. However, the version given here (apparently printed in England) seems to be unique, especially in that it seems to have been adapted to a different audience in the omission of twelve lines near the end of the usual version which especially relate Whitefield to the Countess of Huntingdon, and in the addition of two quatrains and the Conclusion at the end. The "Gentleman of Character in London" to whom this version was sent might have been John Thornton, who was a close supporter of Whitefield and who lived at Clapham, near London (see Wheatley's letters to Thornton). Though Thornton was a friend and supporter of the Countess of Huntingdon, the lines about her which are omitted here probably were in the original version because it was intended for the countess and are dropped here out of deference to Thornton (or by him). Apparently Wheatley did send a copy of the poem (perhaps a printed one) to the

Thy Lessons in unequal'd Accents flow'd,
While Emulation in each Bosom glow'd.
Thou didst, in Strains of Eloquence refin'd,
Inflame the Soul, and captivate the Mind.
Unhappy we thy setting Sun deplore,
Which once was splendid, but it shines no more.
He leaves the Earth for Heaven's unmeasur'd Height,
And Worlds unknown receive him out of Sight.
There *Whitefield* wings with rapid Course his Way,
And sails to *Zion* thro' vast Seas of Day.
When his *Americans* were burthen'd sore,
When Streets were crimson'd with their guiltless Gore,
Wond'rous Compassion in his Breast now strove,
The Fruit thereof was Charity and Love.
Towards *America* what could he more!
Than leave his native Home, the *British* Shore,
To cross the Great *Atlantick* wat'ry Road,
To see *New England's* much-distress'd Abode.
Thy Prayers, great Saint, and thy incessant Cries,
Have often pierc'd the Bosom of the Skies.
Thou, Moon, hast seen, and thou, bright Star of Light,
Hast Witness been of his Requests by Night.
He pray'd for Grace in ev'ry Heart to dwell,
He long'd to see *America* excel.
He charg'd its Youth to let the Grace Divine
Arise, and in their future Actions shine.
He offer'd that he did himself receive:
A greater Gift not God himself could give.
He urg'd the Need of Him to ev'ry one,
It was no less than God's co-equal Son.
Take him, ye Wretched, for your only Good;

---

countess with a letter to her of October 25, 1770. (For the more typical, American broadside version, see the poem preceding this one.) Robinson, *Her Writings*, has facsimiles of this broadside (p. 372) and of a typical illustrated Boston broadside (p. 370). Heartman, *Phillis Wheatley*, also has a foldout photocopy of the latter; and Kaplan, *Black Presence*, p. 154, has a copy of it too.

Take him, ye hungry Souls, to be your Food;
Take him, ye Thirsty, for your cooling Stream;
Ye Preachers, take him for your joyful Theme;
Take him, my dear *Americans*, he said,
Be your Complaints in his kind Bosom laid;
Take him, ye *Africans*, he longs for you,
Impartial Saviour is his Title due.
If you will walk in Grace's heavenly Road,
He'll make you free, and Kings, and Priests to God.
No more can he exert his lab'ring Breath,
Seiz'd by the cruel Messenger of Death.
What can his dear *America* return,
But drop a Tear upon his happy Urn.
Thou, Tomb, shalt safe retain thy sacred Trust,
Till Life Divine reanimate his Dust.

Our *Whitefield* the Haven has gain'd,
   Outflying the Tempest and Wind;
His Rest he has sooner obtain'd,
   And left his Companions behind.

With Songs let us follow his Flight,
   And mount with his Spirit above;
Escap'd to the Mansions of Light,
   And lodg'd in the *Eden* of Love.

THE CONCLUSION.

May *Whitefield's* Virtues flourish with his Fame,
And Ages yet unborn record his Name.
All Praise and Glory be to God on High,
Whose dread Command is, That we all must die.
To live to Life eternal, may we emulate
The worthy Man that's gone, e'er tis too late.

Printed and sold for the Benefit of a poor Family burnt out a few Weeks since
near *Shoreditch Church*, that lost all they possessed, having nothing insur'd.
   Price a Penny apiece, or 5 s. a Hundred to those that sell them again.

To Mrs. LEONARD, *on the Death of her* HUSBAND.[21]

GRIM Monarch! see depriv'd of vital breath,
A young Physician in the dust of death!
Dost thou go on incessant to destroy:
The grief to double, and impair the joy?
Enough thou never yet wast known to say,
Tho' millions die thy mandate to obey.
Nor youth, nor science nor the charms of love,
Nor aught on earth thy rocky heart can move.
The friend, the spouse, from his dark realm to save,
In vain we ask the tyrant of the grave.

    Fair mourner, there see thy own LEONARD spread,
Lies undistinguish'd from the vulgar dead;
Clos'd are his eyes, eternal slumbers keep,
His senses bound in never-waking sleep,
Till time shall cease; till many a shining world,
Shall fall from Heav'n, in dire confusion hurl'd:
Till dying Nature in wild torture lies;
Till her last groans shall rend the brazen skies!
And not till then, his active Soul shall claim,
Its body, now, of more than mortal frame.
But ah! methinks the rolling tears apace,
Pursue each other down the alter'd face.
Ah! cease ye sighs, nor rend the mourner's heart:
Cease thy complaints, no more thy griefs impart.
From the cold shell of his great soul arise!
And look above, thou native of the skies!
There fix thy view, where fleeter than the wind
Thy LEONARD flies, and leaves the earth behind.

---

21. From a Boston 1771 broadside at the Historical Society of Pennsylvania. This poem is in her 1772 Proposals and in her book, revised and titled "To a Lady on the Death of Her Husband." Thankfull Leonard was the daughter of Thomas Hubbard. Therefore, see also the poem to him on the death of his daughter. She had married Dr. Thomas Leonard (1744–71) on October 4, 1770. He died on June 21, 1771. Robinson, *Her Writings*, p. 374, has a facsimile of this broadside. Also, Heartman, *Phillis Wheatley*, contains a foldout photocopy of it.

Thyself prepare to pass the gloomy night,
To join forever in the fields of light;
To thy embrace, his joyful spirit moves,
To thee the partner of his earthly loves;
He welcomes thee to pleasures more refin'd
And better suited to the deathless mind.

Phillis Wheatley.

❧

ON THE DEATH OF DR. SAMUEL MARSHALL[22]

Thro' thickest glooms, Look back, immortal Shade;
On that confusion which thy flight hath made.
Or from Olympus height, look down, and see,
A Town involv'd in grief, bereft of thee.
His Lucy sees him mix among the Dead,
And rends the gracefull tresses from her head.
Frantic with woe, with griefs unknown, oppress'd,
Sigh follows Sigh, and heaves the downy breast;
Too quickly fled, ah! whither art thou gone?
Ah! lost forever to thy wife and son!
The hapless child, thy only hope, and heir,
Clings round the neck, and weeps his Sorrows there
The loss of thee, on Tyler's Soul returns.
And Boston too, for her Physician mourns.
When Sickness call'd for Marshall's kindly hand,
Lo! how with pitty would his heart expand!
The Sire, the friend in him we oft have found;
With gen'rous friendship, did his Soul abound.
Could Esculapius then no Longer stay,
To bring his lingring Infant in to Day?
The Babe unborn, in dark confiens is toss'd

22. From the manuscript at the Connecticut Historical Society. This is the earliest version of this poem which we have. It has not previously been known to Wheatley scholars and has not been published before. See the version that follows this one.

And Seems in anguish for its Father Lost.
Gone is Apollo! from his house of earth!
And leaves the memorial of his worth.
From yonder worlds unseen he Comes no more,
The common parent, whom we thus deplore:
Yet in our hopes, immortal Joys attend,
The Sire, the Spouse, the universal freind.

ॐ

On the Death of Doctor SAMUEL MARSHALL.[23]

Thro' thickest glooms, look back, immortal Shade!
On that confusion which thy flight has made.
Or from Olympus' height look down, and see
A Town involv'd in grief for thee:
His *Lucy* sees him mix among the dead.
And rends the graceful tresses from her head:
Frantic with woe, with griefs unknown, oppres'd,
Sigh follows sigh, and heaves the downy breast.

Too quickly fled, ah! whither art thou gone!
Ah! lost for ever to thy Wife and Son!
The hapless child, thy only hope and heir,
Clings round her neck, and weeps his sorrows there.

23. From the *Boston Evening-Post* of October 7, 1771, p. 3, unsigned. This poem was in her
1772 Proposals and was revised and included in her book. Samuel Marshall (1735–71) was a
Harvard graduate (1754), studied medicine in hospitals in London, and returned to Boston in
1764. On October 14, 1765, he married Lucy Tyler, and Wheatley's poem was published one
week before their sixth wedding anniversary, following his death on September 29. The obitu-
ary in the *Boston Evening-Post* of September 30, p. 3, noted that he was held in high esteem, "a
very skillful Physician, Surgeon, and Man Midwife" whose death was to be much lamented,
not only in regard to his professional skills but also for "his many social Virtues, and agreeable,
obliging Disposition." It also stated that he had been "suddenly seized with an Apoplectic Fit
and died in a few minutes." Lucy Marshall had become a member of Boston's Old South
Church on August 18, 1771, the same day that Wheatley had (see *An Historical Catalogue of the
Old South Church (Third Church) Boston*, pp. 50–51, published in Boston in 1883). Also, Dr.
Marshall was a relative of Susanna Wheatley, Phillis's mistress. See the version of this poem
that precedes this one.

The loss of thee on *Tyler's* soul returns,
And *Boston* too, for her Physician mourns.
When sickness call'd for *Marshall's* kindly hand,
Lo! how with pity would his heart expand!
The sire, the friend, in him we oft have found,
With gen'rous friendship did his soul abound.

Could Esculapius then no longer stay?
To bring his ling'ring infant into day!
The babe unborn, in dark confines is toss'd
And seems in anguish for it's father lost.

Gone, is Apollo! from his house of earth,
And leaves the sweet memorials of his worth.
From yonder world unseen, he comes no more,
The common parent, whom we thus deplore:
Yet, in our hopes, immortal joys attend
The Sire, the Spouse, the universal Friend.

∾

To the AUTHOR *of the* LONDON MAGAZINE.[24]

Boston, in New-England, Jan. 1, 1772.

SIR,

As your Magazine is a proper repository for any thing valuable or curious, I hope you will excuse the communicating the following by one of your subscribers.

L.

There is in this town a young *Negro woman*, who left *her* country at ten years of age, and has been in *this* eight years. She is a compleat sempstress, an

24. From the letter and the accompanying poem in the "Poetical Essays" section of the *London Magazine: Or, Gentleman's Monthly Intelligencer* for March 1772 (41:134–35). The poem does not appear in her 1772 Proposals, though it might have been sent for London publication in relation to the 1772 Proposals, which were appearing during that same period. Indeed, the "L." who sent the cover letter and enclosures might have been either the Reverend John Lathrop or his wife Mary, the daughter of John and Susanna Wheatley and Phillis's good friend and tutor. (Mary, only ten years Phillis's senior, seems the more likely possibility, given the contents of the letter.) The "A.M." of the dedication might have been Abigail May, who be-

accomplished mistress of her pen, and discovers a most surprising genius. Some of her productions have seen the light, among which is a poem on the death of the Rev. Mr. George Whitefield.—The following was occasioned by her being in company with some young ladies of family, when one of them said she did not remember, among all the poetical pieces she had seen, ever to have met with a poem upon RECOLLECTION. The *African* (so let me call her, for so in fact she is) took the hint, went home to her master's, and soon sent what follows.

"MADAM,

"Agreeable to your proposing *Recollection* as a subject proper for me to write upon, I enclose these few thoughts upon it; and, as you was the first person who mentioned it, I thought none more proper to dedicate it to; and, if it meets with your approbation, the poem is honoured, and the authoress satisfied. I am, Madam,

Your very humble servant,

PHILLIS."

RECOLLECTION.

To Miss A—— M——, humbly inscribed by the Authoress.

MNEME, begin; inspire, ye sacred Nine!
Your vent'rous *Afric* in the deep design.

---

came a member of Boston's Old South Church in the same year that Phillis did—Abigail in February and Phillis in August of 1771. One is tempted to imagine the conversation cited in the letter and the resultant poem as being related to struggles with the catechism and the fervent preaching in Old South. Robinson (*Her Writings*, p. 377) has pointed out that Wheatley forgot that Mneme (or Mnemosyne) was the *goddess* of memory, not male—which was ironic given the subject of the poem. The error was corrected in the revised version in her book. This earlier version was reprinted in the *Massachusetts Gazette and Post Boy and Advertiser* (March 1, 1773), the *Essex Gazette* (March 16–23, 1773), and (without the two letters) *The Annual Register, or a View of the History, Politics, and Literature for the Year 1772* (London: J. Dodsley, 1773— and subsequent editions at least through a fifth in 1795). Robinson, *Her Writings*, pp. 377–78, has a facsimile of the *Annual Register* format, which did not give her name and had a headnote saying only: "Verses by a young African Negro Woman, at Boston in New-England; who did not quit her own country till she was ten years old, and has not been above eight in Boston." The poem's appearances in 1773 might have been intended to help whet interest in her 1773 volume, which was advertised in Boston papers in April (Robinson, *Her Writings*, p. 317). In fact, the book version of the poem was reprinted in the London *Gentleman's Magazine* for September 1773 (43:456) with a note saying, "This piece is taken from a small collection of Poems on Various Subjects, just published, written by Phillis Wheatley, a negro of Boston."

Do ye rekindle the cœlestial fire,
Ye god-like powers! the glowing thoughts inspire,
Immortal Pow'r! I trace thy sacred spring,
Assist my strains, while I *thy* glories sing.
By *thee*, past acts of many thousand years,
Rang'd in due order, to the mind appears;
The *long-forgot* thy gentle hand conveys,
Returns, and soft upon the fancy plays.
Calm, in the visions of the night he pours
Th' exhaustless treasures of his secret stores.
Swift from above he wings his downy flight
Thro' *Phœbe's* realm, fair regent of the night.
Thence to the raptur'd poet gives his aid,
Dwells in his heart, or hovers round his head;
To give instruction to the lab'ring mind,
Diffusing light cœlestial and refin'd.
Still he pursues, unweary'd in the race,
And wraps his senses in the pleasing maze.
The Heav'nly Phantom *points* the actions done
In the past worlds, and tribes beneath the sun.
He, from his throne in ev'ry human breast,
Has *vice* condemn'd, and ev'ry *virtue* bless'd.
Sweet are the sounds in which thy words we hear,
Cœlestial musick to the ravish'd ear.
We hear thy voice, resounding o'er the plains,
Excelling Maro's sweet Menellian strains.
But awful *Thou*! to that perfidious race,
Who scorn thy warnings, nor the good embrace;
By *Thee* unveil'd, the horrid crime appears,
Thy mighty hand redoubled fury bears;
The time mis-spent augments their hell of woes,
While through each breast the dire contagion flows.
Now turn and leave the rude ungraceful scene,
And paint fair Virtue in immortal green.
For ever flourish in the glowing veins,
For ever flourish in poetick strains.
Be *Thy* employ to guide my early days,

And *Thine* the tribute of my youthful lays.

Now **eighteen years* their destin'd course have run,
In due succession, round the central sun;
How did each folly unregarded pass!
But sure 'tis graven on eternal brass!
To *recollect*, inglorious I return;
'Tis mine past follies and past crimes to mourn.
The *virtue*, ah! unequal to the *vice*,
Will scarce afford small reason to rejoice.

Such, RECOLLECTION! is thy pow'r, high-thron'd
In ev'ry breast of mortals, ever own'd.
The wretch, who dar'd the vengeance of the skies,
At last awakes with horror and surprise.
By *Thee* alarm'd, he sees impending fate,
He howls in anguish, and repents too late.
But oft *thy* kindness moves with timely fear
The furious rebel in his mad career.
Thrice bless'd the man, who in *thy* sacred shrine
Improves the REFUGE from the wrath divine.
* Her age.

꘎

To the Rev. Mr. *Pitkin*, on the DEATH of his LADY.²⁵

WHERE Contemplation finds her sacred Spring;
Where heav'nly Music makes the Centre ring;
Where Virtue reigns unsulled, and divine;
Where Wisdom thron'd, and all the Graces shine;

25. From the broadside of this poem in the Rare Book and Special Collections Division of the Library of Congress. As revised, this poem is in her book, with the title "To a Clergyman on the Death of His Lady." Timothy Pitkin (1727–1812) was a son of Governor William Pitkin of Connecticut. For much of his life he was closely associated with Yale, but he also was a trustee of Dartmouth College (1769–73) and worked with Christian Indian ministers, including Samson Occom. Pitkin was wealthy and patriotic and was a classical scholar. From 1752 to 1785 he was a Congregationalist minister in Farmington, Connecticut. A letter to him is included in Wheatley's 1779 Proposals. In 1752 he married Temperance Clap, daughter of the president of Yale, the Reverend Thomas Clap, and sister to Mary Clap Wooster (see Wheat-

There sits thy Spouse, amid the glitt'ring Throng;
There central Beauty feasts the ravish'd Tongue;
With recent Powers, with recent glories crown'd,
The Choirs angelic shout her Welcome round.
  The virtuous Dead, demand a grateful Tear—
But cease thy Grief a-while, thy Tears forbear,
Not thine alone, the Sorrow I relate,
Thy blooming Off-spring feel the mighty Weight;
Thus, from the Bosom of the tender Vine,
The Branches torn, fall, wither, sink supine.
  Now flies the Soul, thro' Æther unconfin'd.
Thrice happy State of the immortal Mind!
Still in thy Breast tumultuous Passions rise,
And urge the lucent Torrent from thine Eyes.
Amidst the Seats of Heaven, a Place is free
Among those bright angelic Ranks for thee.
For thee, they wait—and with expectant Eye,
Thy Spouse leans forward from th' ethereal Sky,
Thus in my Hearing, "Come away," she cries,
"Partake the sacred Raptures of the Skies!
"Our Bliss divine, to Mortals is unknown,
"And endless Scenes of Happiness our own;
"May the dear Off-spring of our earthly Love,
"Receive Admittance to the Joys above!
"Attune the Harp to more than mortal Lays,
"And pay with us, the Tribute of their Praise
"To Him, who died, dread Justice to appease,
"Which reconcil'd, holds Mercy in Embrace;
"Creation too, her MAKER'S Death bemoan'd,

---

ley's poem "On the Death of General Wooster" and her earlier letter to Wooster). Temperance
Clap Pitkin died on May 19, 1772, in childbirth. The manuscript, in Wheatley's hand, from
which this broadside was set (including its endnote in her hand also) is in the Connecticut
Historical Society. It has not previously been known to Wheatley scholars. It is not printed here
because the differences between the manuscript and the broadside versions are few and insig-
nificant, involving primarily a few spelling corrections and capitalization changes by the printer,
his adding the few indentations, and his moving the quotation marks inside the left margin. In
general he was very faithful to the copy she had given him, with no change in wording.
(Heartman, *Phillis Wheatley*, has a foldout photocopy of the broadside of this poem.)

"Retir'd the Sun, and deep the Centre groan'd.
"He in his Death slew ours, and as he rose,
"He crush'd the Empire of our hated Foes.
"How vain their Hopes to put the GOD to flight,
"And render Vengence to the Sons of Light!"
   Thus having spoke she turn'd away her Eyes,
Which beam'd celestial Radiance o'er the Skies.
Let Grief no longer damp the sacred Fire,
But rise sublime, to equal Bliss aspire;
Thy Sighs no more be wafted by the Wind,
Complain no more, but be to Heav'n resign'd.
'Twas thine to shew those Treasures all divine,
To sooth our Woes, the Task was also thine.
Now Sorrow is recumbent on thy Heart,
Permit the Muse that healing to impart,
Nor can the World, a pitying tear refuse,
They weep, and with them, ev'ry heavenly Muse.

                              Phillis Wheatley.
Boston, June 16th, 1772.

   The above *Phillis Wheatley*, is a Negro Girl, about 18 Years old, who has
been in this Country 11 Years.

~

A POEM ON THE DEATH OF <u>CHARLES ELIOT</u>, AGED 12
MONTHS[26]

Thro' airy realms, he wings his instant flight,
To purer regions of celestial light;
Unmov'd he sees unnumber'd systems roll.

---

26. From the manuscript at the Massachusetts Historical Society. In the Houghton Library
at Harvard University there is another manuscript version, apparently the first stage of the
poem, written somewhat hastily and sent to Samuel Eliot (the child's father). It was folded sev-
eral times, sealed with red wax, and addressed to him by Wheatley. However, with the same ti-
tle, date, and signature, it differs relatively little and not significantly from the version above,
with most changes here being in spelling, punctuation, capitalization, and indentation, mostly
for the better. The version above is more polished, in a very neat and more careful version of

Beneath his feet, the universal whole
In just succession run their destin'd round,
And circling wonders spread the dread profound;
Th' etherial now, and now the starry skies,
With glowing splendors, strike his wond'ring eyes.
   The heav'nly legions, view, with joy unknown,
Press his soft hand, and seat him on the throne,
And smiling, thus: "To this divine abode,
"The seat of Saints, of Angels, and of GOD:
"Thrice welcome thou."—— The raptur'd babe replies,
"Thanks to my God, who snatch'd me to the skies,
"Ere vice triumphant had possess'd my heart;
"Ere yet the tempter claim'd my better part;
"Ere yet on sin's most deadly actions bent;
"Ere yet I knew temptation's dread intent;
"Ere yet the rod for horrid crimes I knew,
"Not rais'd with vanity, or press'd with wo;
"But soon arriv'd to heav'n's bright port assign'd.
"New glories rush on my expanding mind;
"A noble ardor now, my bosom fires,
"To utter what the heav'nly muse inspires!"
   Joyful he spoke—exulting cherubs round
Clap loud their pinions, and the plains resound.
Say, parents! why this unavailing moan?
Why heave your bosoms with the rising groan?
To CHARLES, the happy subject of my song,
A happier world, and nobler strains belong.

---

her handwriting, undoubtedly written after the Houghton manuscript. Especially the place-
ment of the quotation marks in each supports this sequence. On September 22, John Andrews,
a Boston merchant and patriot who was interested in Wheatley and her poems, with a letter to
his brother-in-law William Barrell (apparently also interested in Wheatley), enclosed a copy of
this poem, which was provided by Andrews's wife, Ruthy, but copied by someone else. (In a
letter on September 3 Andrews already had told Barrell of the death of Charles Eliot.
Charles's mother was the sister of Andrews's wife and of Barrell, who was a merchant in Phila-
delphia.) Andrews says that the poem is addressed to the boy's father and that Andrews thinks
it "a masterly performance." (Wheatley, her poems, and her publication plans are mentioned in
a number of 1772–74 letters between the two men which are at the Massachusetts Historical
Society.) The poem was revised before its inclusion in her book. Robinson, *Her Writings*,
pp. 381–84, has facsimiles of both manuscripts. (See the note to her 1772 Proposals.)

Say, would you tear him from the realms above? [sic]
Or make less happy, frantic in your love?
Doth his beatitude increase your pain,
Or could you welcome to this earth again
The son of bliss?—No, with superior air,   ⎫
Methinks he answers with a smile severe,   ⎬
"Thrones and dominions cannot tempt me there!" ⎭
  But still you cry, "O Charles! thy manly mind,
"Enwrap our souls, and all thy actions bind;
"Our only hope, more dear than vital breath,
"Twelve moons revolv'd, and sunk in shades of death!
"Engaging infant! Nightly visions give
"Thee to our arms, and we with joy recieve:
"We fain would clasp the phantom to our breast,
"The phantom flies, and leaves the soul unblest!"
  Prepare to meet your dearest infant friend
Where joys are pure, and glory's without end.

Boston, Sept.ʳ 1.ˢᵗ 1772.   Phillis Wheatley.

ॐ

TO THE RIGHT HON! WILLIAM EARL OF DARTMOUTH,
HIS MAJESTY'S SECRETARY OF STATE FOR NORTH AMERICA
&.ᶜ &.ᶜ &.ᶜ 27

Hail! happy day! when Smiling like the Morn,
Fair Freedom rose, New England to adorn.
The northern clime, beneath her genial ray,

27. From the manuscript in the papers of Lord Dartmouth in the Staffordshire Records Office in Stafford, England. (Robinson, *Her Writings*, pp. 385–87, has a facsimile of the manuscript.) The poem was revised and included in her book. On June 3, 1773, the *New-York Journal* printed in its "Poet's Corner" the above version of this poem, with a number of changes in word choice, spelling, punctuation, capitalization, and indentation and with the omission of lines thirteen and fourteen. Also printed were her letter to Dartmouth of October 10, 1772, with which the poem was enclosed, and a headnote in which it was said: "*A Gentleman who had seen several of the Pieces ascribed to* [Wheatley], *thought them so much superior to her Situation, and Opportunities of Knowledge, that he doubted their being genuine—And in order to be satisfied, went to*

Beholds, exulting, thy Paternal Sway,
For big with hope, her race no longer mourns,
Each Soul expands, each ardent bosom burns,
While in thy hand, with pleasure, we behold
The Silken reins, and Freedom's charms unfold!
Long lost to Realms beneath the northern Skies,
She Shines supreme, while hated Faction dies,
Soon as he Saw the triumph long desir'd
Sick at the view, he languish'd and expir'd.
Thus from the Splendors of the rising Sun.
The Sickning Owl explores the dark unknown.

No more of grievance unredress'd complain;
Or injur'd Rights, or groan beneath the chain,
Which Wanton Tyranny with lawless hand,
Made to enslave, O Liberty! thy Land.
My Soul rekindles at thy glorious name
Thy beams essential to the vital Flame.

The Patrio'ts' breast, what Heav'nly virtue warms! [sic]
And adds new lustre to his mental charms;
While in thy Speech, the Graces all combine;
Apollos too, with Sons of Thunder Join,
Then Shall the Race of injur'd Freedom bless

---

her Master's House, told his Doubts, and to remove them, desired that she would write something before him. She told him she was then busy and engaged for the Day, but if he would propose a Subject, and call in the Morning, she would endeavour to satisfy him. Accordingly he gave for a Subject, The Earl of Dartmouth, and calling the next Morning, she wrote in his Presence, as follows" (the letter and poem). In the papers of Lord Dartmouth there is a November 24, 1772, letter to him from Thomas Wooldridge in New York (see Rawley, "World") in which this Englishman traveling in the American colonies for Dartmouth says: "While in Boston, I heard of a very Extraordinary female Slave, who had made some verses on our mutually dear deceased Freind [Whitefield]; I visited her mistress, and found by conversing with the African, that she was no Impostor; I asked if she could write on any Subject; she said Yes; we had just heard of your Lordships Appointment; I gave her your name, which she was well acquainted with. She, immediately, wrote a rouʒh Copy of the inclosed Address & Letter, which I promised to convey or deliver. I was astonishd, and could hardly believe my own Eyes. I was present while she wrote, and can attest that it is her own production; she shewd me her Letter to Lady Huntington [sic], which, I dare say, Your Lordship has seen; I send you an Account signed by her master of her Importation, Education &.c they are all wrote in her own hand." (The account actually is not signed by John Wheatley but bears the name of his son Nathaniel and the date October 12, 1772.) Dartmouth must have received these items by early 1773. (Isani, in "Early Versions," p. 152, thinks

The Sire, the Friend, and messenger of Peace.

While you, my Lord, read o'er th' advent'rous Song
And wonder whence Such daring boldness Sprung:
Hence, flow my wishes for the common good
By feeling hearts alone, best understood.

From Native clime, when Seeming cruel fate
Me snatch'd from Afric's fancy'd happy Seat
Impetuous.——Ah! what bitter pangs molest
What Sorrows labour'd in the Parent breast!
That more than Stone, ne'er Soft compassion mov'd
Who from its Father Seiz'd his much belov'd.
Such once my case.—Thus I deplore the day
When Britons weep beneath Tyrannic sway.
To thee, our thanks for favours past are due,
To thee, we still Solicite for the new;
Since in thy pow'r as in thy Will before,
To Sooth the griefs which thou didst then deplore.

May heav'nly grace, the Sacred Sanction give

Wheatley was responsible for changes in her letter before its publication in the *Journal* and that she probably provided the poem and letter to it. Robinson, in *Her Writings*, p. 388, speaks of the changes from the manuscript to the *Journal* version of the poem as made by a "copyist." I suspect that he is correct and that Wheatley did not see the quickly written items again after giving them to Wooldridge and that she was not aware of the *Journal* publication of them before it occurred (she was at sea going to London May 8–June 17). The poem probably was published by the *Journal* in response to the growing awareness of Wheatley's poems and of her trip to England. Another (briefer) variant of this poem was published during her lifetime, in the London *Arminian Magazine* for July 1784 (see the note for her poem "On Imagination" in this volume).

William Legge (1731–1801), second Earl of Dartmouth, in August 1772 became secretary of state for the colonies and president of the Board of Trade and Foreign Plantations in Lord North's administration, which appointment he retained until November 1775. Wheatley's political hopes (and those of many others) turned out to have been misplaced, as he proved to be a minister not in sympathy with the events that occurred in New England in the following months. However, Dartmouth was a friend of the Countess of Huntingdon (see the dedication to Wheatley's book) and to the Methodist movement, of which the Wheatleys, George Whitefield, John Thornton, Samson Occom (and various others whose names also show up in relation to Phillis Wheatley in letters and poems) also were supporters. While Wheatley was in England she had "near half an hour's conversation" with Dartmouth, and he gave her money with which to purchase books, which she did. (See her letter to David Wooster, October 18, 1773, the note to John Wheatley's letter at the front of her 1773 book, and the note to her first letter to the Countess of Huntingdon. Also see B. D. Bargar, *Lord Dartmouth and the American Revolution* [Columbia, S.C., 1965].)

To all thy works, and thou for ever live,
Not only on the wing of fleeting Fame,
(Immortal Honours grace the Patriots' name!)
Thee to conduct to Heav'ns refulgent fane;
May feiry coursers sweep th' ethereal plain!
Thou, like the Prophet, find the bright abode
Where dwells thy Sire, the Everlasting God.

~

To the Hon'ble Thomas Hubbard, *Esq; On the Death of*
Mrs. Thankfull Leonard.[28]

WHILE thus you mourn beneath the Cypress shade
That hand of Death, a kind conductor made
To her whose flight commands your tears to flow
And wracks your bosom with a scene of wo:
Let Recollection bear a tender part
To sooth and calm the tortures of your heart:
To still the tempest of tumultous grief;
To give the heav'nly Nectar of relief;
Ah! cease, no more her unknown bliss bemoan!
Suspend the sigh, and check the rising groan.
Her virtues shone with rays divinely bright,
But ah! soon clouded with the shades of night.
How free from tow'ring pride, that gentle mind!
Which ne'er the hapless indigent declin'd,

28. From a broadside at the Historical Society of Pennsylvania. (Robinson, *Her Writings*, p. 390, has a facsimile of the broadside, and Heartman, *Phillis Wheatley*, has a foldout photocopy of it.) The poem was in Wheatley's 1772 Proposals and as revised was in her book. Thomas Hubbard was for twenty years treasurer of Harvard College and was a distinguished citizen and merchant, very active in public affairs. He was for many years a deacon in the Old South Church, and in his will he left a sizable sum for the poor of Boston. The Hubbards were at one time neighbors of the Wheatleys. Hubbard was one of those who signed the letter "To the PUBLICK," which was printed at the front of her book. His daughter Thankfull Hubbard Leonard died in 1772. (Also see Wheatley's earlier poem to Thankfull Leonard on the death of her husband, who is referred to in this poem.) Another variant of this poem was published during Wheatley's lifetime, in the London *Arminian Magazine* for February 1784 (see the note for her poem "On Imagination" in this volume).

Expanding free, it sought the means to prove
Unfailing Charity, unbounded Love!

She unreluctant flies, to see no more
Her much lov'd Parents on Earth's dusky shore,
'Till dark mortality shall be withdrawn,
And your bless'd eyes salute the op'ning morn.* } * Meaning the
Impatient heav'n's resplendent goal to gain   Resurrection.
She with swift progress scours the azure plain,
Where grief subsides, where passion is no more
And life's tumultous billows cease to roar,
She leaves her earthly mansions for the skies
Where new creations feast her won'dring eyes.
To heav'n's high mandate chearfully resign'd
She mounts, she flies, and leaves the rolling Globe behind.
She who late sigh'd for LEONARD to return
Has ceas'd to languish, and forgot to mourn.
Since to the same divine dominions come
She joins her Spouse, and smiles upon the Tomb:
And thus addresses;—(let Idea rove)—
Lo! this the Kingdom of celestial Love!
Could our fond Parents view our endless Joy,
Soon would the fountain of their sorrows dry;
Then would delightful retrospect inspire,
Their kindling bosoms with the sacred fire!
Amidst unutter'd pleasures, whilst I play,
In the fair sunshine of celestial day:
As far as grief affects a deathless Soul,
So far doth grief my better mind controul:
To see on Earth, my aged Parents mourn,
And secret, wish for THANKFULL to return!
Let not such thought their latest hours employ
But as advancing fast, prepare for equal Joy.

Boston, January 2.   *Phillis Wheatley.*
1773.

BOSTON, MAY 10, 1773[29]   Saturday last Capt. Calef sailed for London, in [with] whom went Passengers Mr. Nathaniel Wheatley, Merchant; also, Phillis, the extraordinary Negro Poet, Servant to Mr. John Wheatley.

FAREWELL TO AMERICA.
To Mrs. S—— W——. By Phillis Wheatley.

ADIEU New England's smiling Meads;
  Adieu the flow'ry Plain,
I leave thy opening Charms, O Spring!
  To try the Azure Reign.
In vain for me the Flow'rets rise
  And show their gawdy Pride,
While here beneath the Northern Skies
  I mourn for Health deny'd.
Thee, charming Maid! while I pursue
  In thy luxuriant Reign;
And sigh and languish, thee to view,
  Thy Pleasures to regain.
Susanna mourns, nor can I bear
  To see the Christal Show'r
Fast falling—the indulgent Tear
  In sad Departure's Hour.
Not unregarding lo! I see

29. From number 3632 of the *Massachusetts Gazette: and the Boston Weekly News-Letter*, for Thursday, May 13, 1773, p. 4. (Robinson, *Her Writings*, pp. 392–93, has a facsimile of this publication of the poem.) Isani, in "Wheatley's Departure," reports other newspaper publication of this poem during May, usually accompanied by some information about her departure for England, which collectively helps us know that (accompanied by Nathaniel Wheatley, son of her mistress) she sailed on Saturday, May 8 (the day after the date given with the revised version of this poem in her book) on the Wheatley-owned *London Packet* of Captain Robert Calef (a friend of the Wheatley family, who in 1772 had become involved in trying to get her book published in England). On May 10, 13, and 27 this poem was published in four different Boston newspapers, in mid-May in a Salem one, and later in the same month in a Hartford one (see Isani, who says, p. 123, that these publications may have made this poem her best-known one before the publication of her book, except for her earlier poem on the death of Whitefield). This version of the poem also was published in the *London Chronicle* for July 1–3, 1773. Although the body of the poem differs insignificantly among its several May printings, in the London printing "S W" in the dedication is expanded to "Susanna W." Some of the newspa-

Thy Soul with Grief oppress'd;
Ah! curb the rising Groan for me,
   Nor Sighs disturb thy Breast.
In vain the feather'd Songsters sing,
   In vain the Garden Blooms,
And on the Bosom of the Spring,
   Breaths out her sweet Perfumes.
While for Britannia's distant Shore,
   We sweep the liquid Plain,
Till Aura to the Arms restore
   Of this belov'd Domain.
Lo! Health appears! Celestial Dame,
   Complacent and serene,
With Hebe's Mantle o'er her Frame,
   With Soul-delighting Mein.
Deep in a Vale where London lies,
   With misty Vapours crown'd,
Which cloud Aurora's thousand Dyes,
   And Veil her Charms around.
Why Phœbus! moves thy Car so slow,
   So slow thy rising Ray;
Nor gives the mantled Town to View
   Thee glorious King of Day!

---

pers indicated that the poem was being published by request, and clearly it was part of a pub-
licity campaign in anticipation of the publication of Phillis's book, which finally was published
in early September after she was back in Boston. It also was a fitting tribute from Phillis to Su-
sanna Wheatley, her mistress, who had done so much for her personally and to encourage her
writing (and whose approaching death would cause Phillis to return from England earlier than
she had planned). Also, two of the Boston printings and the Salem one included "To the Em-
pire of AMERICA, beneath the Western Hemisphere" preceding the poem's title, suggesting
broader intentions as well. Nathaniel was traveling to England on business and to accompany
her. She was making the trip to try to improve her frail health, but also in relation to her writ-
ing and publication of her book and probably secondarily for educational and religious pur-
poses. He stayed on in England when she returned home because of his mother's serious ill-
ness. Had she also thought, as she was leaving Boston, that perhaps her own health and other
circumstances might keep her from returning? (Compare her "An Elegy on leaving ——,"
which also has the less neoclassical four-line stanza arrangement to which she changed this
poem for its book version, a version which Isani, p. 125, finds to have gained in "clarity, vigor,
and directness.") See the Introduction to this volume.

But late from Orient Skies, behold!
  He Shines benignly bright,
He decks his native Plains with Gold,
  With chearing Rays of Light.
For thee Britannia! I resign
  New-England's smiling Face,
To view again her Charms divine,
  One short reluctant Space.
But thou Temptation! hence, away,
  With all thy hated Train
Of Ills—nor tempt my Mind astray
  From Virtue's sacred Strain.
Most happy! who with Sword and Shield
  Is screen'd from dire Alarms,
And fell Temptation, on the Field,
  Of fatal Power disarms.
But cease thy Lays, my Lute forbear
  Nor frown my gentle Muse,
To see the secret falling Tear,
  Nor pitying look refuse.

❧

An ELEGY, To Miss. Mary Moorhead, on the DEATH of her Father,
The Rev. Mr. JOHN MOORHEAD.³⁰

INVOLV'D in Clouds of Wo, *Maria* mourns,
And various Anguish wracks her Soul by turns;
See thy lov'd Parent languishing in Death,

---

30. From a broadside at the Massachusetts Historical Society. This poem is not included in
her 1779 Proposals. A native of Ireland and educated in Scotland, John Moorhead came to
Boston in 1730. He became the popular pastor of a Scotch Presbyterian church not far from
the Wheatley house, which he established as the Church of the Presbyterian Strangers not
long after his arrival. He was one of those who signed the letter "To the PUBLICK" printed at
the front of her book. Mary Moorhead had been born in 1732 and had two brothers. (Also see
Wheatley's poem to S[cipio] M[oorhead] in her book.) Note the mention of Moorhead in the
letter from Susanna Wheatley to Samson Occom in the Introduction to this volume.

His Exit watch, and catch his flying Breath;
"Stay happy Shade," distress'd *Maria* cries;
"Stay happy Shade," the hapless Church replies;
"Suspend a while, suspend thy rapid flight,
"Still with thy Friendship, chear our sullen Night;
"The sullen Night of Error, Sin, and Pain;
"See Earth astonish'd at the Loss, complain;"
Thine, and the Church's Sorrows I deplore;
Moorhead is dead, and Friendship is no more;
From Earth she flies, nor mingles with our Wo,
Since cold the Breast, where once she deign'd to glow;
Here shone the heavenly Virtue, there confess'd,
Celestial Love, reign'd joyous in his Breast;
Till Death grown jealous for his drear Domain,
Sent his dread Offspring, unrelenting Pain.
With hasty Wing, the Son of Terror flies,
Lest *Moorhead* find the Portal of the Skies;
Without a Passage through the Shades below,
Like great *Elijah*, Death's triumphant Foe;
Death follows soon, nor leaves the Prophet long,
His Eyes are seal'd, and every Nerve unstrung;
Forever silent is the stiff'ning Clay,
While the rapt Soul, explores the Realms of Day.
Oft has he strove to raise the Soul from Earth,
Oft has he travail'd in the heavenly Birth;
Till JESUS took possession of the Soul,
Till the new Creature liv'd throughout the whole.
    When fierce conviction seiz'd the Sinner's Mind,
The Law-loud thundering he to Death consign'd;
JEHOVAH'S Wrath revolving, he surveys,
The Fancy's terror, and the Soul's amaze.
Say, what is Death? The Gloom of endless Night,
Which from the Sinner, bars the Gates of Light:
Say, what is Hell? In Horrors passing strange;
His Vengeance views, who seals his final Change;
The winged Hours, the final Judgment brings,

Decides his Fate, and that of Gods and Kings;
Tremendous Doom! And dreadful to be told,
To dwell in Tophet 'stead of shrines of Gold.
"Gods! Ye shall die like Men," the Herald cries,
"And stil'd no more the Children of the Skies."
  Trembling he sees the horrid Gulf appear,
Creation quakes, and no Deliverer near;
With Heart relenting to his Feelings kind,
See *Moorhead* hasten to relieve his Mind.
See him the Gospel's healing Balm impart,
To sooth the Anguish of his tortur'd Heart.
He points the trembling Mountain, and the Tree,
Which bent beneath th' incarnate Deity,
How God descended, wonderous to relate,
To bear our Crimes, a dread enormous Weight;
Seraphic Strains too feeble to repeat,
Half the dread Punishment the GOD-HEAD meet.
Suspended there, (till Heaven was reconcil'd,)
Like MOSES' Serpent in the Desert wild.
The Mind appeas'd what new Devotion glows,
With Joy unknown, the raptur'd Soul o'erflows;
While on his GOD-like Savior's Glory bent,
His Life proves witness of his Heart's intent.
Lament ye indigent the Friendly Mind,
Which oft relented, to your Mis'ry kind.
  With humble Gratitude he render'd Praise,
To Him whose Spirit had inspir'd his Lays;
To Him whose Guidance gave his Words to flow,
Divine instruction, and the Balm of Wo:
To you his Offspring, and his Church, be given,
A triple Portion of his Thirst for Heaven;
Such was the Prophet; we the Stroke deplore,
Which let's us hear his warning Voice no more.
But cease complaining, hush each murm'ring Tongue,
Pursue the Example which inspires my Song.
Let his Example in your Conduct shine;

Own the afflicting Providence, divine;
So shall bright Periods grace your joyful Days,
And heavenly Anthems swell your Songs of Praise.

Boston, Decem. ⎫
  15 1773. ⎬   *Phillis Wheatley.*

    Printed from the Original Manuscript, and Sold by WILLIAM
M'ALPINE, at his Shop in *Marlborough-Street,* 1773.

❧

[TO A GENTLEMAN OF THE NAVY.][31]
For the ROYAL AMERICAN MAGAZINE.

By particular request we insert the following Poem addressed, by Philis [sic]*, (a
young* Affrican*, of surprising genius) to a gentleman of the navy, with his
reply.*
*By this single instance may be seen, the importance of education.—Uncultivated
nature is much the same in every part of the globe. It is probable* Europe
and Affrica *would be alike* savage *or polite in the same circumstances;
though, it may be questioned, whether men who have no* artificial *wants, are
capable of becoming so ferocious as those, who by faring* sumptuously *every
day, are reduced to a habit of thinking it necessary to their happiness, to
plunder the whole human race.*

Celestial muse! for sweetness fam'd inspire
My wondrous theme with true poetic fire,
Rochfort, for thee! And Greaves deserve my lays
The sacred tribute of ingenuous praise.
For here, true merit shuns the glare of light,
She loves oblivion, and evades the sight.

31. From the "Poetical Essays" section of Boston's *Royal American Magazine* 1 (December
1774): 173–74, whose editor was Joseph Greenleaf. It was followed on pages 474–75 by a re-
ply, which also is reprinted here, though it is not by Wheatley. In the next number of the same

At sight of her, see dawning genius rise
And stretch her pinions to her native skies.
  Paris, for Helen's bright resistless charms,
Made Illion bleed and set the world in arms.
Had you appear'd on the Achaian shore
Troy now had stood, and Helen charm'd no more.
The Phrygian hero had resign'd the dame
For purer joys in friendship's sacred flame,
The noblest gift, and of immortal kind,
That brightens, dignifies the manly mind.
  Calliope, half gracious to my prayer,
Grants but the half and scatters half in air.
  Far in the space where ancient Albion keeps
Amidst the roarings of the sacred deeps,
Where willing forests leave their native plain,
Descend, and instant, plough the wat'ry main.
Strange to relate! with canvas wings they speed
To distant worlds; of distant worlds the dread.
The trembling natives of the peaceful plain,
Astonish'd view the heroes of the main,
Wond'ring to see two chiefs of matchless grace,
Of generous bosom, and ingenuous face,
From ocean sprung, like ocean foes to rest,
The thirst of glory burns each youthful breast.
  In virtue's cause, the muse implores for grace,
These blooming sons of Neptune's royal race;

---

magazine she responded to the reply, which response is reprinted here too. Her 1779 Propos-
als include poems: "To Lieut R——— of the Royal Navy" followed by "To the same," which ap-
parently are these two poems by her. Vice-Admiral Samuel Graves had become commander in
chief of the North American station, at Boston, in the summer of 1774. A good many men in
the Royal Navy in the eighteenth century, including Samuel Graves, had served along the coast
of Africa because of the trading done by the English in the Senegambia and Gold Coast areas
(see Eveline C. Martin, "The English Establishments on the Gold Coast in the Second Half of
the Eighteenth Century," *Transactions of the Royal Historical Society*, 4th ser., 5 [1922]: 167–208).
Apparently, the lieutenant of these poems was attached to Graves's command, may have seen
service on the coast of Africa, and was an admirer of Milton and Newton. (See also her letter
to John Thornton of this same date.)

Cerulean youths! your joint assent declare,
Virtue to rev'rence, more than mortal fair,
A crown of glory, which the muse will twine,
Immortal trophy! Rochfort shall be thine!
Thine too O Greaves! for virtue's offspring share,
Celestial friendship and the muse's care.
Yours is the song, and your's the honest praise,
Lo! Rochfort smiles, and Greaves approves my lays.

BOSTON; October 30th. 1774.

❧

THE ANSWER.[32]

Celestial muse! sublimest of the nine,
Assist my song, and dictate every line:
Inspire me once, nor with imperfect lays,
To sing this great, this lovely virgins praise:
But yet, alas! what tribute can I bring,
WH—TL-Y but smiles, whilst I thus faintly sing,
    Behold with reverence, and with joy adore;
The lovely daughter of the Affric shore,
Where every grace, and every virtue join,
That kindles friendship and makes love divine;
In hue as diff'rent as in souls above;
The rest of mortals who in vain have strove,
Th' immortal wreathe, the muse's gift to share,
Which heav'n reserv'd for this angelic fair.
    Blest be the guilded shore,[33] the happy land,
Where spring and autumn gently hand in hand;
O'er shady forests that scarce know a bound,
In vivid blaze alternately dance round:
Where cancers torrid heat the soul inspires;

---

32. See the preceding poem and the one that follows this one.
33. The Gold Coast of west Africa.

With strains divine and true poetic fires;
(Far from the reach of Hudson's chilly bay)
Where cheerful phœbus makes all nature gay;
Where sweet refreshing breezes gently fan;
The flow'ry path, the ever verdent lawn,
The artless grottos, and the soft retreats;
"At once the lover and thee muse's seats."
Where nature taught, (tho' strange it is to tell,)
Her flowing pencil Europe to excell.
Britania's glory long hath fill'd the skies;
Whilst other nations, tho' with envious eyes,
Have view'd her growing greatness, and the rules,
That's long been taught in her untainted schools:
Where great Sir Isaac! whose immortal name;
Still shines the brightest on the seat of fame;
By ways and methods never known before;
The sacred depth of nature did explore:
And like a God, on philosophic wings;
Rode with the planets thro' their circling rings:
Surveying nature with a curious eye,
And viewing other systems in the sky.
    Where nature's bard with true poetic lays,
The pristine state of paradise displays,
And with a genius that's but very rare
Describes the first the only happy pair
That in terrestial mansions ever reign'd,
View'd hapiness now lost, and now regain'd,
Unravel'd all the battles of the Gods,
And view'd old night below the antipodes.
On his imperious throne, with awful sway,
Commanding regions yet unknown today,
    Or where those lofty bards have dwelt so long,
That ravish'd Europe with their heavenly song,
    But now this blissful clime, this happy land,[34]
That all the neighbouring nations did command;

34. England.

Whose royal navy neptunes waves did sweep,
Reign'd Prince alone, and sov'reign of the deep:
No more can boast, but of the power to kill,
By force of arms, or diabolic skill.
For softer strains we quickly must repair
To Wheatly's song, for Wheatly is the fair;
That has the art, which art could ne'er acquire:
To dress each sentence with seraphic fire.
    Her wondrous virtues I could ne'er express!
To paint her charms, would only make them less.

December 2nd. 1774.

❧

PHILIS'S [sic] Reply to the Answer in our last by the Gentleman in the Navy.[35]

For one bright moment, heavenly goddess! shine,
Inspire my song and form the lays divine.
Rochford, attend. Beloved of Phœbus! hear,
A truer sentence never reach'd thine ear;
Struck with thy song, each vain conceit resign'd
A soft affection seiz'd my grateful mind,
While I each golden sentiment admire
In thee, the muse's bright celestial fire.
The generous plaudit 'tis not mine to claim,
A muse untutor'd, and unknown to fame.
    The heavenly sisters pour thy notes along
And crown their bard with every grace of song.
My pen, least favour'd by the tuneful nine,
Can never rival, never equal thine;
Then fix the humble Afric muse's seat

---

35. From the "Poetical Essays" section of the *Royal American Magazine* 2 (January 1775): 34–35. (See the preceding two poems.)

At British Homer's and Sir Isaac's feet.[36]
Those bards whose fame in deathless strains arise
Creation's boast, and fav'rites of the skies.

   In fair description are thy powers display'd
In artless grottos, and the sylvan shade;
Charm'd with thy painting, how my bosom burns!
And pleasing Gambia on my soul returns,
With native grace in spring's luxuriant reign,
Smiles the gay mead, and Eden blooms again,
The various bower, the tuneful flowing stream,
The soft retreats, the lovers golden dream,
Her soil spontaneous, yields exhaustless stores;
For phœbus revels on her verdant shores.
Whose flowery births, a fragrant train appear,
And crown the youth throughout the smiling year,
   There, as in Britain's favour'd isle, behold
The bending harvest ripen into gold!
Just are thy views of Afric's blissful plain,
On the warm limits of the land and main.

   Pleas'd with the theme, see sportive fancy play,
In realms devoted to the God of day![37]

   Europa's bard, who the great depth explor'd,
Of nature, and thro' boundless systems soar'd,
Thro' earth, thro' heaven, and hell's profound domain,
Where night eternal holds her awful reign.
But, lo! in him Britania's prophet dies,
And whence, ah! whence, shall other *Newton's* rise?
Muse, bid thy Rochford's matchless pen display
The charms of friendship in the sprightly lay.

36. Milton and Newton, from the preceding poem. Although she owned Pope's translation
of Homer (see her letter to David Wooster), here she calls Milton the British Homer. How-
ever, she also had her own handsome copy of Milton's *Paradise Lost*.

37. According to letters at the Medford Historical Society, Timothy Fitch, the owner of the
slave ship *Phillis*, on which Wheatley arrived at Boston, often instructed its captain, Peter
Gwin, to get slaves from the Senegal-Gambia region or as far south on the west African coast
as Sierra Leone. Certainly Wheatley here is one of the earliest American black poets to write
in such a romantic vein about Africa (see Isani, " 'Gambia on My Soul' ").

Queen of his song, thro' all his numbers shine,
And plausive glories, goddess! shall be thine.
With partial grace thou mak'st his verse excel,
And *his* the glory to describe so well.
Cerulean bard! to thee these strains belong,
The Muse's darling and the prince of song.

DECEMBER 5th, 1774.

❧

TO HIS EXCELLENCY GENERAL WASHINGTON.[38]

The following LETTER *and* VERSES, *were written by the famous* Phillis
Wheatley, *the African Poetess, and presented to his Excellency Gen.* Washington.

SIR,

I Have taken the freedom to address your Excellency in the enclosed poem,
and entreat your acceptance, though I am not insensible of its inaccuracies.

38. This poem and letter were printed in the "Poetical Essays" section of the *Pennsylvania Magazine* 2 (April 1776): 193, while Thomas Paine was its editor, from which printing this was taken. (Kaplan, *Black Presence*, p. 164, has a photograph of it.) Almost simultaneously, the poem and letter also were printed in the *Virginia Gazette* for March 30, 1776 (p. 1), printed by John Dixon and William Hunter. The poem (but not the letter) was in Wheatley's 1779 Proposals, from which the title for the poem is taken. An examination of the very few differences in spelling and punctuation between the Pennsylvania and Virginia printings, and comparison of them with Wheatley's usual practices, suggests that the Pennsylvania printing was set from Wheatley's manuscript and the Virginia one from a copy sent to the printers, "Mess. Dixon & Hunter," with a note asking them to "*Pray insert the enclosed letter and verses, written by the famous* Phillis Wheatley, *the African poetess, in your next gazette,*" as was printed above them in the Virginia printing.

In a letter to Colonel Joseph Reed (his close friend and former military secretary, former president of the second Provincial Congress, and now a member of the Congress and adjutant general of the Continental army), dated Cambridge, February 10, 1776, which begins with concern over the public's opinion of him, Washington says: "I recollect nothing else worth giving you the trouble of, unless you can be amused by reading a letter and poem addressed to me by Mrs. or Miss Phillis Wheatley. In searching over a parcel of papers the other day, in order to destroy such as were useless, I brought it to light again;—at first with a view of doing justice to her great poetical genius, I had a great mind to publish the poem, but not knowing whether it might not be considered rather as a mark of my own vanity than as a compliment to her, I laid it aside, till I came across it again in the manner just mentioned" (William B. Reed, ed., *Reprint of the Original Letters from Washington to Joseph Reed, during the American Revolution* [Philadelphia, 1852], p. 69). Note that Washington did not find the Wheatley items "useless" and appropriate for destruction.

Your being appointed by the Grand Continental Congress to be Generalissimo of the armies of North America, together with the fame of your virtues, excite sensations not easy to suppress. Your generosity, therefore, I presume, will pardon the attempt. Wishing your Excellency all possible success in the great cause you are so generously[39] engaged in. I am,

Your Excellency's most obedient humble servant,

PHILLIS WHEATLEY.

Providence, Oct. 26, 1775.
His Excellency Gen. Washington.

In my paper at the Phillis Wheatley Conference I tried to put this poem in the full context of the political and military situations both in the Boston area and nationally, contending that they importantly affected both the form and content of the poem and letter and also the handling of them both by Washington and by Reed, who was then in Philadelphia and undoubtedly made the decision to publish the letter and poem that had been sent to him by Washington. When Wheatley sent the poem to Washington she was not in Boston, but in Providence, Rhode Island, probably living with her friend and former tutor, Mary Wheatley Lathrop, and her husband, the strongly patriotic Rev. John Lathrop. She was a refugee from her home in Boston, where conditions were drastically bad because of the British control of the city, and many had fled. Washington had been appointed commander in chief of the Continental Army on June 15, 1775, and had arrived at Cambridge, near Boston, on July 2 and assumed command, offering new hope for Boston and the country. Wheatley's poem should be read as a plea and challenge from a Boston refugee, rather than primarily as a poem of praise. Indeed, both Washington and his army had done little yet to deserve such praise, but praise is offered as possible reward if he is successful in the endeavors on which he is newly embarked, even then trying to decide whether to attack Boston. The poem also expresses local pride as a result of the local battles before Washington arrived and expresses encouragement to the army and its leader, who are seen as the only hope if the refugee is to be able to return to her home soon. (See the Introduction to this volume.)

From Cambridge on February 28, 1776, Washington replied to Wheatley: "[Miss] Phillis, Your favour of the 26th of October did not reach my hands 'till the middle of December. Time enough, you will say, to have given an answer ere this. Granted. But a variety of important occurrences, continually interposing to distract the mind and withdraw the attention, I hope will apologize for the delay, and plead my excuse for the seeming, but not real neglect. [par.] I thank you most sincerely for your polite notice of me, in the elegant Lines you enclosed; and however undeserving I may be of such encomium and panegyrick, the style and manner exhibit a striking proof of your great poetical Talents. In honour of which, and as a tribute justly due to you, I would have published the Poem, had I not been apprehensive, that, while I only meant to give the World this new instance of your genius, I might have incurred the imputation of Vanity. This and nothing else, determined me not to give it place in the public Prints. [par.] If you should ever come to Cambridge, or near Head Quarters, I shall be happy to see a person so favoured by the Muses, and to whom Nature has been so liberal and beneficent in her dispensations. I am, with great Respect, etc." (John C. Fitzpatrick, ed., *The Writings of George Washington from the Original Manuscript Sources, 1745–1799* [Washington, D.C., 1931], 4:360–61).

CElestial choir! enthron'd in realms of light,
Columbia's scenes of glorious toils I write.
While freedom's cause her anxious breast alarms,
She flashes dreadful in refulgent arms.
See mother earth her offspring's fate bemoan,
And nations gaze at scenes before unknown!
See the bright beams of heaven's revolving light
Involved in sorrows and the veil of night!
    The goddess comes, she moves divinely fair,
Olive and laurel binds her golden hair:
Wherever shines this native of the skies,
Unnumber'd charms and recent graces rise.
    Muse! bow propitious while my pen relates
How pour her armies through a thousand gates:
As when Eolus heaven's fair face deforms,
Enwrapp'd in tempest and a night of storms;
Astonish'd ocean feels the wild uproar,
The refluent surges beat the sounding shore;

By the time Washington had written to Reed about the poem, the situation had begun to im-
prove at Boston; and by the time he wrote to Wheatley, he had reason to believe that he might
be as successful as she had implored and challenged him to be. Benson J. Lossing's *Field Book
of the Revolution* (New York, 1860), 1:556, says that Wheatley accepted Washington's invitation
and visited him "a few days before the British evacuated Boston" and was courteously received
by him and his Cambridge staff. The patriots had taken Dorchester Heights on March 4, and
the British evacuated Boston on March 17. Apparently, after hearing of Washington's continu-
ing successes at Boston in the face of his first significant test as commander in chief, Reed de-
cided that it was time to use Wheatley's poem, both because present circumstances would
cause it to seem more appropriate than it would have before (though he kept the earlier date)
and it could ride the tide of Washington's success and help contribute to awareness of it, and
also because politically it would be helpful in relation to Washington's detractors, particularly in
Philadelphia. Although it was also published in Washington's home state, apparently circum-
stances in Boston at the time of Reed's decision did not make it seem appropriate to send the
poem there for publication too. Indeed, allowing for travel time for mail from Philadelphia to
Virginia and advance time needed for publishing, Reed probably made his decision on March
15 after receiving that day Washington's somewhat exuberant March 7 letter to him with the
good news about Dorchester Heights, but Reed's decision preceded the now expected removal
of the British from Boston, which finally did take place two days later on March 17. (Compare
this poem's attitude toward Britain with that in Wheatley's earlier "America." Also compare her
Liberty and Peace.)
    39. This may refer to the widely publicized fact that Washington had volunteered to serve
without pay, except for official expenses.

Or thick as leaves in Autumn's golden reign,[40]
Such, and so many, moves the warrior's train.
In bright array they seek the work of war,
Where high unfurl'd the ensign waves in air.
Shall I to Washington their praise recite?
Enough thou know'st them in the fields of fight.
Thee, first in place and honours,—we demand
The grace and glory of thy martial band.
Fam'd for thy valour, for thy virtues more,
Hear every tongue thy guardian aid implore!
    One century scarce perform'd its destin'd round,
When Gallic powers Columbia's fury found;
And so may you, whoever dares disgrace
The land of freedom's heaven-defended race!
Fix'd are the eyes of nations on the scales,
For in their hopes Columbia's arm prevails.
Anon Britannia droops the pensive head,
While round increase the rising hills of dead.
Ah! cruel blindness to Columbia's state!
Lament thy thirst of boundless power too late.
    Proceed, great chief, with virtue on thy side,[41]
Thy ev'ry action let the goddess guide.
A crown, a mansion, and a throne that shine,
With gold unfading, WASHINGTON! be thine.

❧

ON THE CAPTURE OF GENERAL LEE[42]

The following thoughts on his Excellency Major General Lee being betray'd
into the hands of the Enemy by the treachery of a pretended Friend; To the

---

40. Compare John Milton, *Paradise Lost*, Bk. 1, lines 301–2: "His [Satan's] legions . . . /
Thick as autumnal leaves that strew the brooks."
41. Compare the lines about Washington near the end of Wheatley's "On the Capture of
General Lee."
42. From the manuscript of the poem at Bowdoin College's library. The manuscript is in-
scribed to "The Honourable James Bowdoin Esqr." This poem was in her 1779 Proposals,

Honourable James Bowdoin Esqr are most respectfully Inscrib'd, By his
most obedient and devoted humble Servant.

PHILLIS WHEATLEY.

The deed perfidious, and the Hero's fate,
In tender strains, celestial Muse! relate.
The latent foe to friendship makes pretence
The name assumes without the sacred sense!
He, with a rapture well dissembl'd, press'd
The hero's hand, and fraudful, thus address'd.
  "O friend belov'd! may heaven its aid afford,
"And spread yon troops beneath thy conquering sword!
"Grant to America's united prayer
"A glorious conquest on the field of war.
"But thou indulgent to my warm request
"Vouchsafe thy presence as my honour'd guest:
"From martial cares a space unbend thy soul
"In social banquet, and the sprightly bowl."
  Thus spoke the foe; and warlike Lee reply'd,
"Ill fits it me, who such an army guide;
"To whom his conduct each brave soldier owes
"To waste an hour in banquets or repose:
"This day important, with loud voice demands
"Our wisest Counsels, and our bravest hands."

---

from which we get the title. (Also see the poem "A Rebus" by Bowdoin in Wheatley's book.)
Wheatley's patriotism is appropriate, and she may be remembering that Lee had served under
Washington during the seige of Boston; however, she has Lee speak words near the end of the
poem which hardly are in keeping with his great desire to replace Washington in command.
Probably that is why the better-informed Bowdoin never published the poem (see *Proceedings of
the Massachusetts Historical Society* 7 (1863–64): 165–67, where the poem was first published,
from this manuscript, which had been found in Bowdoin's papers). However, Wheatley was a
civilian far from the place where Lee had been captured, and she therefore was likely to en-
counter many rumors. Lee was taken prisoner on the night of December 13, 1776, in a New
Jersey tavern by men from the same British regiment he had led in the Seven Years' War, and
she tries to imagine the devices of that capture in the first part of the poem, as well as the likely
contempt of the British for one who now fought on the other side from them. Charles Lee
(1731–82) was a flamboyant officer, who in his actions often modified or ignored orders given
to him and eventually, after Valley Forge, would be court-martialed and found guilty of dis-
obeying orders and of disrespect to Washington. (Also see her poem to Washington.)

Thus having said he heav'd a boding sigh.
The hour approach'd that damps Columbia's Joy.
Inform'd, conducted, by the treach'rous friend
With winged speed the adverse train attend
Ascend the Dome, and seize with frantic air
The self surrender'd glorious prize of war!
On sixty coursers, swifter than the wind
They fly, and reach the British camp assign'd.
Arriv'd, what transport touch'd their leader's breast!
Who thus deriding, the brave Chief address'd.
"Say, art thou he, beneath whose vengeful hands
"Our best of heroes grasp'd in death the sands?
"One fierce regard of thine indignant eye
"Turn'd Brittain pale, and made her armies fly;
"But Oh! how chang'd! a prisoner in our arms
"Till martial honour, dreadful in her charms,
"Shall grace Britannia at her sons' return,
"And widow'd thousands in our triumphs mourn."
While thus he spoke, the hero of renown
Survey'd the boaster with a gloomy frown
And stern reply'd. "Oh arrogrance of tongue!
"And wild ambition, ever prone to wrong!
"Believ'st thou Chief, that armies such as thine
"Can stretch in dust that heaven-defended line?
"In vain allies may swarm from distant lands
"And demons aid in formidable bands.
"Great as thou art, thou shun'st the field of fame
"Disgrace to Brittain, and the British name!
"When offer'd combat by the noble foe,
"(Foe to mis-rule,) why did thy sword forgo
"The easy conquest of the rebel-land?
"Perhaps too easy for thy martial hand.
"What various causes to the field invite!
"For plunder you, and we for freedom fight:
"Her cause divine with generous ardor fires,
"And every bosom glows as she inspires!
"Already, thousands of your troops are fled

"To the drear mansions of the silent dead:
"Columbia too, beholds with streaming eyes
"Her heroes fall—'tis freedom's sacrifice!
"So wills the Power who with convulsive storms
"Shakes impious realms, and nature's face deforms.
"Yet those brave troops innum'rous as the sands
"One soul inspires, one General Chief commands
"Find in your train of boasted heroes, one
"To match the praise of Godlike Washington.
"Thrice happy Chief! in whom the virtues join,
"And heaven-taught prudence speaks the man divine!"
He ceas'd. Amazement struck the warrior-train,
And doubt of conquest, on the hostile plain.

BOSTON. Dec.ʳ 30, 1776

❧

ON THE DEATH OF GENERAL WOOSTER[43]

Madam

I recᵈ your favour by Mr Dennison inclosing a paper containing the Character of the truely worthy General Wooster. It was with the most sensible regret that I heard of his fall in battle, but the pain of so afflicting a dispensation of Providence must be greatly alleviated to you and all his friends in the consideration that he fell a martyr in the Cause of Freedom——

---

43. From the copy of the manuscript at the Massachusetts Historical Society in the Hugh Upham Clark Papers. This poem is listed in her 1779 Proposals, from which we derive a title for it. It was first published by Isani in *Modern Philology*. The letter is to Mary Wooster at New Haven, Connecticut, the widow to whom the poem about her late husband, General David Wooster, also is addressed (see the poem's last six lines). Mary Clap Wooster was sister to Temperance Clap Pitkin, wife of Timothy Pitkin (see Wheatley's poem to him on the death of his wife). (Also see Wheatley's earlier letter to Wooster.) Wooster died on May 2, 1777, having been mortally wounded during Tryon's raid on Danbury on April 27. (See the *Dictionary of American Biography*.) Isani points out that Wheatley's mention of twelve shillings lawful money in the letter suggests a fair demand for her book even five years after its publication, as she continued her financial concerns and efforts (changes in the worsening economy would help to account for some of the increase beyond the earlier advertised few shillings). Though she had become Phillis Peters in April, to Mrs. Wooster, whom she had not met, Phillis would have

From this the muse rich consolation draws
He nobly perish'd in his Country's cause
His Country's Cause that ever fir'd his mind
Where martial flames, and Christian virtues join'd.
How shall my pen his warlike deeds proclaim
Or paint them fairer on the list of Fame—
Enough great Cheif—now wrapt in shades around
Thy grateful Country shall thy praise resound
Tho' not with mortals' empty praise elate
That vainest vapour to th' immortal State
Inly serene the expiring hero lies
And thus (while heav'nward roll his swimming eyes)
Permit, great power while yet my fleeting breath
And Spirits wander to the verge of Death—
Permit me yet to paint fair freedom's charms
For her the Continent shines bright in arms
By thy high will, celestial prize she came—
For her we combat on the feild of fame
Without her presence vice maintains full sway
And social love and virtue wing their way
O still propitious be thy guardian care
And lead Columbia thro' the toils of war.
With thine own hand conduct them and defend
And bring the dreadful contest to an end—
For ever grateful let them live to thee
And keep them ever virtuous, brave, and free—
But how, presumptuous shall we hope to find
Divine acceptance with th' Almighty mind—
While yet (O deed ungenerous!) they disgrace
And hold in bondage Afric's blameless race?
Let virtue reign—And thou accord our prayers
Be victory our's, and generous freedom theirs.

---

been known still as Wheatley. The poem is notable not only for its patriotism and praise of
Wooster but even more for the strong lines concerning slavery which she puts into the hero's
dying prayer.

The hero pray'd—the wond'ring Spirit fled
And Sought the unknown regions of the dead—
Tis thine fair partner of his life, to find
His virtuous path and follow close behind—
A little moment steals him from thy Sight
He waits thy coming to the realms of light
Freed from his labours in the ethereal Skies
Where in Succession endless pleasures rise!

You will do me a great favour by returning to me by the first oppy those books
that remain unsold and remitting the money for those that are sold—I can
easily dispose of them here for 12/Lm? each—I am greatly obliged to you for
the care you show me, and your condescention in taking so much pains for
my Interest—I am extremely Sorry not to have been honour'd with a personal
acquaintance with you—if the foregoing lines meet with your acceptance and
approbation I shall think them highly honour'd. I hope you will pardon the
length of my letter, when the reason is apparent—fondness of the Subject
&—the highest respect for the deceas'd—I sincerely sympathize with you in
the great loss you and your family Sustain and am Sincerely

Your friend & very humble Servt

Phillis Wheatley

Queenstreet
Boston July—
15th 1778

❧

AN ELEGY, SACRED TO THE MEMORY OF THAT GREAT DIVINE,
THE REVEREND AND LEARNED DR. SAMUEL COOPER,[44] *Who de-
parted this Life December 29, 1783, ÆTATIS 59.* BY PHILLIS PETERS.
BOSTON: *Printed and Sold by E. Russell, in Essex-Street, near Liberty-Pole,*
M,DCC,LXXXIV.

To the CHURCH *and* CONGREGATION *assembling in Brattle-Street, the
following* ELEGY, *Sacred to the* MEMORY *of their late Reverend and Worthy*

---

44. This poem was first published in an eight-page pamphlet which included at the end the
words for the anthem (set to music by William Billings) used at Cooper's funeral on January 2,

PASTOR, *Dr.* SAMUEL COOPER, *is, with the greatest Sympathy, most respectfully inscribed by their Obedient,*

> Humble Servant,
>
> PHILLIS PETERS.

BOSTON, Jan. 1784.

O THOU whose exit wraps in boundless woe,
  For Thee the tears of various Nations flow:
For Thee the floods of virtuous sorrows rise
From the full heart and burst from streaming eyes,
Far from our view to Heaven's eternal height,
The Seat of bliss divine, and glory bright;
Far from the restless turbulence of life,
The war of factions, and impassion'd strife.
From every ill mortality endur'd,
Safe in celestial *Salem's* walls secur'd.

  E'ER yet from this terrestrial state retir'd,
The Virtuous lov'd Thee, and the Wise admir'd.
The gay approv'd Thee, and the grave rever'd;
And all thy words with rapt attention heard!
The Sons of Learning on thy lessons hung,
While soft persuasion mov'd th' illit'rate throng.
Who, drawn by rhetoric's commanding laws,
Comply'd obedient, nor conceiv'd the cause.

1784. This is from the pamphlet at the Massachusetts Historical Society. Because of its use of "performed at the funeral of" in the anthem's headnote, the pamphlet seems to have been printed after the funeral. It is possible that Wheatley's poem had been used at the funeral, as had the anthem. (Cooper died on Monday, December 29, but the funeral was not held until Friday.) The *Boston Magazine* for December 1783 reported in his obituary that Cooper "had been confined to his chamber with a disorder of the lethargic kind for upwards of six weeks" before he died, so she might have even anticipated his death in her composition. Cooper was graduated from Harvard in 1743 and was minister at the same church from 1744 until his death. He was a Whig and an open patriot, a scholar, an attractive and popular preacher, a frequent contributor to the newspapers, a friend of Benjamin Franklin, John Adams, and John Hancock, a friend to literature, a patron to Harvard, one of the founders of the American Academy of Arts and Sciences, and one of those who signed the letter "To the PUBLICK," which was printed at the front of Wheatley's book. He was chosen as president of Harvard in 1774 but he declined. His D.D. was from the University of Edinburgh. When Wheatley was

Thy every sentence was with grace inspir'd,
And every period with devotion fir'd;
Bright Truth thy guide without a dark disguise,
And penetration's all-discerning eyes.

THY COUNTRY mourn's th' afflicting Hand divine
That now forbids thy radiant lamp to shine,
Which, like the sun, resplendent source of light
Diffus'd its beams, and chear'd our gloom of night.

WHAT deep-felt sorrow in each *Kindred* breast
With keen sensation rends the heart distress'd!
Fraternal love sustains a tenderer part,
And mourns a BROTHER with a BROTHER'S heart.

THY CHURCH laments her faithful PASTOR fled
To the cold mansions of the silent dead.
There hush'd forever, cease the heavenly strain,
That wak'd the soul, but here resounds in vain.
Still live thy merits, where thy name is known,
As the sweet Rose, its blooming beauty gone
Retains its fragrance with a long perfume:
Thus COOPER! thus thy death-less name shall bloom
Unfading, in thy *Church* and *Country's* love,
While Winter frowns, or spring renews the grove.
The hapless Muse, her loss in COOPER mourns,
And as she sits, she writes, and weeps, by turns;
A Friend sincere, whose mild indulgent grace
Encourag'd oft, and oft approv'd her lays.

WITH all their charms, terrestrial objects strove,
But vain their pleasures to attract his love.

---

baptized in 1771, the Old South Church temporarily had been without a minister, so Cooper
was called upon from his Congregational church on Brattle Street to perform the sacrament
for her. (There is a manuscript copy of this poem at the Massachusetts Historical Society, but
it is not in Wheatley's hand, misspells her last name, and includes the marginal line numbering
used in the pamphlet, from which apparently it was copied. For someone else's poem on Coo-
per's death in the same vein, see the *Boston Magazine* for January 1784, pp. 114–15.) Also see
Charles Akers, *The Divine Politician: Samuel Cooper and the American Revolution in Boston* (Bos-
ton, 1982) and the Introduction to this volume.

Such COOPER was—at Heaven's high call he flies;
His task well finish'd, to his native skies.
Yet to his fate reluctant we resign,
Tho' our's to copy conduct such as thine:
Such was thy wish, th' observant Muse survey'd
Thy latest breath, and this advice convey'd.

⌘

LIBERTY AND PEACE, A POEM.[45] *By* PHILLIS PETERS. BOSTON:
Printed by WARDEN *and* RUSSELL, *At Their Office in Marlborough-Street.*
M,DCC,LXXXIV.

LO! Freedom comes. Th' prescient Muse foretold,
    All Eyes th' accomplish'd Prophecy behold:
Her Port describ'd, "*She moves divinely fair,*
"*Olive and Laurel bind her golden Hair.*"
She, the bright Progeny of Heaven, descends,
And every Grace her sovereign Step attends;
For now kind Heaven, indulgent to our Prayer,
In smiling *Peace* resolves the Din of *War*.
Fix'd in *Columbia* her illustrious Line,
And bids in thee her future Councils shine.
To every Realm her Portals open'd wide,
Receives from each the full commercial Tide.
Each Art and Science now with rising Charms
Th' expanding Heart with Emulation warms.
E'en great *Britannia* sees with dread Surprize,
And from the dazzl'ing Splendors turns her Eyes!
Britain, whose Navies swept th' *Atlantic* o'er,
And Thunder sent to every distant Shore:
E'en thou, in Manners cruel as thou art,
The Sword resign'd, resume the friendly Part!
For *Galia's* Power espous'd *Columbia's* Cause,

45. *Liberty and Peace* was first published in 1784 as a four-page pamphlet, and this is based on the pamphlet at the New-York Historical Society. In lines 3–4 Wheatley proudly quotes her

And new-born *Rome* shall give *Britannia* Law,
Nor unremember'd in the grateful Strain,
Shall princely *Louis'* friendly Deeds remain;
The generous Prince th' impending Vengeance eye's,
Sees the fierce Wrong, and to the rescue flies.
Perish that Thirst of boundless Power, that drew
On *Albion's* Head the Curse to Tyrants due.
But thou appeas'd submit to Heaven's decree,
That bids this Realm of Freedom rival thee!
Now sheathe the Sword that bade the Brave attone
With guiltless Blood for Madness not their own.
Sent from th' Enjoyment of their native Shore
Ill-fated—never to behold her more!
From every Kingdom on *Europa's* Coast
Throng'd various Troops, their Glory, Strength and Boast.
With heart-felt pity fair *Hibernia* saw
Columbia menac'd by the Tyrant's Law:
On hostile Fields fraternal Arms engage,
And mutual Deaths, all dealt with mutual Rage;
The Muse's Ear hears mother Earth deplore
Her ample Surface smoak with kindred Gore:
The hostile Field destroys the social Ties,
And ever-lasting Slumber seals their Eyes.
Columbia mourns, the haughty Foes deride,
Her Treasures plunder'd, and her Towns destroy'd:
Witness how *Charlestown's* curling Smoaks arise,[46]
In sable Columns to the clouded Skies!
The ample Dome, high-wrought with curious Toil,
In one sad Hour the savage Troops despoil.[47]

---

own description of Columbia from her 1775 poem to Washington (see that poem and her ear-
lier "America" for general comparison). In February Boston celebrated the advent of peace
with a festive occasion. Perhaps this poem was intended to be part of that context.

46. Apparently a reference to the burning by the British of Charlestown, northward across
the river from Boston.

47. Apparently a reference to the battle of Bunker's Hill on Charlestown peninsula on June
7, 1775, and the fierceness of the fighting, which was focused on the earthworks fortifications
there. In effect, she is asking the reader to remember the beginnings of the war now that it is
over and to remember how hard have been the paths to liberty and peace.

Descending *Peace* the Power of War confounds;
From every Tongue celestial *Peace* resounds:
As from the East th' illustrious King of Day,
With rising Radiance drives the Shades away,
So Freedom comes array'd with Charms divine,
And in her Train Commerce and Plenty shine.
Britannia owns her Independent Reign,
Hibernia, *Scotia*, and the Realms of *Spain*;
And great *Germania's* ample Coast admires
The generous Spirit that *Columbia* fires.
Auspicious Heaven shall fill with fav'ring Gales,
Where e'er *Columbia* spreads her swelling Sails:
To every Realm shall *Peace* her Charms display,
And Heavenly *Freedom* spread her golden Ray.

❧

An ELEGY *on leaving* ——.[48]

FAREWEL! ye friendly bowėrs, ye streams adieu,
    I leave with sorrow each sequesterėd seat:
The lawns, where oft I swept the morning dew,
    The groves, from noon-tide rays a kind retreat.

Yon wood-crownėd hill, whose far projecting shade,
    Inverted trembles in the limpid lake:
Where wrapt in thought I pensively have strayėd,
    For crowds and noise, reluctant, I forsake.

48. From the *Arminian Magazine* 7 (July 1784): 395–96. Although first published during the last year of her life, this is the most recently added poem in the Wheatley canon, through its publication by Isani in *American Literature* in December 1986, before which it had been unknown to those now interested in her and her writings. Published in London, the *Arminian* was the first magazine of the Methodist movement, and it published a number of Wheatley's poems, all of them variants of previously published poems by her except for this previously unpublished one (see the note for her poem "On Imagination" in this volume). Isani says (p. 612) that the primary interest of this poem is that it is one of only a small number of poems published in the last decade of her life, which was more than half of her life as a poet. More specific contexts for the poem's content and composition are not known. (Compare her poem "A Farewel to America," including form.)

The solemn pines, that, winding through the vale.
   In graceful rows attract the wandėring eye,
Where the soft ring-dove pours her soothing tale,
   No more must veil me from the fervid sky.

Beneath yon aged oak's protecting arms,
   Oft-times beside the pebblėd brook I lay;
Where, pleasėd with simple Nature's various charms,
   I passėd in grateful solitude the day.

Rapt with the melody of Cynthio's strain,
   There first my bosom felt poetic flame;
Mute was the bleating language of the plain,
   And with his lays the wanton fawns grew tame.

But, ah! those pleasing hours are ever flown;
   Ye scenes of transport from my thoughts retire;
Those rural joys no more the day shall crown,
   No more my hand shall wake the warbling lyre.

But come, sweet Hope, from thy divine retreat,
   Come to my breast, and chase my cares away,
Bring calm Content to gild my gloomy seat,
   And cheer my bosom with her heavėnly ray.

❧

To Mr. and Mrs.——, on the Death of their Infant Son,   *By Phillis Wheatly* [sic].[49]

O DEATH! whose sceptre, trembling realms obey,
And weeping millions mourn thy savage sway;
Say, shall we call thee by the name of friend,
Who blasts our joys, and bids our glories end?
Behold, a child who rivals op'ning morn,

---

49. This is from the "Poetical Essays" section of the *Boston Magazine* for September 1784, page 488, only a few months before her own death and that of her last living child. It was the last item written by her published during her lifetime, though its being signed with her maiden

When its first beams the eastern hills adorn;
So sweetly blooming once that lovely boy,
His father's hope, his mother's only joy,
Nor charms nor innocence prevail to save,
From the grim monarch of the gloomy grave!
Two moons revolve when lo! among the dead
The beauteous infant lays his weary head:
For long he strove the tyrant to withstand,
And the dread terrors of his iron hand;
Vain was his strife, with the relentless power,
His efforts weak; and this his mortal hour;
He sinks—he dies—celestial muse, relate,
His spirit's entrance at the sacred gate.
Methinks I hear the heav'nly courts resound,
The recent theme inspires the choirs around.
His guardian angel with delight unknown,
Hails his bless'd charge on his immortal throne;
His heart expands at scenes unknown before,
Dominions praise, and prostrate thrones adore;
Before the Eternal's feet their crowns are laid,
The glowing seraph vails his sacred head.
Spirits redeem'd, that more than angels shine,
For nobler praises tune their harps divine:
These saw his entrance; his soft hand they press'd,
Sat on his throne, and smiling thus address'd,
"Hail: thou! thrice welcome to this happy shore,

---

name may suggest its composition before her marriage in April 1778, in which case it could be
the poem called "To P.N.S. & Lady on the death of their infant son" in the 1779 Proposals.
There was an editorial note on page 462 of this same number of the *Boston Magazine*: "The
Poem, in page 488, of this Number, was selected from a manuscript Volume of Poems, written
by PHILLIS PETERS, formerly Phillis Wheatly [sic]—and is inserted as a Specimen of her
Work: should this gain the Approbation of the Publick, and sufficient encouragement be given,
a Volume will be shortly Published, by the Printers hereof, who receive subscriptions for said
Work." (Greenleaf and Freeman were listed as the printers and publishers of the magazine.)
Unfortunately, Wheatley died on December 5. The proposed book was never published, and
the second attempt for a second volume of her poems also was not successful (see the 1779
Proposals). It also was the third time she unsuccessfully proposed the publication of a book in
Boston (see also the 1772 Proposals).

Born to new life where changes are no more;
Glad heaven receives thee, and thy God bestows,
Immortal youth exempt from pain and woes.
Sorrow and sin, those foes to human rest,
Forever banish'd from thy happy breast."
Gazing they spoke, and raptur'd thus replies,
The beauteous stranger in the etherial skies.
"Thus safe conducted to your bless'd abodes,
With sweet surprize I mix among the Gods;
The vast profound of this amazing grace,
Beyond your search, immortal powers, I praise;
Great Sire, I sing thy boundless love divine,
Mine is the bliss, but all the glory thine."
    All heav'n rejoices as your . . . . sings,
To heavenly airs he tunes the sounding strings;
Mean time on earth the hapless parents mourn,
"Too quickly fled, ah! never to return."
Thee, the vain visions of the night restore,
Illusive fancy paints the phantom o'er;
Fain would we clasp him, but he wings his flight;
Deceives our arms, and mixes with the night;
But oh! suppress the clouds of grief that roll,
Invading peace, and dark'ning all the soul.
Should heaven restore him to your arms again,
Oppress'd with woes, a painful endless train,
How would your prayers, your ardent wishes, rise,
Safe to repose him in his native skies.

Letters and Proposals

Although we now have twenty-two of Wheatley's letters, we know that she wrote others because they are mentioned here and there or are listed in her 1779 Proposals. For example, according to the letter from John Wheatley at the front of her 1773 book, she wrote a letter to Samson Occom in 1765 (more likely in 1766 because Occom did not sail from Boston until December 23, 1765) after he had gone to England to raise money; but we do not have that letter. We also know that she received a good number of letters, but almost all of that side of her correspondence seems to have escaped preservation (but see George Washington's letter to her, to be found with her poem to him, and there also her letter to him). Three of her letters (to "Madam," 1771; to George Washington, October 26, 1775; and to Mary Wooster, July 15, 1778) are printed with the poems they accompanied, rather than in this section of prose. We do have an interesting variety of letters (for example, to her black friend Obour Tanner, to persons of high station in England, to Samuel Hopkins, to George Washington); and if we think of many of her poems as letters in verse, as in effect they were because of their very often occasional nature, then the variety is even greater. Nevertheless, in regard to number, chronological span, fullness, and continuity of correspondence as a whole or with individuals, what we have leaves much to be desired. But the letters we do have provide a good bit of what we know about her and her life—her relationships with those close to her (except, notably, for her husband), the business aspects of her book, the suggestion that she become an African missionary, when she was freed, and so forth. In a few, especially in the letter to David Wooster, we learn a great many facts and a great deal about her personality—occasionally we can even see how she handles the same subject differently, depending on the addressee and on what she is trying to accomplish. Indeed, without the letters we would know so much less than the far from enough we do know about her. Despite the good intentions she expresses to the contrary, it is my impression that she was not a prolific correspondent and that not a great many of the letters she wrote are missing. The largest number we have to one person is the seven to Obour Tanner, and that over a seven-year period, an average of one per year. I do not think we are missing any letters from Wheatley to Tanner, for Tanner seems to have valued her letters from Wheatley and to have preserved them carefully together to be passed on for further preservation. Most of the letters we have could be called business letters, at least letters of purpose (to benefit her to one degree or another). She was not a casual or light correspondent. As much as her poetry, her letters often seem occasional in nature; even with Tanner she is more a responder than an initiator, from the first letter to the last. Sixteen of the twenty-two letters we have are from only three years (four from 1772, five from 1773, and seven from 1774)—and twelve of those in one way or another are about her trip to England and its aftermath (June 1773–October 1774), including Mrs. Wheatley's death and selling her volume of poems. From the letters we have we learn little of the last ten years of her life, during the war and her marriage—and nothing at all of the last five and one-half years. On the other hand, we should be glad for those we do have and that they focus on that rich and productive period of her life, rather than having only a few letters focusing on some much less interesting period in relation to her poetry; and we must remember that the letters are of interest to us first of all because she was a poet.

Three of her Proposals for book publishing are included here because of the valuable information and insights they provide. (The fourth is with the poem it accompanied in 1784, the last one in this volume.) Who wrote them is not known, but the chances are good that she wrote the 1772 and 1779 ones—certainly she cooperated in their conception and contents.

The items in this section are in chronological order. For each letter, the first information given (preceding the salutation and date) as to addressee and that person's location (and by whom the letter is delivered) is from (when it has been available) the "envelope," actually that part of the paper on which the letter is written (or on an extra sheet of paper) which was left exposed, with this address information showing, when the paper was folded for protection of the letter itself and for privacy, in the usual eighteenth-century fashion. The same type of information found elsewhere with the letter is from the letter itself, inside the folded sheet of paper. (Arbour Tanner and Obour Tanner are the same person.)

❧

TO THE RT. HON'BLE THE COUNTESS OF HUNTINGDON[1]

Most noble Lady,
 The Occasion of my addressing your Ladiship will, I hope, Apologize for

---

1. From the original in the Countess of Huntingdon's Papers of the Cheshunt Foundation at Westminster College in Cambridge, England, as are the other two letters from Wheatley to the

this my boldness in doing it: it is to enclose a few lines on the decease of your worthy Chaplain, the Rev'd Mr. Whitefield, in the loss of whom, I Sincerely sympathize with your Ladiship: but your great loss which is his Greater gain, will, I hope, meet with infinite reparation, in the presence of God, the Divine Benefactor whose image you bear by filial imitation.

The Tongues of the learned, are insufficient, much less the pen of an untutor'd African, to paint in lively characters, the excellencies of this Citizen of Zion! I beg an Interest in your Ladiship's Prayers, and Am

> With great humility
> your Ladiship's most Obedient
> Humble Servant

[Boston Oct. 25, 1770]   Phillis Wheatley

Countess of Huntingdon in this volume. (Also see the three versions of Wheatley's poem on the death of George Whitefield, the 1769 version of her poem on the death of Dr. Sewall, and the note to her poem "On Imagination"; and see Jackson, "Letters of Phillis Wheatley and Susanna Wheatley.")

Selina Hastings (1707–91), Countess of Huntingdon, in 1739 joined the Methodist movement and became one of its strong supporters, though she eventually would side with Whitefield and the Calvinistic Methodists instead of with the Wesleys. In 1748 she made Whitefield her chaplain and from that time till his death gave great support to his work both in England and in America. An influential group with interests in evangelical Methodism, to which she gave a center and encouragement, was called "The Countess of Huntingdon's Connection," or "Connexion." In 1768 she established a college at Trevecca in Talgarth in South Wales for the purpose of educating ministers who would follow her evangelical and Methodist persuasion. At her death she left sixty-four Methodist chapels for which she had been responsible. Among those who shared her concerns were the Earl of Dartmouth and John Thornton, whose names are also associated with Phillis Wheatley. The Wheatleys were among those in America who shared the countess' interests and concerns. Liking Phillis's poems, the countess agreed to allow Wheatley's book to be dedicated to her and asked that a portrait of the author be provided for a frontispiece. When Wheatley visited England she and the countess hoped to meet, but the countess was in Wales, and before Wheatley could accept her invitation to visit there she was called back to Boston because of the serious illness of her mistress and had to cut short her stay in Britain. Among those who had prepared the way with good accounts of Wheatley in letters to the countess were Wheatley's mistress and Richard Cary of nearby Charlestown, Massachusetts, letters from both of whom are in the countess' papers. On April 30, 1773, Susanna Wheatley reported to the countess that Phillis's poor health had led the doctors to advise the sea for her and that Phillis would be coming to England with Mrs. Wheatley's son, Nathaniel, who was going on business. She asked the countess to advise both of the young travelers. On May 25, 1772, Cary had written to the countess: "The Negro Girl of Mr. Wheatley's, by her virtuous Behaviour and Conversation in Life gives Reason to believe, she's a Subject of Divine Grace—remarkable for her Piety, of an extraordinary Genius, and in full Communion with one of the Churches; the Family, & Girl, was Affected at the kind enquiry your Ladyship

For Printing By Subscription,

A Collection of POEMS, wrote at several times, and upon various occasions, by PHILLIS, a Negro Girl, from the strength of her own Genius, it being but a few Years since she came to this Town an uncultivated Barbarian from *Africa*. The Poems having been seen and read by the best judges, who think them well worthy of the Publick View; and upon critical examination, they find that the declared Author was capable of writing them. The Order in which they were penned, together with the Occasion, are as follows;

On the Death of the Rev. Dr. *Sewell*, when sick, 1765—On Virtue, 166

---

made after her." On April 3, 1773, he wrote to her, concerning men of her acquaintance who were coming to Boston, that "I shall not omit bringing [them] to an acquaintance with Phillis, the Christian Poetess, who continues in well doing." And when Wheatley left for England she carried with her a letter from Cary for the countess, dated May 3, which, unfortunately, she was not able to deliver in person, as had been intended, but which eventually reached the countess anyway. In it he praised Wheatley for her "Humility, modesty and Spirituall minded-ness" and said, "[I] hope she will continue an ornament to the Christian name and profession, as she grows older and has more experience, I doubt not her Writtings will run more in an Evangelicall Strain. I think your Ladyship will be pleas'd with her." Cary was one of those who had signed the letter "To the PUBLICK" to be used at the front of her book.

When Whitefield died in 1770, Wheatley's poem about him was addressed to the countess. In the countess' papers in England, the copy of that poem mentioned in the letter above is not to be found. Many have presumed that Wheatley refers to a manuscript copy of it, but as the poem was already in print by the time the letter was written, it might have been a broadside that was sent, which might have been even more impressive than a manuscript and might well have been placed apart from correspondence after it arrived, perhaps even displayed.

In the countess' papers there is another manuscript of the letter above, which differs from it inconsequentially. It appears to be a draft but could be a careless copy. Fortunately, it is dated, from which we get a date for the neater and more "artistic" (but undated) version used above. (Robinson, *Her Writings*, p. 399, has a facsimile of the dated version.)

Also see the Introduction to this volume and Wheatley's 1773 and 1779 Proposals.

2. From the *Boston Censor* for Saturday, February 29, 1772 (vol. 1, no. 15). It also was printed in the *Censor* for March 14 and April 11. It did not generate enough response, so efforts were begun to try to have the book published in England (see her 1773 Proposals). (The abbreviation "do." is for "ditto," the same.) One of the persons who did subscribe for her book in 1772 was the Boston merchant John Andrews, who wrote from Boston to his brother-in-law William Barrell in Philadelphia on May 29, 1772: "Its above two months since I subscribed for Phillis's poems, which I expected to have sent you long ago, but the want of spirit to carry on any thing of the kind here has prevented it, as they are not yet publish'd." On February 24, 1773, almost a year from the first publication of the Proposals above, Andrews wrote to Barrell: "In regard to Phillis's poems they will originate from a London press, as she was blamd by her friends for printg them here & made to exp[ect] a large emolument if she sent ye copy home [to England], which inducd her to remand it of ye printer & dld [delivered] it Capt Calef, who [later] could not sell it [in England] by reason of their not crediting ye performance

[sic]—On two Friends, who were cast away, do. To the University of Cambridge, 1767.—An Address to the Atheist, do.—An Address to the Deist, do.—On America, 1768—On the King, do.—On Friendship, do.—Thoughts on being brought from Africa to America, do.—On the Nuptials of Mr. *Spence* to Miss *Hooper*, do.—On the Hon. Commodore Hood, on his pardoning a Deserter, 1769.—On the Death of the Reverend Dr. *Sewell*, do.—On the Death of Master *Seider*, who was killed by *Ebenezer Richardson*, 1770.— On the Death of the Rev. *George Whitefield*, do.—On the Death of a young Miss, aged 5 years, do. On the Arrival of the Ships of War, and landing of the Troops.—On the Affray in King-Street, on the Evening of the 5th of March.—On the death of a young Gentleman.—To *Samuel Quincy*, Esq; a Panegyrick.—To a Lady on her coming to America for her Health.—To Mrs. *Leonard*, on the Death of her Husband.—To Mrs. Boylston and Children, on the Death of her Son and their Brother.—To a Gentleman and Lady on the

---

to be by a Negro, since which she has had a paper drawn up & signed by the Gov. Council, Ministers & most of ye people of note in this place, certifying the authenticity of it; which paper Capt. Calef carried last fall, thefore we may expect it in print by the Spring ships" (see the letter "To the PUBLICK" at the front of her book). (This correspondence is in the Massachusetts Historical Society.) Even though the book was not published in 1772 in Boston, there was direct continuity from the Proposals above to the book that would be published in 1773 in London (even though the contents differ in several ways from those announced above); and presumably the Bostonians, such as Andrews, who wanted to buy her book in 1772 also bought it in 1773 and later—and they were joined by many others in that city and in other New England communities. Andrews wrote to Barrell on January 28, 1774: "After so long a time, have at last got Phillis's poems in print, which will be dld you by Capt Dunn . . . these dont seem to be near all her productions . . . I believe [she] intends to have ye benefit of another volume." (See the Introduction to this volume, her 1779 Proposals, and her poem on the death of Charles Eliot.)

These Proposals are useful in dating poems, in further confirming authorship of them, in clarifying some subjects in poems, in knowing of poems we do not have, and as partial evidence about how publishing the book in England instead of in Boston (for a very different audience) led her to change it in various ways. Some of the poems listed in the Proposals were too American, too politically oriented in sensitive times, for England and the Wheatleys' friends there, so they were omitted. Others were changed some in light of the same concerns but were retained. Others were added. Some were simply made more generic for an audience for whom many of the local names would mean nothing (though in the Proposals for Boston publication they are emphasized). The total number of poems increased by approximately one-fourth, and the book as a whole took on an even more religious cast, one not unsuited to the woman to whom it now was dedicated and her friends. We have variants for some of the 1773 book poems which illustrate the directions of her revisions for the 1773 book, and we have some of the poems she did not include. A few of the poems listed above we do not have (as far as I know), but some of their titles tell something about their focuses. For example, the first poem in the list apparently comes from a period when Sewall was ill and was thought near

Death of their Son, aged 9 Months.—To a Lady on her remarkable Deliverance in a Hurricane.—To *James Sullivan*, Esq; and Lady on the Death of her Brother and Sister, and a Child *Avis*, aged 12 Months.—*Goliah* [sic] of Gath.—On the Death of Dr. *Samuel* Marshall.

It is supposed they will make one small Octavo Volume, and will contain about 200 Pages.

They will be printed on Demy Paper, and beautiful Types.

The Price to Subscribers, handsomely bound and lettered, will be Four Shillings.—Stitched in blue, Three Shillings.

It is hoped Encouragement will be given to this Publication, as a reward to a very uncommon Genius, at present a Slave.

This Work will be put to the Press as soon as three Hundred Copies are subscribed for, and and [sic] shall be published with all Speed.

Subscriptions are taken in by E. Russell, in Marlborough Street.

TO JOHN THORNTON IN LONDON[3]

Boston April 21st, 1772

Hon'd, Sir

I rec'd your instructive fav^r. of Feb. 29, for which, return you ten thousand thanks, I did not flatter myself with the tho'ts of your honouring me with an Answer to my letter, I thank you for recommending the Bible to be my cheif Study, I find and Acknowledge it the best of Books, it contains an endless

---

death (its date tells us that as early as about age twelve, only four years after arriving in Boston, she was writing poetry—the statement above about her being capable of writing the poems involved age as well as background). And the fifth of March poem clearly must focus on the famous Boston Massacre of that date in 1770, also the year of the landing of the troops in the preceding title (see Robinson, *Her Writings*, p. 455, for some anonymous verse on the Massacre, from the Boston *Evening Post* for March 12, 1770). For some of the poems listed with no date, we have dates from elsewhere—for example, 1771 for the Samuel Marshall poem. Ezekiel Russell (at the end of the Proposals) published the *Censor*, in which this appeared. He had published a broadside of her poem on Whitefield in 1770 and later would publish her poem on Samuel Cooper and her *Liberty and Peace*. (See Isani, "The First Proposed Edition.") The *Censor* was a paper with Tory sympathies.

3. From the original (GD 26/13/663) in the Scottish Record Office in Edinburgh, as are the other three Wheatley letters to Thornton in this volume. They are not listed in her 1779 Proposals. Occasionally in some of Wheatley's letters to Thornton there are defective places in the letters which have caused problems in clarity, indicated here by brackets. (See Silverman,

treasure of wisdom, and knowledge. O that my eyes were more open'd to see the real worth, and true excellence of the word of truth, my flinty heart Soften'd with the grateful dews of divine grace and the Stubborn will, and affections, bent on God alone their proper object, and the vitiated palate may be corrected to relish heav'nly things. It has pleas'd God to lay me on a bed of Sickness, and I knew not but my deathbed, but he has been graciously pleas'd to restore me in a great measure. I beg your prayers, that I may be made thankful for his paternal corrections, and that I may make a proper use of them to the glory of his grace. I am Still very weak & the Physicians, seem to think there is danger of a consumpsion. And O that when my flesh and my heart fail me God would be my strength and portion for ever. that I might put my whole trust and Confidence in him, who has promis'd never to forsake those who Seek him with the whole heart. You could not, I am sure have express greater tenderness and affection for me, than by.being a welwisher to my Soul, the friends of Souls bear Some resemblance to the father of Spirits and are made partakers of his divine Nature.

I am affraid I have entruded on your patient, but if I had not tho't it ungrateful to omit writing in answer to your favour Should not have troubl'd you, but I can't expect you to answer this,

I am Sir with greatest respect,
your very hum. sert.
Phillis Wheatley

"Four New Letters," the note to Wheatley's poem "On Imagination," and her letters to David Wooster and to the Countess of Huntingdon.) John Thornton (1720–90), merchant and philanthropist, annually dispensed sizable amounts of money for charity and religious purposes, including help to missionaries. His home in Clapham, near London, became a center for mission activities, and the presence of other similarly minded persons in that community gave rise to the term "The Clapham Sect." Their social reform interests encompassed both poverty and slavery. Although an Anglican, Thornton shared many causes and friends with the Countess of Huntingdon, including George Whitefield and Samson Occom (see Wheatley's poem on Whitefield and her letter to Occom). John and Susanna Wheatley disbursed funds which Thornton sent for Indian missions and kept him informed accordingly. Thornton was somewhat wary that Wheatley's growing reputation might be an impediment to her religious life. Her life, however, no matter how genuine her piety, was also one of literature and related interests, and she could not accept the directions in which he would have it move, no matter how grateful she might feel for his concern and good intentions.

Dear Sister   Boston May 19th 1772

I rec'd your favour of February 6th for which I give you my sincere thanks, I greatly rejoice with you in that realizing view, and I hope experience, of the Saving change which you So emphatically describe. Happy were it for us if we could arrive to that evangelical Repentance, and the true holiness of heart which you mention. Inexpressibly happy Should we be could we have a due Sense of the Beauties and excellence of the Crucified Saviour. In his Crucifixion may be seen marvellous displays of Grace and Love, Sufficient to draw and invite us to the rich and endless treasures of his mercy, let us rejoice in and adore the wonders of God's infinite Love in bringing us from a land Semblant of darkness itself, and where the divine light of revelation (being obscur'd) is as darkness. Here, the knowledge of the true God and eternal life are made manifest; But there, profound ignorance overshadows the Land, Your observation is true, namely, that there was nothing in us to recommend us to God. Many of our fellow creatures are pass'd by, when the bowels of divine love expanded towards us. May this goodness & long Suffering of God lead us to unfeign'd repentance

It gives me very great pleasure to hear of so many of my Nation, Seeking with eagerness the way to true felicity, O may we all meet at length in that happy mansion. I hope the correspondence between us will continue, (my being much indispos'd this winter past was the reason of my not answering yours before now) which correspondence I hope may have the happy effect of improving our mutual friendship. Till we meet in the regions of consummate blessedness, let us endeavor by the assistance of divine grace, to live the life, and we Shall die the death of the Righteous. May this be our happy case and of those who are travelling to the region of Felicity is the earnest request of your affectionate

Friend & hum. Sert.   Phillis Wheatley

4. From the original of this letter in the Roberts Autograph Collection in the Quaker Collection of the Haverford College Library. The other six letters from Wheatley to Tanner are from the originals at the Massachusetts Historical Society. At one time the six were in the hands of Mrs. William H. Beecher, who had received them from Tanner herself, and who described Tanner as very dark, pious, sensible, intelligent, and respected (see *Proceedings of the Massachusetts Historical Society* 7 [November 1863]: 267–79, which includes all seven letters; and 15 [December 1877]: 386). Tanner was a servant in the home of James Tanner of Newport,

To the care of Mr. Pease's Servant.

My dear friend   Boston July 19th 1772

I rec'd your kind Epistle a few days ago; much disappointed to hear that you had not rec'd my answer to your first letter.* I have been in a very poor state of health all the past winter and spring, and now reside in the country for the benefit of its more wholesome air. I came to town this morning to spend the Sabbath with my master and mistress: Let me be interested in yr. Prayers that God would please to bless to me the means us'd for my recovery, if agreeable to his holy Will. While my outward man languishes under weakness and pa[in], may the inward be refresh'd and Strengthend more abundantly by him who declar'd from heaven that his strength was made perfect in weakness! may he correct our vitiated taste, that the meditation of him may be delightful to us. No longer to be so excessively charm'd with fleeting vanities: But pressing forward to the fix'd mark f[or] the prize. How happy that man who is prepar'd for that Nig[ht] Wherein no man can work! Let us be mindful of our high calling, continually on our guard, lest our treacherous hearts Should give the adversary an advantage over us. O! who can think without horror of the Snares of the Devil. Let us, by freque[nt] meditation on the eternal Judgment prepare for it. May the Lord bless to us these thoughts; and teach us by his Spirit to live to him alone, and when we leave this world may We be his: That this may be our happy case, is the sincere desire
                    Of,
                        your affectionate friend, & humble Servt.
* I sent the letter   Phillis Wheatley
to Mr. Whitwell's who said he
would forward it.

Rhode Island. She was baptized in the First Congregational Church in Newport on July 10, 1768; she married Barra Tanner on November 14, 1789; and she died in Newport on June 21, 1835. In 1793 she was recorded as free, but how long she had been free is not known (see Robinson, *Her Writings*, pp. 42 and 314). (In some places in some of Wheatley's letters to Tanner the manuscripts are slightly defective from wear, particularly on the right side of the page, to the very edge of which she usually wrote. There is little or no doubt as to the few letters missing in these cases, but such defects have been indicated here by brackets.) Letters to Tanner are not listed in Wheatley's 1779 Proposals. (Arbour Tanner and Obour Tanner are the same person.)

5. See the note to Wheatley's letter to Tanner of May 19, 1772. Judging from the contents of

TO THE RIGHT HON'BLE THE EARL OF DARTMOUTH &.^c &.^c &.^c pr. favour of Mr. Wooldridge.[6]

My Lord,

The Joyful occasion which has given me this Confidence in addressing your Lordship in the enclos's Peice, will, I hope, Sufficiently apologize for this freedom from an African, who with the (now) happy America, exults with equal transport, in the view of one of its greatest advocates Presiding, with the Special tenderness of a Fatherly heart, over the American department.

Nor can they, my Lord, be insensible of the Friendship so much exemplified in your endeavors in their behalf, during the late unhappy disturbances.[7] I sincerely wish your Lordship all Possible Success, in your undertakings for the Interest of North America.

That the united Blessings of Heaven and Earth, may attend you here,

---

that letter and this one, it would seem that the first contact between these two women was in a letter from Tanner to Wheatley and that Wheatley's response on May 19 was her first letter to Tanner. William Whitwell was a Boston merchant and a member of the Old South Church, of which Wheatley was also a member.

6. From the original in the papers of Lord Dartmouth in the Staffordshire Records Office in Stafford, England. See the note to Wheatley's poem to Lord Dartmouth. A letter to Lord Dartmouth was listed in her 1779 Proposals. There exist two slightly but not significantly variant versions of this letter. One is with the variant of her Dartmouth poem in the *New-York Journal* and the other is in manuscript at the Massachusetts Historical Society (MHS). (Robinson, *Her Writings*, reprints the former on p. 402 and provides a facsimile of the latter on pp. 400–401.) Aside from not unusual minor differences in spelling, punctuation, and capitalization among the three versions, the nature of their close similarity and some of their other slight differences poses a puzzle. The wording of the *Journal* version is that of the MHS version with "in an African," "that Department," and "10th" instead of "10," but is like the version above with the plural "undertakings" and *and* spelled out in "Heaven and Earth" instead of an ampersand. The version above is the only one to include "& devoted" in the closing; and the number of paragraphs is different in each (paragraph two above is two paragraphs in the MHS version, and the *Journal* version has the same first paragraph as above and all else in a second paragraph). The above version is clearly the one sent to Dartmouth by Wheatley, and the *Journal* version presumably was taken from the one above, via Wooldridge. But what is the MHS version (which clearly is not in Wheatley's hand, despite a nineteenth-century statement to the contrary)—is it some sort of draft or a copy? Is it a copy from the above (with changes) for the *Journal*, which then made the other changes? This last seems the most likely explanation.

7. Apparently a reference to the unhappiness with the Stamp Act and then its repeal.

and the endless Felicity of the invisible State, in the presence of the Divine Benefactor, may be your portion here after, is the hearty desire
Of, My Lord,
Boston, N.E. Oct. 10. 1772
Your Lordship's most Obt. & devoted Huml. Servt.
Phillis Wheatley

PROPOSALS[8]

For Printing in *London* by SUBSCRIPTION,
A Volume of POEMS,
Dedicated by Permission to the Right Hon. the
Countess of Huntingdon.
Written by PHILLIS,
A Negro Servant to Mr. Wheatley of *Boston*
in New-England.
Terms of Subscription.

I. The Book to be neatly printed in 12 mo. on a new
Type and a fine Paper, adorned with an elegant
Frontispiece, representing the Author.
II. That the Price to Subscribers shall be Two Shillings
Sewed or Two Shillings and Six-pence neatly bound.
II. [sic] That every Subscriber deposit One Shilling at the
Time of subscribing; and the Remainder to be paid
on the Delivery of the Book.

$*_*^*$ Subscriptions are received by Cox & Berry,
in *Boston*.

8. From the *Massachusetts Gazette and the Boston News-Letter* for Friday, April 16, 1773 (no. 3628). With a few insignificant minor changes, it also was published in the *Massachusetts Gazette and Boston Post Boy and Advertiser* for April 19 and 22. Having failed to gain enough support to publish her book in Boston (see the 1772 Proposals), Mrs. Wheatley, her mistress, through her husband's business connections and her own Methodist connections in England, began attempts to have it published in London. By the time these Proposals appeared, the decision for publication there had already been made and a publisher secured, for the countess

THE RIGHT HONOURABLE   THE COUNTESS OF HUNTINGTON
[sic]. AT TALGARTH   SOUTH WALES.—⁹

London
Madam   June 27th 1773

It is with pleasure I acquaint your Ladyship of my safe arrival in London
after a fine passage of 5 weeks, in the Ship London, with my young Master:
(advis'd by my Physicians for my Health.) have Brought a letter from Richd.
Carey Esqr. but was disappointed by your absence of the honour of waiting
upon your Ladyship with it. I woud have inclos'd it, but was doubtful of the
safety of the conveyance.

I should think my self very happy in Seeing your Ladyship, and if you was
So desirous of the Image of the Author as to propose it for a Frontispiece I
flatter myself that you would accept the Reality

I conclude with thanking your Ladyship for permitting the Dedication of
my Poems to you; and am not insensible, that, under the patronage of your
Ladyship, not more eminent in the Station of Life than in your examplary
Piety and Virtue, my feeble efforts will be Shielded from the Severe trials of
unpitying Criticism and, being encourag'd by your Ladyship's Indulgence, I
the more freely resign to the world these Juvenile productions, And Am,
Madam, with greatest humility, your Dutiful Huml Sert.

Phillis Wheatley

THE RIGHT HON'BLE   THE COUNTESS   OF HUNTINGDON¹⁰

Madam

I rec'd with the mix'd sensations of pleasure & disappointment your
Ladiship's message favored by Mr. Rien Acquainting us with your pleasure

---

had allowed the book to be dedicated to her and had insisted on a portrait of Phillis as a fron-
tispiece, thereby lending her own considerable reputation and contacts toward the book's suc-
cess. Therefore, by this time the subscription process was no longer a prerequisite for the pub-
lication of this book (though prepublication commitment to purchase a book is always helpful
and welcome); and Phillis's letters after its publication are full of interest and activity in secur-
ing new sales of it hither and yon with the help of anyone who was willing, though there had
been some subscriptions also. (See Wheatley's letters to the Countess of Huntingdon and the
Introduction to this volume.)

9. See the note for Wheatley's letter to the Countess of Huntingdon, October 25, 1770.
10. See the note for Wheatley's letter to the Countess of Huntingdon, October 25, 1770.

that my Master & I Should wait upon you in So. Wales, delighted with your Ladiship's Condescention to me so unworthy of it. Am sorry [to a]cquaint your Ladiship that the Ship is certainly to Sail next Thurs[day on] which I must return to America. I long to see my Friends there, [I am ex]tremely reluctant to go without having first Seen your Ladiship.

It gives me very great satisfaction to hear of an African[11] so worthy to be honour'd with your Ladiship's approbation & Friendship as him whom you call your Brother. I rejoice with your Ladiship in that Fund of mental Felicity which you cannot but be possessed of, in the consideration of your exceeding great reward. My great opinion of your Ladiship's goodness, leads to believe, I have an interest in your most happy hours of communion, with your most indulgent Father and our great and common Benefactor. With greatest humility I am,

most dutifully

London July 17   your Ladiship's Obedt. Sert
     1773   Phillis Wheatley.

My master is yet undetermined about going home, and Sends his dutiful respects to your Ladiship[12]

TO COL. DAVID WORCESTER [WOOSTER] IN NEW HAVEN, CON-
NECTICUT.[13] favour'd by Mr.
       Badcock's Servant.

Sir

Having an opportunity by a Servant of Mr. Badcock's who lives near you, I am glad to hear you and your Family are well, I take the Freedom to transmit to you, a short Sketch of my voyage and return from London where I went for

---

The original of the letter above is missing a small area of one edge; therefore conjectured words are in brackets here.

11. Probably James Albert Ukawsaw Gronniosaw, whose dictated *Narrative* (1770) was dedicated to the countess with her permission.

12. Captain Robert Calef's *London*, with Phillis on board, had sailed for Boston by the end of July, but Nathaniel remained in London with business interests, and in November married Mary Enderby and remained a London resident the rest of his life, dying there in 1783. He did bring his wife to visit Boston in the fall of 1774, some months after his mother's death.

13. From the copy of the letter at the Massachusetts Historical Society in the Hugh Upham Clark Papers. This letter is not listed in her 1779 Proposals. This remarkable letter, full of all

the recovery of my health as advisd by my Physician, I was reciev'd in England with such kindness[,] Complaisance, and so many marks of esteem and real Friendship as astonishes me on the reflection, for I was no more than 6 weeks there.—Was introduced to Lord Dartmouth and had near half an hour's conversation with his Lordship, with whom was Alderman Kirkman,—Then to Lord Lincoln, who visited me at my own Lodgings with the Famous Dr. Solander, who accompany'd Mr. Banks in his late expedition round the World.

Then to Lady Cavendish, and Lady Carteret Webb,—Mrs. Palmer a Poetess. an accomplishd Lady.—Dr. Thos. Gibbons, Rhetoric Proffesor, To Israel Mauduit Esqr. Benjamin Franklin Esqr. F.R.S. Grenville [sic] Sharp Esqr. who attended me to the Tower & Show'd the Lions, Panthers, Tigers, &c. The Horse Armoury, Sma[ll] Armoury. the Crowns, Sceptres, Diadems, the Font for christin[in]g the Royal Family, Saw Westminster Abbey. British Museum[,] Coxe's Museum, Saddler's wells. Greenwich Hospital, Park and Chapel, The royal Observatory at Greenwich, &c. &c. too many things & Places to trouble you with in a Letter.—The Earl of Dartmouth made me a

---

kinds of helpful and interesting information about her, was first published by Isani in 1979 in "Phillis Wheatley in London." As he says (p. 255), "It describes her London visit, her emancipation, and her financial preoccupations" while they were still fresh in her mind. David Wooster (1711–77) was a Yale graduate (1738), who had served in several military contexts before becoming a merchant in New Haven, and he continued to serve when needed and gradually rose in rank. In 1763 he became collector of customs in New Haven. In 1775 he would be made a major-general of six Connecticut regiments. Despite his varied experience, he seems not to have been a good commander. Nevertheless, he would continue to see sporadic service until he was killed in action. (See Wheatley's poem on his death.) The 1773 letter is almost as tightly packed as were the days she spent in England. (Compare her letters to Obour Tanner of October 30 and to John Thornton of December 1.) She must not have known Wooster well to misspell his name, but somehow she knew him (or knew about him) well enough to engage him in the business of her book, and she understood that he (unlike the more pious Tanner and Thornton) was a person who could appreciate such worldly excitement as leaps from her frenetic account of her London activities during her not lengthy visit (June 17–ca. July 26). This is the letter of a young lady of about twenty, who has been made much of in the city of London and has seen "the world," and she still finds that heady enough to boast of even after having to return sooner than had been expected, enduring being at sea from ca. July 26 until September 13, and finding her friend and mistress (the nearest to a mother she had) seriously ill. She needed someone to share this experience with who would understand it because despite her disappointment at not seeing the Countess of Huntingdon or the king, there had been much to remember. Appropriate to the letter's contents and its recipient, it is one of her most personal and secular in tone. As Isani says (p. 258), "She was precocious and extraordinarily mature for her years, but she also had a breadth of interest and an inquiring mind" and "the weight of her prestige and piety did not inhibit [her] . . . from tasting of the novel and the profane."

Compliment of 5 guineas, and desird me to get the whole of Mr. Pope's Works, as the best he could recommend to my perusal, this I did, also got Hudibrass, Don Quixot, & Gay's Fables—was presented with a Folio Edition of Milton's Paradise Lost, printed on a Silver Type. so call'd from its elegance, (I suppose) By Mr. Brook Watson Mercht. whose Coat of Arms is prefix'd.—Since my return to America my Master, has at the desire of my friends in England given me my freedom, The Instrument is drawn, so as to secure me and my property from the hands of the Exectutrs. administrators, &c. of my master, & secure whatsoever Should be given me as my Own, a Copy is Sent to Isra. Mauduit Esqr. F.R.S.

I expect my Books which are publishd in London in Capt. Hall, who will be here I believe in 8 or 10 days. I beg the favour that you would honour the enclos'd Proposals, & use your interest with Gentlemen & Ladies of your acquaintance to subscribe also, for the more subscribers there are, the more it will be for my advantage as I am to have half the Sale of the Books, This I am the more Solicitous for, as I am now upon my own footing and whatever I get by this is entirely mine, & it is the Chief I have to depend upon. I must also request you would desire the Printers in New Haven, not to reprint that

<hr>

As the *Dictionary of National Biography*, Isani's article, and Robinson's notes for this letter in *Her Writings* (pp. 34–37, 322–23) collectively show, the people she met in London were a varied group of political, religious, artistic, scientific, scholarly, and abolitionist interests. Israel Mauduit in 1763 had become agent in London for Massachusetts Bay and perhaps was one of those who felt it suitable to express English concern that Wheatley was still a slave. Both he and Franklin appear in her 1779 Proposals. (F.R.S. stands for Fellow of the Royal Society.) Concerning Dartmouth, see her letter and poem to him. Also varied were the sights she toured, including the Tower of London, the museum of the famous jeweler James Cox, and Sadler's Wells with its spa and shows. Most of the books she mentions acquiring are extant— the five volumes of Pope's translation of *The Iliad* are at Dartmouth College and his four-volume translation of *The Odyssey* and the nine volumes of Pope's own writings are at the University of North Carolina at Charlotte (each one of the handsome eighteen volumes identified by her as from Dartmouth's gift to her); volume 2 of Smollett's translation of *Don Quixote* is in the Schomburg Center in New York; and *Paradise Lost* is at Harvard's Houghton Library. However, there is a book which she acquired during her London visit which is not mentioned in this letter or elsewhere by her, but which has now turned up at the Essex Institute—a copy of Granville Sharp's *Remarks on Several Very Important Prophecies, in Five Parts* (London, 1768), in which she wrote "To Phillis Wheatley from the Author" and he wrote his name and "London July 21." (Also see the Introduction to this volume.) This letter lets us narrow the time of her manumission to between September 13 and October 18, and her emphasis on sales of her books and related matters reflects her now more independent situation and its concerns. In this and other letters she appears alertly active and apparently astute in the business of selling her books and both promoting and protecting her own work and interests.

Book, as it will be a great hurt to me, preventing any further Benefit that I might so recieve from the Sale of my Copies from England. The price is 2/6.$^{\underline{d}}$ Bound or 2 Sterling Sewed.—If any should be so ungenerous as to reprint them the Genuine Copy may be known, for it is sign'd in my own handwriting. My dutiful respects attend your Lady and Children and I am

ever respectfully your oblig'd Huml Sert.

Boston October

18th 1773   Phillis Wheatley

I found my mistress very sick on my return
But she is some what better, we wish we could depend on it.
She gives her Compliments to you & your Lady.

TO OBOUR TANNER IN NEW PORT[14]

Dear Obour   Boston Oct. 30, 1773

I rec'd your most kind Epistles of Augt. 27th, & Oct 13th by a young man of your Acquaintance, for which I am obligd to you. I hear of your welfare with pleasure; but this acquaints you that I am at present indisposd by a cold. & Since my arrival have been visited by the asthma.—

Your observations on our dependence on the Deity, & your hopes that my wants will be supply'd from his fulness which is in Christ Jesus, is truely worthy of your self.—I can't say but my voyage to England has conduced to the recovery (in a great measure) of my Health. The Friends I found there among the Nobility and Gentry. Their Benevolent conduct towards me, the unexpected, and unmerited civility and Complaisance with which I was treated by all, fills me with astonishment, I can scarcely Realize it.—This I

---

14. See the note to Wheatley's letter to Tanner of May 19, 1772. For more information about her recent trip to England, see her letter to David Wooster and her poem "Farewell to America." The young man mentioned at the beginning and end of this letter may have been John Peters, whom Wheatley would marry in April 1778. (See the Introduction to this volume.) Miss West probably was Elizabeth West, whom Tanner's minister, Samuel Hopkins, had met at Wheatley's Old South Church at least as early as 1764. During the Revolution West left Boston for the country, where she met various people from Rhode Island, who persuaded her to open a boarding school for girls at Newport after the war. In 1794 she would become Hopkins's second wife. (See Edwards A. Park, *Memoir of the Life and Character of Samuel Hopkins, D.D.* [Boston, 1854], pp. 240–41. Also see Wheatley's two letters to Hopkins.)

humbly hope has the happy Effect of lessning me in my own Esteem. Your Reflections on the sufferings of the Son of God, & the inestimable price of our immortal Souls, Plainly dem[on]strate the sensations of a Soul united to Jesus. What you observe of Esau is true of all mankind, who, (left to themselves) would sell their heavenly Birth Rights for a few moments of sensual pleasure whose wages at last (dreadful wages!) is eternal condemnation. Dear Obour let us not sell our Birth right for a thousand worlds, which indeed would be as dust upon the Ballance.—The God of the Seas and dry Land, has graciously Brought me home in safety. Join with me in thanks to him for so great a mercy, & that it may excite me to praise him with chearfulness, to Persevere in Grace & Faith, & in the Knowledge of our Creator and Redeemer,—that my heart may be filld with gratitude. I should have been pleasd greatly to see Miss West, as I imagine she knew you. I have been very Busy ever since my arrival or should have, now wrote a more particular account of my voyage, But must submit that satisfaction to some other Opportunity, I am Dear friend,

most affectionately ever yours.

Phillis Wheatley

my mistress has been very sick above 14 weeks & confind to her Bed the whole time. but is I hope s[om]e what Better, now

The young man by whom this is handed you seems to me to be a very clever man knows you very well & is very Complaisant and agreable.—

P.W.

I enclose Proposals for my Book, and beg youd use your interest to get Subscriptions as it is for my Benefit.

TO JOHN THORNTON ESQRE. MERCHANT LONDON[15]

Hon'd Sir

It is with great satisfaction, I acquaint you with my experience of the goodness of God in safely conducting my passage over the mighty waters, and

15. See the note for Wheatley's letter to Thornton of April 21, 1772. (See also Wheatley's letter to the Countess of Huntingdon of July 17, 1773.) Wheatley arrived back in Boston on September 13. Mrs. Wilberforce was Thornton's sister and the aunt of the future abolitionist

returning me in safety to my American Friends. I presume you will Join with them and m[e] in praise to God for so distinguishing a favour, it was amazing Mercy, altogether unmerited by me: and if possible it is augmented by the consideration of the bitter r[e]verse, which is the deserved wages of my evil doings. The Apostle Paul, tells us that the wages of Sin is death. I don't imagine he excepted any sin whatsoever being equally hateful in its nature in the sight of God, who is essential Purity.

Should we not sink hon'd Sir, under this Sentence of Death, pronounced on every Sin, from the comparatively least to the greatest, were not this blessed Co[n]trast annexed to it, "But the Gift of God is eternal Life, through Jesus Christ our Lord? It is his Gift. O let us be thankful for it! What a load is taken from the Sinner's Shoulder when he thinks that Jesus has done that work for him which he could never have done, and Suffer'd, that punishment of his imputed Rebellions, for which a long Eternity of Torments could not have made sufficient expiation. O that I could meditate continually on this work of wonde[r] in Deity itself. This, which Kings & Prophets have desir'd to see, & have not See[n.] This, which Angels are continually exploring, yet are not equal to the search,—Millions of Ages shall roll away, and they may try in vain to find out to perfection, the sublime mysteries of Christ's Incarnation. Nor will this desir[e] to look into the deep things of God, cease, in the Breasts of glorified Saints & Angels. It's duration will be coeval with Eternity. This Eternity how dreadf[ul,] how delightful! Delightful to those who have an interest in the Crucifi[ed] Saviour, who has dignified our Nature, by seating it at the Right Hand of the divine Majesty.—They alone who are thus interested have Cause to rejoi[ce] even on the brink of that Bottomless Profound: and I doubt not (without the [lea]st Adulation) that you are one of that happy number. O pray that I may be one also, who Shall Join with you in Songs of praise at the Throne of him, who is no respecter of

---

and statesman William Wilberforce. (Is the letter to her which is mentioned here the one to "Mrs. W——e" listed in Wheatley's 1779 Proposals?) Re John Moorhead see Wheatley's poem to his daughter Mary. Thornton replied to the above letter, probably in January. A copy of his letter is in his papers in Scotland; though the only date on it has been misread as "75," it actually says "74," which fits the several direct responses in it to specific items in Wheatley's December 1, 1773, letter, including her letter's date and her return journey to Boston from England. This, then, probably is his letter which included one to be passed on to Samson Occom which is mentioned in Wheatley's March 29, 1774, letter to Thornton, which also says that

Persons: being equally the great Maker of all:—Therefor disdain not to be called the Father of Humble Africans and Indians; though despisd on earth on account of our colour, we have this Consolation, if he enables us to deserve it. "That God dwells in the humble & contrite heart." O that I were more & more possess'd of this inestimable blessing; to be directed by the immediate influence of the divine Spirit in my daily walk & Conversation.

Do you, my hon'd Sir, who have abundant Reason to be thankful for the great Share you possess of it, be always mindful in your Closet, of those who want it—of me in particular.—

When I first arrivd at home my mistress was so bad as not to be expected to live above two or three days, but through the goodness of God She is still alive, but remains in a very weak & languishing Condition, She begs a continued interest in your most earnest prayers, that she may be surly prepar'd for that great Change which [She] is likely Soon to undergo; She intreats you, as her Son is Still in England, that you would take all opportun[i]ties to advise & counsel him; She says she is going to leave him & desires you'd be a Spiritual Fath[er] to hi[m]. She will take it very kind. She thanks you heartily for the kind notice you took of me while in England. Pleas[e] to give my best Respects to Mrs. & miss Thornton, and masters Henry and Robert who held with me a long conversation on many subjects which Mrs. Drinkwater knows very well, I hope she is in better Health than when I left her. Please to remember me to your whole family & I than[k] them for their kindness to me. begging Still an interest in your best hours
I am Hon'd Sir

     most respectfully your Humble Servt.
Boston Dec: 1. 1773   Phillis Wheatley

I have written to Mrs. Wilberforce, Sometime since Please to give my duty to her; Since writing the above the Rev'd Mr. Moorhead has made his Exit from this world, in whom we lament the loss of the Zealous Pious & true christian

---

Thornton's letter included one to Susanna Wheatley which arrived "above a fortnight" after she died on March 3, 1774.

pr Post

Rev'd Sir   Boston Feb: 9th 1774.—

I take with pleasure this opportunity by the Post, to acquaint you of the arrl. of my books from London, I have Seal'd up a package, containing 17 for you 2 for Mr. Tanner and one for Mrs. Mason, and only wait for you to appoint some proper person by whom I may convey them to you, I recd. some time ago 20/ sterling, upon them by the hands of your Son in a Letter from Obour Tanner; I recd. at the same time a paper by which I understood there are two Negro men who are desirous of returning to their native Country, to preach the Gospel; But being much indispos'd by the return of my Asthmatic complaint, besides, the sickness of my mistress who has been long confin'd to her bed, & is not expected to live a great while; all these things render it impracticable for me to do anything at present with regard to that paper. but what I can do in influencing my Christian friends and acquaintance, to promote this laudable design shall not be wanting. Methinks Rev'd Sir, this is the beginning of that happy period foretold by the Prophets, when all shall

---

16. From the original at the Historical Society of Pennsylvania. No letters to Hopkins are listed in her 1779 Proposals. The *Pennsylvania Freeman* for May 9, 1839, printed this same letter with only minor differences. It had been sent by the abolitionist Joshua Coffin to John Greenleaf Whittier, Quaker abolitionist and writer, then editor of the *Freeman*. Coffin said that he had found the letter, in Wheatley's hand, in the papers of the Reverend W. B. Sprague. (Robinson, *Her Writings*, pp. 406–7 provides a facsimile of that printing.) Samuel Hopkins (1721–1803) was pastor of the First Congregational Church in Newport. He had graduated from Yale in 1741 and served at several other places (including more than twenty-five years at Great Barrington) before coming to Newport in 1770. (During 1769 he preached several times at Boston's Old South Church, where he probably met Wheatley.) When the British took Newport in December 1776, Hopkins fled for his safety, not returning until 1780. In 1790 Brown University conferred a D.D. degree upon him. In 1770 he had begun various efforts in opposition to slavery and with intentions to Christianize Africa, which he continued the rest of his life. The two Africans mentioned in the letter above were Bristol Yamma and John Quamine, who had been brought to Newport from Africa as children, but who had retained their native language. They eventually were able to buy their freedom from slavery. Each was married and had a child. They already were communicants in Hopkins's church when he arrived in Newport and learned of their interest in returning to Africa as missionaries. Hopkins and others were successful in raising money to help educate them further toward that end, which efforts are probably what Wheatley is referring to here. Hopkins may have been the link in the establishment of first contact between Wheatley and his church's communicant Obour Tanner, perhaps in relation to his African projects, after he came to Newport in 1770. (See Robinson, *Her Writings*, p. 329, and Wheatley's letters to Hopkins [May 6, 1774], to John Thornton [October 30, 1774], and to Obour Tanner.) Susanna Wheatley, Phillis's mistress, died on March 3.

know the Lord from the least to the greatest, and that without the assistance of human Art & Eloquence. my heart expanded, with sympathetic Joy, to see at distant time the thick cloud of ignorance dispersing from the face of my benighted Country; Europe and America have long been fed with the heavenly provision, and I fear they loathe it, while Africa is perishing with a Spiritual Famine. O that they could partake of the crumbs, the precious crumbs, Which fall from the table, of these distinguishd children of the Kingdome

Their minds are unprejudiced against the truth therefore tis to be hoped they woud. recieve it with their Whole heart, I hope that which the divine royal Psalmist Says by inspiration is now on the point of being Accomplish'd, namely. Ethiopia Shall Soon Stretch forth her hands Unto God, of this Obour Tanner (and I trust many others within your knowledge are living witnesses, Please to give my love to her & I intend to write to her soon, my best respects attend every kind inquirer after your obligd Humble Servant.   Phillis Wheatley

TO SAMSON OCCOM

The following is an extract of a Letter from Phillis, a Negro Girl of Mr. Wheatley's, in Boston, to the Rev. Samson Occom, which we are desired to insert as a Specimen of her Ingenuity.—It is dated 11th Feb., 1774.[17]

"Rev'd and honor'd Sir,
I have this Day received your obliging kind Epistle, and am greatly satisfied with your Reasons respecting the Negroes, and think highly reasonable what you offer in Vindication of their natural Rights: Those that invade them cannot be insensible that the divine Light is chasing away the thick Darkness

---

17. From the *Connecticut Gazette; and the Universal Intelligencer* for Friday, March 11, 1774 (vol. 11, no. 539), published in New-London, near where Occom had been born and still lived. With minor differences it also appeared in the *Massachusetts Gazette* (March 21) and the *Massachusetts Spy* in Boston, in the *Essex Gazette* in Salem, and in various other New England newspapers during March and April. This protest by a firm Christian and former slave, now freed, was Wheatley's strongest and most direct publication against slavery. (It is not known whether she knew the letter would be published. It is not in her 1779 Proposals.) Occom (1723–92) was a Mohegan Indian and a Presbyterian minister who was a friend of the Wheatleys, who were interested in many of the same causes in which he was interested. He stayed in the Wheatley home on at least one occasion when he was preaching in Boston, and he not only

which broods over the Land of Africa; and the Chaos which has reign'd so long, is converting into beautiful Order, and [r]eveals more and more clearly, the glorious Dispensation of civil and religious Liberty, which are so inseparably united, that there is little or no Enjoyment of one without the other: Otherwise, perhaps, the Israelites had been less solicitous for their Freedom from Egyptian slavery; I do not say they would have been contented without it, by no means, for in every human Breast, God has implanted a Principle, which we call Love of Freedom; it is impatient of Oppression, and pants for Deliverance; and by the Leave of our modern Egyptians I will assert, that the same Principle lives in us. God grant Deliverance in his own Way and Time, and get him honour upon all those whose Avarice impels them to countenance and help forward the Calamities of their fellow Creatures. This I desire not for their Hurt, but to convince them of the strange Absurdity of their Conduct whose Words and Actions are so diametrically opposite. How well the Cry for Liberty, and the reverse Disposition for the exercise of oppressive Power over others agree,—I humbly think it does not require the Penetration of a Philosopher to determine."—

TO MISS OBOUR TANNER   NEW PORT.[18]

Dear Obour,

I recd. your obliging Letter, enclosd, in your revd. Pastor's & handed me by his Son. I have lately met with a great trial in the death of my mistress, let us imagine the loss of a Parent, Sister or Brother the tenderness of all these were united in her.—I was a poor little outcast & a stranger when she took me in. not only into her house but I presently became, a sharer in her most tender

---

corresponded with Phillis but also sold her book for her in Connecticut. At one time he joined some others in thinking that she might go to Africa as a missionary, which idea she firmly rejected. (See her letters of March 29 and October 30, 1774, to John Thornton.) The success of Occom's visit to England and Scotland in 1766–67 may have lent support to the idea of Wheatley's visit to England in 1773. In her letter above she seems to be responding to a protest and challenge to ministers who owned slaves and also preached Christianity and freedom and liberty which had been written by Occom (see Robinson, *Her Writings*, p. 44). Also see Akers, "'Our Modern Egyptians,'" and John Wheatley's letter at the front of her 1773 book. A letter from Susanna Wheatley to Occom is found in the Introduction to this volume.

18. See the note to Wheatley's letter to Tanner of May 19, 1772. Tanner's pastor at this time was Samuel Hopkins (see Wheatley's two letters to him this same year). Wheatley's mistress,

affections, I was treated by her more like her child than her Servant, no opportunity was left unimprov'd, of giving me the best of advice, but in terms how tender! how engaging! this I hope ever to keep in remembrance. Her exampl[?]ly life was a greater monitor than all her precepts and Instruction, thus we may observe of how much greater force example is than Instruction. To alleviate our sorrows we had the satisfaction to se[e] her depart in inexpresible raptures, earnest longings & impatient thirstings for the upper Courts of the Lord. Do, my dear friend, remember me & this family in your Closet. that this afflicting dispensation may be sanctify'd to us. I am very sorry to hear that you are indispo[s'd] but hope this will find you in better health; I have been unwell the great Part of the winter, but am much better as the Spring approache[s.] Pray excuse my not writing to you so long before, for I have been so busy lately, that I could not find leizure. I shall send the 5 Books you wrote for, the first convenient, Opportunity. if you want more, they Shall be ready for you I am very affectionately your Friend

Boston March 21. 1774.   Phillis Wheatley

JOHN THORNTON ESQR   MERCHANT   AT CLAPHAM   NEAR LONDON[19]   Pr Capt Hood

Much honoured Sir,

I should not so soon have troubled you with the 2d. Letter, but the mournful Occasion will sufficiently Apologize. It is the death of Mrs. Wheatley. She has been labouring under a languishing illness for many months past and has at length took her flight from hence to those blissful

---

Susanna Wheatley, died March 3, 1774, at the age of sixty-five (see the letter that follows this one). Kaplan, *Black Presence*, p. 168, has a photograph of this letter; and there also is a facsimile of it in the *Proceedings of the Massachusetts Historical Society* 15 (December 1877): between pp. 386 and 387. (The Rare Book and Special Collections Division of the Library of Congress has a facsimile of the manuscript of this letter that was printed as a separate item, perhaps to be sold or distributed by the Massachusetts Historical Society as a broadside of the manuscript.)

19. See the note for Wheatley's letter to Thornton of April 21, 1772. Susanna Wheatley died on March 3. (See Wheatley's letter to Obour Tanner of March 21, 1774, and Wheatley's poem to Mary Moorhead.) Thornton received this letter on May 25, and he replied at the beginning of August. (See her next letter to him.) Wheatley's remarks about Nathaniel Wheatley in the letter above are in response to Thornton's letter responding to her letter to him of December 1, 1773 (see the note to that letter).

regions, which need not the light of any, but the Sun of Righteousness. O could you have been present, to See how She long'd to drop the tabernacle of Clay, and to be freed from the cumbrous Shackles of a mortal Body, which had so many Times retarded her desires when Soaring upward. She has often told me how your Letters hav[e] quicken'd her in her Spiritual Course: when She has been in darkness of mind they have rais'd and enliven'd her insomuch, that She went on, with chearfuln[ess] and alacrity in the path of her duty. She did truely, run with patience the race that was Set before her, and hath, at length obtained the celestial Goal. She is now Sure, that the afflictions of this present time, were not worthy to be compared to the Glory, which is now, revealed in her, Seeing they have wrought out for her, a far more exceeding and eternal weight of Glory: This, Sure, is Sufficient encouragement under the bitterest Sufferings, which we can endure.—About half an hour before her Death, She Spoke with a more audible voice, than She had for 3 months before. She calld. her friends & relations around her, and charg'd them not to leave their great work undone till that hour, but to fear God, and keep his Commandments. being ask'd if her faith faild her She answer'd, No. Then Spr[ead] out her arms crying come! come quickly! come, come! O pray for an eas[y] and quick Passage! She eagerly longed to depart to be with Christ. She retaind her Senses till the very last moment when "fare well, fare well." with a very low voice, were the last words She utter'd. I sat the whole time by her bed Side, and Saw with Grief and Wonder, the Effects of Sin on the human race. Had not Christ taken away the envenom'd Sting, where had been our hopes? what might we not have fear'd, what might we not have expectd from the dreadful King of Terrors? But this is matter of endless praise, to the King eternal immortal, invisible, that, it is finished. I hope her Son will be interested in Your Closet duties, & that the prayers which she was continually putting up, & wch. are recorded before God, in the Book of his remembrance for her Son & for me may be answer'd, I can Scarcely think that an Object of so many prayers, will fail of the Blessings implor'd for him ever Since he was born. I intreat the same Interest in your best thoughts for my Self, that her prayers, in my behalf, may be favour'd with an Answer of Peace. We received and forwarded your Letter to the rev'd Mr. Occom, but first, took the freedom to peruse it, and am exceeding glad, that you have order'd him to draw immediately for £25. for I really think he is in absolute necessity for that and as much more, he is so loth to run in debt for fear he Shall not be able to repay, that he has not the Least

Shelter for his Creatures to defend them from the inclemencies of the weather, and he has lost some already for want of it, His hay is quite as defenceless, thus the former are in a fair way of being lost, and the latter to be wasted; It were to be wished that his <u>dwelling house</u> was like the Ark, with appartments, to contain the beasts and their provision; He Said Mrs. Wheatley and the rev'd Mr. Moorhead were his best friends in Boston, But alass! they are gone. I trust gone to recieve the rewards promis'd to those, who Offer a Cup of cold water in the name & for the sake of Jesus—They have both been very instrum[ental in meetin]g the wants of that child of God, Mr. Occom—but I fear your pa[tience has been] exhausted, it remains only that we thank you for your kind Letter to my mistress it came above a fortnight after her Death.—Hoping for an interest in your prayers for these Sanctificiation [sic] of this bereaving Providence, I am hon'd Sir with dutiful respect ever your obliged

and devoted Humble Servant   Phillis Wheatley

Boston

  N England March 29th

1774.

John Thornton Esqr.

TO THE REV'D MR. SAML. HOPKINS   NEW PORT   RHODE ISLAND[20]   fav'd. by Mr. Pemberton

Rev'd Sir

    I recieved your kind letter last Evening by Mr. Pemberton, by whom also this is to be handed you. I have also recd. the money for the 5 Books I sent Obour, & 2/6 more for another. She had wrote me, but the date is 29 April. I am very sorry to hear, that Philip Quaque has very little or no <u>apparent</u> Success in his mission—Yet, I wish that what you hear respecting him, may be only a misrepresentation—Let us not be discouraged, but still hope that

20. From the original in the Chamberlin Collection of the Boston Public Library. See Wheatley's letter to Hopkins of February 9, 1774. Pemberton might have been the Reverend Ebenezer Pemberton who was a signer of the letter "To the PUBLICK" used at the front of her book. Philip Quaque was an English-educated African who was the first African to be an Anglican priest. He was working in Africa as a chaplain and as master of a mission school, with all the problems attendant thereto (see Phillip D. Curtin, ed., *Africa Remembered* [Madison, 1968], pp. 99–139). Hopkins was corresponding with Quaque.

God will bring about his great work, that Philip may not be the Instrument in the Divine Hand to perform this work of wonder, turning the Africans "from darkness to light." Possibly, if Philip would introduce himself properly to them, (I don't know the reverse) he might be more Successful; and in setting a good example which is more powerfully winning than Instruction. I Observe your Reference to the Maps of Guinea & Salmon's Gazetteer, and shall consult them. I have recd. in some of the last Ships from London 300 more copies of my Poems, and wish to dispose of them as Soon as Possible. If you know of any being wanted I flatter myself you will be pleas'd to let me know it, which will be adding one more to the many Obligations already confer'd on her, who is, with a due Sense of your kindness,

Your most humble,

Boston   And Obedient Servant,

     May 6, 1774.   Phillis Wheatley

The revd S. Hopkins

TO MISS OBOUR TANNER   NEW PORT   RHODE ISLAND.[21]   favd.

by Mr. Pemberton

Dear Obour

I recd. last evening your kind & friendly Letter, and am not a little animated thereby.   I hope ever to follow your good advices and be resigned to the afflicting hand of a Seemingly frowning Providence. I have recd. the money you sent for the 5 Books & 2/6 more for another, which I now Send & wish safe to hand. Your tenderness for my welfare demands my gratitu[de] Assist me, dear Obour! to Praise our great benefactor, for the innumerable Benefits continually pour'd upon me, that while he strikes one Comfort dead he raises up another. But O, that I could dwell on, & delight in him alone above every other Object! While the world hangs loose about us we Shall not be in painful anxiety in giving up to God, that which he first gave to us. Your

---

21. See the note to Wheatley's letter to Tanner of May 19, 1772. Mr. Pemberton here may be the Reverend Ebenezer Pemberton, who was one of those who signed the letter "To the PUBLICK" at the front of her book.

letter came by Mr. Pemberton who brings you the book you wrote for, I shall wait upon Mr. Whitwell with your Letter, and am,

Dear Sister, ever Affectionately, your

I have recd by some of the last Ships   Phillis Wheatley
300 more of my Poems.

Boston

May 6, 1774

TO JOHN THORNTON ESQR.   MERCHANT   LONDON[22]

Much hond. Sir

I have the honour of your obliging favour of August 1st by Mr. Wheatley who arriv'd not before the 27th Ultimo after a tedious passage of near two months; the obligations I am under to the family I desire to retain a grateful Sense of, And consequently rejoice in the bountiful dealings of providence towards him—

By the great loss I have Sustain'd of my best friend, I feel like One [fo]rsaken by her parent in a desolate wilderness, for Such the world appears to [me], wandring thus without my friendly guide. I fear lest every step Should lead me [in]to error and confusion. She gave me many precepts and instructions; which I hope I shall never forget, Hon'd Sir, pardon me if after the retrospect of such uncommon tenderness for thirteen years from my earliest youth—such unwearied diligence to instruct me in the principles of

22. See the note for Wheatley's letter to Thornton of April 21, 1772. Nathaniel Wheatley and his bride of the past November (the former Mary Enderby) arrived at Salem on September 22, 1774, the British having closed Boston Harbor in March. Before he returned to London in November, his father transferred to him full ownership of the Wheatley home on King Street. Also, apparently he agreed to let Phillis stay on there with his father (see Robinson, *Her Writings*, p. 339). She had been freed earlier than she says here—sometime between September 13 and October 18 (see her letter to David Wooster). For information concerning Yamma and Quamine see her letter to Samuel Hopkins of February 9, 1774. He was helping them. Anamaboe was a large slave-trading town on the Gold Coast of Africa. Obviously the correct year of this letter is 1774 instead of 1770, which is confirmed by the information on the outside of it which records when it was written, received (January 4, 1775), and replied to by Thornton (April 28). Information with her March 29 letter to Thornton dates his letter of reply to it as August 2, not August 1 as she says in her letter above. (See the note to Wheatley's December 1, 1773, letter to Thornton and her poem "To a Gentleman of the Navy," written

the true Religion, this in some degree Justifies me while I deplore my misery—If I readily Join with you in wishing that you could in these respects Supply her place, but this does not seem probable from the great distance of your residence, However I will endeavour to compensate it by a Strict Observance of hers and your good advice from time to time, which you have given me encouragement to hope for—What a Blessed Source of consolation that our greatest friend is an immortal God whose friendship is invariable! from whom I have all that is in me praise worthy in mental possession. This Consideration humbles me much under encomiums on the gifts of God, the fear that I should not improve them to his glory and the good of mankind, it almost hinders a commendable self estimation (at times) but quite beats down the boldness of presumption. The world is a severe Schoolmaster, for its frowns are far less dang'rous than its Smiles and flatteries, and it is a difficult task to keep in the path of Wisdom[.] I attended, and find exactly true your thoughts on the behaviour of those who seem'd to respect me while under my mistresses patronage: you said right, for Some of those have already put on a reserve; but I submit while God rules; who never forsakes any till they have ungratefully forsaken him——. My old master's generous behaviour in granting me my freedom, and still so kind to me I delight to acknowledge my great obligations to him. this he did about 3 months before the death of my dear mistress & at her desire, as well as his own humanity, of wch. I hope ever to retain a grateful Sense, and treat him with that respect which is ever due to A paternal friendship—If this had not been the Case, yet I hope I should willingly Submit to Servitude to be free in Christ.—But since it thus—Let me be a Servant of Christ and that is the most perfect freedom.——

---

on the same date as the letter above.) From information in and with the extant Phillis Wheatley–John Thornton correspondence, we can establish the following summary of it:

W. to T. at least two months before February 29, 1772 (we do not have it—probably the beginning of the correspondence)

T. to W. February 29, 1772 (we do not have it)

W. to T. April 21, 1772 (we do have it)

W. to T. December 1, 1773 (we do have it)

T. to W. 1774, probably in January (we have a copy only—she received it about March 20)

W. to T. March 29, 1774 (we do have it—he received it May 25)

T. to W. August 1 or 2, 1774 (we do not have it—she received it about September 24 via Nathaniel Wheatley)

W. to T. October 30, 1774 (we do have it—he received it January 4)

T. to W. April 28, 1775 (we do not have it—this probably ended the correspondence).

You propose my returning to Africa with Bristol yamma and John Quamine if either of them upon Strict enquiry is Such, as I dare give my heart and hand to, I believe they are either of them good enough if not too good for me, or they would not be fit for missionaries; but why do you hon'd Sir, wish those poor men so much trouble as to carry me So long a voyage? Upon my arrival, how like a Barbarian Shoud I look to the Natives; I can promise that my tongue shall be quiet for a strong reason indeed being an utter stranger to the Language of Anamaboe. Now to be Serious, This undertaking appears too hazardous, and not sufficiently Eligible, to go—and leave my British & American Friends—I am also unacquainted with those Missionaries in Person. The reverend gentleman who unde[r][ta]kes their Education has repeatedly informd. me by Letters of their pro[gress] in Learning also an Account of John Quamine's family and Kingdo[m] But be that as it will I resign it all to God's all wise governance; I thank you heartily for your generous Offer—With Sincerity—

I am hond. Sir
most gratefully your devoted Servt.
Phillis Wheatley

Boston Oct. 30th 1770 [1774]

MISS OBOUR TANNER   WORCESTER.[23]

Dear Obour   Boston May 29th '78
   I am exceedingly glad to hear from you by Mrs. Tanner, and wish you had timely notice of her departure, so as to have wrote me; next to that is the pleasure of hearing that you are well. The vast variety of Scenes that have pass'd before us these 3 years past will to a reasonable mind serve to convince us of the uncertain duration of all things Temporal, and the proper result of such a consideration is an ardent desire of, & preparation for, a State and enjoyments which are more Suitable to the immortal mind;—You will do me a great favour if you'll write me by every Opp'y—Direct your letters under cover to Mr. John Peters in Queen Street. I have but half an hour's notice; and must apologize for this hasty scrawl, I am most affectionately, my dear Obour your sincere friend   Phillis Wheatley

23. See the note to Wheatley's letter to Tanner of May 19, 1772. Apparently to escape dangers from the continuing activities of the British along the coast of Rhode Island, the Tanners

Dr. Obour

By this opportunity I have the pleasure to inform you that I am well and hope you are so; tho' I have been Silent, I have not been unmindful of you but a variety of hindrances was the cause of my not writing to you—But in time to Come I hope our correspondence will revive—and revive in better times.— pray write me Soon for I long to hear from you—you may depend on constant replies—I wish you much happiness and am

Dr. Obour your friend & Sister

Phillis Peters

Boston May 10. 1779.

PROPOSALS,[25]

FOR PRINTING,

BY SUBSCRIPTION

A VOLUME OF POEMS

AND LETTERS,

ON VARIOUS SUBJECTS,

Dedicated to the Right Honourable,

BENJAMIN FRANKLIN, Esq;

One of the Ambassadors of the United States, at

the Court of France,

By PHILLIS PETERS.

POEMS.	LETTERS.
Thoughts on the Times.	1 To the Right Honorable Wil-
On the Capture of General Lee, to	liam E. of Dartmouth Secre-
I B. Esq;	tary of State for N. America.
To his Excellency General	2 To the Rev. Mr. T.P.
Washington.	Farmington.

---

had retreated to Worcester, Massachusetts, much further inland. See Wheatley's poem to George Washington re "these 3 years past" and her own temporary retreat from Boston because of the British occupation of it. Wheatley and John Peters had married in April.

24. See the note to Wheatley's letter to Tanner of May 19, 1772.

25. From the Boston *Evening Post; and the General Advertiser* for Saturday, October 30, 1779

(vol. 2, no. 55), occupying more than a full column on the front page. It also was published in the same paper on November 6 and 27 and December 4, 11, and 18—with numerous errors in the subsequent printings (see Robinson, *Her Writings*, p. 348). White and Adams also published the *Evening Post*. The proposed book was never published. A second volume of her poems was again proposed in 1784 (see her poem "To Mr. and Mrs. ——, on the Death of their Infant Son"). Of the poems in the list above, we have those on Lee (1776), Washington (1775), Wooster (1778), and Lt. R—— (1774, twice)—clearly, the poems in this list are not in chronological order. She seems not to be including any of the poems in her 1772 Proposals which were not used in her 1773 book, and we have one poem clearly later than the 1772 Proposals and her book (to Mary Moorhead, December 1773) which is not in the above list. Many of the listed titles for which we have no poems are intriguing. For example, could the above "To P.N.S. and Lady on the death of their infant son" be the extant "To Mr. and Mrs. ——, on the Death of their Infant Son"? And though John Montagu was a rear admiral when he was commander in chief of the North American Station in Boston in 1771–74, he was not made an ad-

To Dr. L——d and Lady on the
death of their son aged 5 years.
To Mr. L——g on the death of his
son.
To Capt F——: on the death of
his granddaughter.
To Philandra an Elegy.
Niagara.
Chloe to Calliope.
To Musidora on Florello.
To Sir E. L——. Esq.
To the Hon. John Montague Esq;
Rear Admiral of the Blue.

Messieurs PRINTERS,

The above collection of Poems and Letters was put into my hands by the desire of the ingenious author in order to be introduced to public View.

The subjects are various and curious, and the author a *Female African*, whose lot it was to fall into the hands of a *generous* master and *great* benefactor. The learned and ingenuous as well as those who are pleased with novelty, are invited to incourage the publication, by a generous subscription—the former, that they may fan the sacred fire which, is self enkindled in the breast

---

miral of the blue until April 8, 1782. From the letters we have, the above list seems short. Of it, apparently we have letters 1, 7, 12, 13. Some of the initials given for other letters we can assign with reasonable certainty: Timothy Pitkin (see her poem to him); Thomas Wallcut (see the notes for her poem to the students at Cambridge and the Introduction to this volume); Thomas Hubbard (see her poem to him); Israel Mauduit (see her letter to David Wooster); Susanna Wheatley, her mistress; and possibly Mrs. Wilberforce (see Wheatley's letter to John Thornton, December 1, 1773). Franklin (who as an infant in 1706 had been baptized in Boston's Old South Church, whose congregation Wheatley would become a member of in 1771) had visited Wheatley in London; but he probably would have been surprised to know of the above dedication, for in a July 7, 1773, letter he reported that their encounter had been very brief and inconsequential. Concerning the seemingly exceptionally high price given for this book (which probably quickly turned away prospective subscribers), Isani (" 'On the Death of General Wooster,' " p. 308) has suggested that the typesetter most unfortunately may have mistaken the abbreviation for "twelve shillings lawful money" as meaning twelve pounds, which seems a reasonable possibility since in her letter to Mrs. Wooster on July 15, 1778, she had said that she was selling her 1773 book at "12/Lmo. each" (however, see Robinson, *Her Writings*, p. 349). The phrase "rara avis in terra" is Latin for "rare bird in the land" (i.e., exceptional person among us).

of this *young* African—The ingenuous that they may by reading this collection, have a large play for their imaginations, and be ex[c]ited to please and benefit mankind, by some brilliant production of their own pens—Those who are *always* in search of some *new* thing, that they may obtain a sight of this *rara avis in terra*—And every one, that the ingenious author may be encouraged to improve her own mind, benefit and please mankind.

CONDITIONS.

They will be printed on good Paper and a neat Type; and will Contain about 300 pages in Octavo.

The price to Subscribers will be *Twelve Pounds*, neatly Bound & Lettered, and *Nine Pounds* sew'd in blue paper, one Half to be paid on Subscribing, the other Half, on Delivery of the Books.

The Work will be put to the Press as soon as a sufficient Number of Encouragers offer.

Those who subscribe for Six, will have a Seventh Gratis.

Subscriptions are taken by White and Adams, the Publishers, in School-Street, *Boston*.

A SELECTED LIST OF WORKS FOR FURTHER REFERENCE
(from works referred to, and from other works)

For the nature and purpose of this list see the fourth paragraph of "A Note on the Text." This list does not include poems or plays about Wheatley; books for children about her; and reference works, anthologies, or surveys that include her. For some republications of her works, see the next-to-last paragraph of "A Note on the Text." For some other works about her see the section on her reputation. For sources of her works see the notes to them.

Akers, Charles W. " 'Our Modern Egyptians': Phillis Wheatley and the Whig Campaign against Slavery in Revolutionary Boston." *Journal of Negro History* 60 (July 1975): 399–410. (Also in Robinson, ed., *Critical Essays*, pp. 159–71.)

Barksdale, Richard K. (See the list of Conference papers below.)

Broadsides, Ballads, Etc. Printed in Massachusetts, 1639–1800, Massachusetts Historical Society Collections, vol. 75. Boston: Massachusetts Historical Society, 1922.

Burroughs, Margaret G. "Do Birds of a Feather Flock Together?" *Jackson State Review* 6 (Summer 1974): 61–73. (Also in Robinson, ed., *Critical Essays*, pp. 136–46.)

Collins, Terence. "Phillis Wheatley: The Dark Side of the Poetry." *Phylon* 36 (March 1975): 78–88. (Also in Robinson, ed., *Critical Essays*, pp. 147–58.)

Cook, William W. (See the list of Conference papers below.)

Davis, Arthur P. "Personal Elements in the Poetry of Phillis Wheatley." *Phylon* 13 (2d Quarter 1953): 191–98. (Also in Robinson, ed., *Critical Essays*, pp. 93–101.)

Gates, Henry Louis, Jr. "Phillis Wheatley and the Nature of the Negro." In Gates, *Figures in Black: Words, Signs, and the "Racial" Self*. New York: Oxford University Press, 1987. (Also in Robinson, ed., *Critical Essays*, pp. 215–33.)

Grégoire, Henri. *An Enquiry Concerning the Intellectual and Moral Faculties, and Literature of Negroes; Followed with an Account of the Life and Works of Fifteen Negroes & Mullatoes.* Translated by D. B. Warden. Brooklyn: Thomas Kirk, 1810.

Heartman, Charles F. *Phillis Wheatley (Phillis Peters): A Critical Attempt and a Bibliography of Her Writings.* New York: Heartman, 1915.

Holder, Kenneth R. "Some Linguistic Aspects of the Heroic Couplet in the Poetry of Phillis Wheatley." Ph.D. dissertation, North Texas State University, 1973. (Also see *Dissertation Abstracts International*.)

Huddleston, Eugene L. *"Matilda's 'On Reading the Poems of Phillis Wheatley, the African Poetess.' "* *Early American Literature* 5 (Winter 1971): 57–67. (Also in Robinson, ed., *Critical Essays*, pp. 102–12.)

Isani, Mukhtar Ali. "The British Reception of Wheatley's *Poems on Various Subjects*." *Journal of Negro History* 66 (Summer 1981): 144–49.

_____. "Early Versions of Some Works of Phillis Wheatley." *Early American Literature* 14 (Fall 1979): 148–55.

_____. " 'An Elegy on Leaving—': A New Poem by Phillis Wheatley." *American Literature* 58 (December 1986): 609–13.

————. "Far from 'Gambia's Golden Shore': The Black in Late Eighteenth-Century American Imaginative Literature." *William and Mary Quarterly* 36 (July 1979): 353–72.

————. "The First Proposed Edition of *Poems on Various Subjects* and the Phillis Wheatley Canon." *American Literature* 49 (March 1977): 97–103.

————. " 'Gambia on My Soul': Africa and the African in the Writings of Phillis Wheatley." *MELUS* 6, no. 1 (1979): 64–72.

————. "The Methodist Connection: New Variants of Some Phillis Wheatley Poems." *Early American Literature* 22 (Spring 1987): 108–13.

————. " 'On the Death of General Wooster': An Unpublished Poem by Phillis Wheatley." *Modern Philology* 77 (February 1980): 306–9.

————. "The Original Version of Wheatley's On the Death of Dr. Samuel Marshall." *Studies in Black Literature* 7 (Autumn 1976): 20.

————. "Phillis Wheatley and the Elegaic Mode." In *Critical Essays on Phillis Wheatley*, edited by William H. Robinson, pp. 208–14. Boston: G. K. Hall, 1982.

————. "Phillis Wheatley in London: An Unpublished Letter to David Wooster." *American Literature* 51 (May 1979): 255–60.

————. (See the list of Conference papers below.)

————. "Wheatley's Departure for London and Her 'Farewel to America.' " *South Atlantic Bulletin* 42 (November 1979): 123–29.

Jackson, Sara Dunlap. "Letters of Phillis Wheatley and Susanna Wheatley." *Journal of Negro History* 57 (April 1972): 211–15.

Jackson State Review 6 (Summer 1974)—special issue on the Phillis Wheatley Poetry Festival, November 4–7, 1973.

Jamison, Angelene. "Analysis of Selected Poetry of Phillis Wheatley." *Journal of Negro Education* 43 (Summer 1974): 408–16. (Also in Robinson, ed., *Critical Essays*, pp. 128–35.)

Jordan, Winthrop D. *White over Black: American Attitudes toward the Negro, 1550–1812*. Chapel Hill: University of North Carolina Press, 1968.

Kaplan, Sidney. *The Black Presence in the Era of the American Revolution, 1770–1800*. Greenwich: New York Graphic Society, 1973.

Kuncio, Robert C. "Some Unpublished Poems of Phillis Wheatley." *New England Quarterly* 43 (June 1970): 287–97.

Lapsansky, Phil. "*Deism*—An Unpublished Poem by Phillis Wheatley." *New England Quarterly* 50 (September 1977): 517–20.

Levernier, James A. (See the list of Conference papers below.)

————. "Wheatley's ON BEING BROUGHT FROM AFRICA TO AMERICA." *Explicator* 40 (Fall 1981): 25–26.

Loggins, Vernon. *The Negro Author: His Development in America to 1900*. New York: Columbia University Press, 1931.

Mason, Julian. (See the list of Conference papers below.)

Matson, R. Lynn. "Phillis Wheatley—Soul Sister?" *Phylon* 33 (Fall 1972): 222–30. (Also in Robinson, ed., *Critical Essays*, pp. 113–22.)

[Odell, Margaretta Matilda]. *Memoir and Poems of Phillis Wheatley, A Native African and a Slave*. Boston: G. W. Light, 1834. Boston: Light & Horton, 1835. Boston: Isaac Knapp, 1838 (also includes George Moses Horton's *Poems by a Slave*).

O'Neale, Sondra. "A Slave's Subtle War: Phillis Wheatley's Use of Biblical Myth and Symbol." *Early American Literature* 21 (Fall 1986): 145–65.

Parks, Carole A. "Phillis Wheatley Comes Home." *Black World* 23 (February 1974): 92–95.

Porter, Dorothy. "Early American Negro Writings: A Bibliographical Study." *PBSA* (3d Quarter 1945): 193–268.

_____. "Historical and Bibliographical Data of Phillis Wheatley's Publications." *Jackson State Review* 6 (Summer 1974): 54–60.

_____. *North American Negro Poets: A Bibliographical Checklist of Their Writings, 1760–1944*. Hattiesburg: Book Farm, 1945.

Rawley, James A. "The World of Phillis Wheatley." *New England Quarterly* 50 (December 1977): 666–77.

Redding, Saunders. *To Make a Poet Black*. Chapel Hill: University of North Carolina Press, 1939.

Renfro, G. Herbert. *Life and Works of Phillis Wheatley*. Washington: Robert L. Pendleton, 1916.

Richmond, M[erle] A. *Bid the Vassal Soar: Interpretive Essays on the Life and Poetry of Phillis Wheatley . . . And George Moses Horton. . . .* Washington: Howard University Press, 1974.

Rigsby, Gregory. "Form and Content in Phillis Wheatley's Elegies." *CLA Journal* 19 (December 1975): 248–57.

_____. "Phillis Wheatley's Craft as Reflected in Her Revised Elegies." *Journal of Negro Education* 47 (Fall 1978): 402–13.

Robinson, William H. *Phillis Wheatley: A Bio-Bibliography*. Boston: G. K. Hall, 1981.

_____. *Phillis Wheatley and Her Writings*. New York: Garland Publishing, 1984.

_____. "Phillis Wheatley: Colonial Quandary." *CLA Journal* 9 (September 1965): 25–38.

_____. "Phillis Wheatley in London." *CLA Journal* 21 (December 1977): 187–201.

_____. *Phillis Wheatley in the Black American Beginnings*. Detroit: Broadside Press, 1975.

_____. "Phillis Wheatley: On Black in Boston Lace Gloves." In Robinson, *Black New England Letters: The Uses of Writings in Black New England*, pp. 27–62, 142. Boston: Public Library of the City of Boston, 1977.

_____. (See the list of Conference papers below.)

_____, ed. *Critical Essays on Phillis Wheatley*. Boston: G. K. Hall, 1982.

Rogal, Samuel J. "Phillis Wheatley's Methodist Connection." *Black American Literature Forum* 21 (Spring–Summer 1987): 85–95.

Rowell, Charles H., and Jerry W. Ward. "Ancestral Memories: The Phillis Wheatley Poetry Festival." *Freedomways* 14 (2d Quarter 1974): 127–45.

Scruggs, Charles. "Phillis Wheatley and the Poetical Legacy of Eighteenth-Century

England." *Studies in Eighteenth-Century Culture* 10 (1981): 279–95.

Shields, John C. "Phillis Wheatley and Mather Byles: A Study in Literary Relationships." *CLA Journal* 23 (June 1980): 377–90.

―――. "Phillis Wheatley and the Sublime." In *Critical Essays on Phillis Wheatley*, edited by William H. Robinson, pp. 189–205. Boston: G. K. Hall, 1982.

―――. "Phillis Wheatley's Poetics of Ascent." Ph.D. dissertation, University of Tennessee, Knoxville, 1978. (Also see *Dissertation Abstracts International*.)

―――. "Phillis Wheatley's Struggle for Freedom in Her Poetry and Prose." In *The Collected Works of Phillis Wheatley*, edited by John C. Shields, pp. 229–70, 324–36. New York: Oxford University Press, 1988.

―――. "Phillis Wheatley's Use of Classicism." *American Literature* 52 (March 1980): 97–111.

Shurtleff, Nathaniel B. "Phillis Wheatley, the Negro-Slave Poet." *Proceedings of the Massachusetts Historical Society* 7 (1863–64): 270–72. (Reprinted from the *Boston Daily Advertiser*, December 21, 1863, p. 3.)

Silverman, Kenneth. "Four New Letters by Phillis Wheatley." *Early American Literature* 8 (Winter 1974): 257–71.

Sistrunk, Albertha. "The Influence of Alexander Pope on the Writing Style of Phillis Wheatley." In *Critical Essays on Phillis Wheatley*, edited by William H. Robinson, pp. 175–88. Boston: G. K. Hall, 1982.

―――. "Phillis Wheatley: An Eighteenth-Century Black American Poet Revisited." *CLA Journal* 23 (June 1980): 391–98.

Smith, Eleanor. "Phillis Wheatley: A Black Perspective." *Journal of Negro Education* 43 (Summer 1974): 401–7.

Steele, Thomas J. "The Figure of Columbia: Phillis Wheatley plus George Washington." *New England Quarterly* 54 (June 1981): 264–66.

Stetson, Erlene. (See the list of Conference papers below.)

Thatcher, B[enjamin] B[ussey]. *Memoir of Phillis Wheatley, A Native African and a Slave*. Boston: George W. Light, 1834.

Winsor, Justin, ed. *The Memorial History of Boston*. 4 vols. Boston: J. R. Osgood, 1880–83.

PAPERS FROM THE PHILLIS WHEATLEY CONFERENCE AT
ILLINOIS STATE UNIVERSITY   September 27–28, 1984

(See the last paragraph of the section on Wheatley's reputation, in this volume.)

Barksdale, Richard K. (University of Illinois). "Diction and Style in Selected Poems of Phillis Wheatley."

Cook, William W. (Dartmouth College). "Come You, Phillis, Now Aspire: Phillis Wheatley, Pattern and Paragon."

Isani, Mukhtar Ali (Virginia Polytechnic Institute and State University). "Religion and the Poetry of Phillis Wheatley."

Levernier, James A. (University of Arkansas at Little Rock). " 'Sometimes by Simile a Victory's Won': Intentional Irony in the Poetry of Phillis Wheatley."

Mason, Julian (University of North Carolina at Charlotte). "Phillis Wheatley's Poem to George Washington 'In Context.' "

Robinson, William H. (Rhode Island College). "The One and Several Phillis Wheatleys."

Stetson, Erlene (Indiana University, Bloomington). "Wheatley's Dilemma as a Struggling Black Woman Author."

Index

The index covers both the writings of Wheatley and information about her and her writings. Included are significant personifications in her writings (e.g., Nature, Virtue). Italicized page numbers indicate the text of the poem, Proposal, or letter, instead of discussion of it. Wheatley's poetic works are listed alphabetically at the end of the entry under her name; some of the titles have been shortened. *Poems on Various Subjects, Religious and Moral*, which required further modification, appears following the list of titles.